ACQUISITION
Strategy and Implementation

ACQUISITION
Strategy and Implementation

Nancy Hubbard

Ichor Business Books
An Imprint of
Purdue University Press
West Lafayette, Indiana

First Ichor Business Book edition, 1999.

Published under license from Macmillan Press Ltd, Houndmills, Basingstoke, Hampshire, RG21 6XS

This edition available only in the United States and Canada.

03   02   01   00   99   5   4   3   2   1

Library of Congress Cataloging-in-Publication Data
Hubbard, Nancy, 1963–
    Acquisition strategy and implementation / Nancy Hubbard. — 1st
Ichor Business Book ed.
        p.   cm.
    Includes bibliographical references and index.
    ISBN 1–55753–179–X (cloth)
    1. Consolidation and merger of corporations.   2. Consolidation and
merger of corporations—Great Britain—Case studies.   I. Title.
HD2746.5.H83   1999
658.1'6—dc21   99–30365
                                                                      CIP

Printed in Great Britain

Contents

Acknowledgements

This book is the culmination of inputs from many people and organizations, some of whom I would especially like to mention. I would like to thank the Leverhulme Trust for sponsoring my research and Professor John Purcell for his valuable input and support in conducting that research. I would also like to thank the five companies profiled in the book – while they remain anonymous, they have my heartfelt appreciation. It is a brave management team that allows an outsider to write about their corporate experiences especially when they are not all positive. In conjunction with this, I interviewed literally hundreds of employees and other people, who shared their feelings and insights with me. As this essentially created the material for the book, they deserve a lion's share of the credit. I would like to especially thank Michael Burton-Prateley for his input into the financial elements of this book as well as on the roles and responsibilities of advisors. In preparing the book, I would like to acknowledge the help and guidance I received from Stephen Rutt, Ray Addicott and the team at Macmillan – they made this as painless as possible.

I would like to thank IFR Securities Data for supplying the up-to-date merger transaction data used in Table 1.1. In addition, the following tables have been reproduced with the kind permission of the various copyright holders: Table 3.1 is reproduced from J.W. Hunt et al., *Acquisition: The Human Factor*, London: London Business School–EZI, p. 27; Figure 4.2 is reproduced from L.R. Smeltzer, 'An analysis of strategies for announcing organisation-wide change', *Group & Organisation Studies*, March 1991, 16 (1):5–24, p. 8; Table 4.3 is reproduced from D.M. Schweiger and Y. Weber, 'Strategies for managing human resources during mergers and acquisitions: An empirical investigation', *Human Resource Planning* 1989 12(2):69–86, p. 82.

Every effort has been made to trace all the copyright-holders, but if any have been inadvertently overlooked the publishers will be pleased to make the necessary arrangement at the first opportunity.

The five case studies profiled in this book are real companies involved in real acquisitions. Their names and some relevant information such as industry background, however, have been changed in order to ensure their anonymity. In addition, those individuals named in those case studies, while real people, are given different names; again some information has been changed to ensure they remain anonymous. As it will be seen, the leaders of the case study companies share the same initials with their companies in order to reinforce their fictitious nature. They also appear in the index within quotation marks, so as not to infer they are the real individuals.

Introduction

At least one in three employees will, during the course of their working life, undergo an acquisition or merger. Yet statistics show that roughly half of acquisitions are not successful. In the current drive to enhance shareholder returns, value is consistently being destroyed by companies acquiring and their management not fully understanding how to undertake the process successfully, often making the same mistakes over and over again. This book will offer some best practices for those embarking on acquisition, based upon four years of research into acquisition success and failure, the research of others, as well as personal experiences based upon my consulting career. Included are five true case studies which illustrate not only how one acquires successfully but also what happens when it goes horribly wrong.

This book can be broken into four distinct sections: reasons for success and failure, the psychology of acquiring, a process for acquiring and five case studies which demonstrate how the process works (or doesn't, as the case may be). Because of this, it is easy for the reader to spend time on the sections he or she feels are most beneficial. For those readers interested in understanding why employees react as they do during acquisition, the psychology chapter (Chapter 2) is worth reading. If one is interested only in understanding a process for acquiring, then the chapters outlining the process are appropriate (Chapters 3–6). For those who would like to understand what goes wrong when an acquisition is not handled optimally (as well as when it does), the case studies make interesting reading. Unlike most other books, this book will give examples not only of acquisitions which are well handled but also of those where things have gone wrong in order to highlight the differences.

I should explain the terminology I use throughout the book. I refer to mergers as acquisitions unless specified otherwise. I also use three terms which I found helpful in doing my research to differentiate employees. 'Negotiators' are those senior directors who are 'in charge' of the acquisition. For the most part they have reached the height of their career, serving as directors of the company. 'Enactors' are middle managers who are responsible for enacting or implementing the directives of the negotiators in a day-to-day business environment including acquisitions. They will have career aspirations and complex managerial roles as they must take direction from

1

the top and disseminate it downward to their reporting employees. Interestingly, in acquisitions, target negotiators often become enactors as they are tasked with implementing the acquirer's wishes; this is not necessarily a role they feel comfortable with at this stage in their career. Finally those employees who receive the directives and act upon them are called 'recipients'; they do not have employees working for them and tend to be the hourly paid, administrative support staff and shopfloor employees. They also have distinct concerns throughout acquisition which are discussed in Chapter 2.

I will refer repeatedly to my own research which was conducted in the UK. For the research, I analysed five acquisitions and interviewed 177 people from the companies involved.[1] The breakdown of those companies is shown in Table I.1 below. I have used direct quotes from the interviews which were tape-recorded and I use them throughout the book to illustrate certain points, as the employees involved can describe the acquisition process and their feelings about it much better than those watching from the sidelines.

Table I.1 Case study participants

Company name	Industry	Type of acquisition	Degree of integration	Degree of acquisition success
Anglo-American/Gas Appliances	Assembly manufacturing	Agreed public bid	Change then financial controls	Extremely successful
Service Conglomerate/ Quality Guarding	Service – contracting	Subsidiary sale	Change then financial controls	Not successful
Discovery/ Scottish Yeast	Batch process manufacturing	Subsidiary sale	Change then financial controls	Very successful under the circumstances
Global/ Various acquisitions	Fast-moving consumer good manufacturing	Privately held companies, contested public bid	Full integration	Only partially successful
TeleCable/ Infosys	Service – long-term client sales	Subsidiary sale	Partial integration	Not successful

1. This included 22 background interviews, 23 negotiator, 97 enactor and 35 recipient interviews from a cross-section of employees.

People say, 'Each acquisition is different and one cannot generalize about what works and what doesn't.' While it is true that every acquisition is unique, there are some simple truths which apply to most cases, including a process which can be adapted to the acquisition at hand. Perhaps the most contentious truth, but in my experience – both in researching and in consulting – one that is true, is that people expect change after acquisition. They will, therefore, put up with the most massive change programmes as long as they are kept informed prior to the events occurring and that they are treated fairly when they occur. This includes redundancies, relocations, changes in working practices and company culture. What employees will not tolerate is being kept in the dark, being treated badly or being misled. In essence, the key to acquisition is managing employee expectations: doing adequate planning, telling employees about the future, then implementing the changes as communicated. While the actual process is not quite that simple, the basic premise holds true. While this may suggest that successful acquiring is based summarily on 'soft issues', this is not entirely the case. While it is true that those acquirers who follow the acquisition framework outlined below will address employees' concerns and the transaction's soft issues, they will be doing so in a rigorous project management basis. Indeed, acquisition is a meeting of hard and soft issues – proper business planning communicated and implemented in a professional and fair manner. That is not to say that other aspects are not vitally important to acquisitions and cannot greatly effect the deal's overall success. But as it will be seen in the cases in this book, without following the process, agreed deals with wonderful strategic fit can go horribly wrong due to a poorly implemented process while acquisitions that, on the surface, look doomed can be great successes if the process is followed.

As will be discussed in Chapter 2, research over the years has found acquisition success and failure based on a variety of issues: implementation mayhem, poor communication, insufficient planning, fit issues such as culture or strategy or a lack of attention paid to human or 'soft' issues. By following the acquisition framework (see Figure I.1), acquirers will address most of these issues. Planning, communication and implementation are dealt with in full, as are human issues. Potential fit problems are generally uncovered during the information gathering stage; how the acquirer deals with them is probably more of an influence on acquisition success than the problems themselves. Thus, acquirers who follow the acquisition framework are more likely to alleviate acquisition obstacles and, therefore, increase the likelihood of success.

Pre-acquisition planning has traditionally been an area of difficulty for acquirers. In order to make it easier, I have broken the process down into

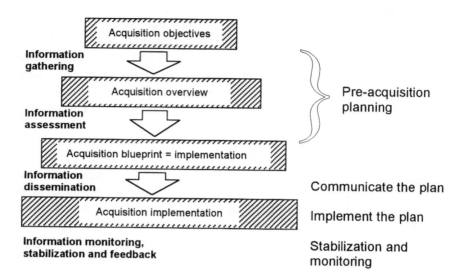

Fig. I.1 *The process of acquiring*

five parts. The difficulty acquirers have traditionally faced in the pre-acquisition planning phase is twofold – having a tested process and having enough time prior to the transaction to conduct it. But bearing in mind the time issues, by the end of the pre-acquisition process, an acquirer following this process should have made the fundamental decisions of how the transaction will progress. These include:

- why the deal is occurring
- how far is the target to be integrated into the acquirer's existing operation?
- what is the timescale for implementing the acquisition plan and any changes?
- the level of employee participation in executing the implementation plan
- are systems (management, operational, information) going to be integrated?
- the degree to which employees are going to be integrated
- the role of the target's senior management team in the new company
- a communication strategy for both internal and external stakeholders
- business topics to be covered by integration teams (if any)
- a written implementation project management plan

- a timescale for delivering the implementation plan
- a process for delivering the implementation plan.

Communication of the plan has been an area which varies greatly between acquirers. Most highly successful acquirers have sophisticated communication strategies and processes for dealing with their target's internal and external stakeholders. Obviously, if an acquirer has not done sufficient pre-acquisition planning, there is not the substance of information to be communicated to employees. Similarly, even if an acquirer has the most well-developed acquisition plan, it is wasted if it is not adequately communicated.

While all elements of the acquisition process are important, the implementation phase is fundamental to its success. Hunt et al. (1987) found an 83 per cent correlation between implementation success and overall acquisition success. Hostile acquisitions can be 'turned around' by a professional and well-handled implementation process while agreed deals can suffer irreparably by botched implementations. An example of this is seen in Infosys (Chapter 11), where a very positive deal was badly soured by a disastrous implementation process; as one target employee said: 'This could have been the perfect acquisition.' The key is the fair handling of a logical process supported by continuous ongoing communication.

The final stage is the stabilization phase which occurs sometime after the major changes related to the acquisition have been made. The time at which this phase begins varies due to the amount of change experienced by affected employees and how employees feel the process has been handled. If the process was well handled, employees adjust more readily; if not, they remain apprehensive for what can be a considerable period of time. This time can be spent constructively appraising how well the acquirer did during the acquisition and what could be done differently next time. Unfortunately, most acquirers fail to assess their actions post-acquisition and consequently have many of the same problems in their next acquisition rather than learning from their mistakes.

Each of the four headings, pre-acquisition planning, communication, implementation and stabilization, will be discussed in separate chapters (Chapters 3–6). The five case studies will then be used to illustrate how the process worked (or didn't, as the case may be) (Chapters 7–11). First we will look at acquisition trends through the years and the reason for acquisition success or failure in Chapter 1, and the psychology of acquiring in Chapter 2.

1 Why History Repeats Itself: Acquisition Trends, Successes and Failures

INTRODUCTION

The current acquisition climate means that history is being rewritten daily with the announcement of each new 'mega-merger', but this is only history repeating itself: in the past, companies have consolidated on national lines; this time it is on a global basis. It will be interesting to see what the success rates will be of these mega-mergers – will they surpass the much touted 50 per cent success rate of the average deal? I think not, for, as we have seen, although there is often a logical strategic fit in these deals, their success relies very heavily on a well-run implementation process and the human resource (HR) function in order to oversee the raft of redundancies, relocations and reprocessing which is inherent to an economies of scale acquisition. Most acquirers do not give this element of the transaction the time or importance it deserves. As will be discussed in this chapter, perhaps this is why poor implementation and HR issues account for such a large percentage of acquisition failures. First, let us look at the history of acquisition trends.

A DEFINITION OF ACQUISITION

There are four types of corporate takeovers: mergers, acquisitions which can be friendly or hostile, proxy contests and leveraged buyouts. Mergers, legally defined, involve similar-sized entities: both companies' shares are exchanged for shares in a new corporation. As such, there is no cash element in the transaction. While a merger appears with some frequency based on this legalese definition, in actuality true mergers are quite rare indeed. There are psychological differences between acquisitions and mergers as the latter involve two partners of relatively equal size and power and a genuine attempt is made to meld the two entities into a culturally new one. Acquisitions, conversely, have clear winners and losers, where power is not negotiable.

6

Examples of mergers in recent times include: Smith Kline/Beecham, Grand Metropolitan and Guinness to create Diageo, and Asea and Brown Boveri to become ABB.

Acquisitions are takeovers in which the bidder negotiates directly with the target company's board of directors; the purchase can be based on a consideration of cash, paper, or a combination of the two. The deal goes to the shareholders with the board of directors' approval (an agreed bid) or without the support of the target board (a contested bid). A contested bid can become an agreed bid at a later time for a variety of reasons, including an increase in the purchase price to a level which is acceptable to the board. The actual percentage of hostile bids versus agreed bids is small, accounting for less than 7 per cent of all UK public bids and a tiny percentage of all UK transactions. Tender offers are American phenomena and refer to those takeovers in which the bidder takes the decision directly to the target company shareholders by circumventing the target board. A proxy contest is when there is an attempt to gain control of the target company's board of directors via a shareholder vote, thus removing the incumbent management from decision making power. Finally, a leveraged buyout, sometimes in the form of a management buyout, is a purchase of shareholder equity by a group usually including incumbent management and is financed by debt, venture capital or both.

GLOBAL MERGER TRENDS AND NUMBERS

The history of merger trends in the US is well documented (Barnatt and Wong, 1992) and has been mirrored in other developed nations. The global markets are in the midst of the fifth major merger wave, with acquirers pursuing different acquisition objectives and creating different types of organization.

Historical trends

The first merger wave occurred in the US between 1889 and 1901 in which buyers pursued horizontal integration in an attempt to create monopolies in specific industries. Examples of this were the amalgamation of US Steel and the consolidation of the railways. The second wave of activity occurred in the late 1920s where the majority of US mergers prompted moves towards vertical integration, most notably in the automobile and other manufacturing industries as well as in new industries such as radio. During this time the UK was also experiencing a wave of mergers which, in intent, paralleled the horizontal American wave of the 1900s of horizontal integration. ICI was formed in 1926 by the merger of four UK chemical companies: United Alkali, British Dyestuffs, Brunner Mond, and Nobel Industries highlighting the trend.

Anti-trust legislation limiting competition, as well as adverse sentiment against acquisitions occurred during the 1930s through the 1950s. This, as well as the Great Depression and the Second World War, caused the lull in acquisition activity until the 1960s when the next great wave of mergers resulted in the formation of conglomerates, both in the US and in parts of Europe. These acquisitions were primarily into related or concentric industries where there was hope of attaining some kind of strategic synergy through diversification (aided in advances in information and communication technology) which enhanced the ability to institute tighter financial controls and, as a consequence, broader organizational structures.

The fourth great merger wave occurred during the late 1980s and was caused, in part, by a rethinking of corporate strategy in which attempts were made to maximize shareholder value. This led to divestments of peripheral or non-core businesses many of which ironically were acquired in the 1960 merger wave. In doing so, companies took full advantage of relaxing anti-trust legislation, industry deregulation and the creation of innovative forms of finance, most notably junk bonds, to expand into related areas of business. Merger activity reached its pinnacle during this period in the US with over $200 billion worth of deals led by Kohlberg, Kravis and Roberts' acquisition of RJR Nabisco for $24.7 billion (£15 billion), completed in 1989.

Like the US, the 1980s merger boom in the UK was also fuelled by the divestiture of many 1960s acquisitions. The 'merger mania' which occurred in the US spread to the UK and Europe with transatlantic activity peaking in 1988 and declining in volume thereafter. The European market, however, continued to expand through 1989, with brisk intra-European cross border activity in anticipation of the relaxation of market regulations in 1992.

Although the acquisition market remained flat for much of the early 1990s, the decade's close has seen a massive resurgence in merger activity. Activity in the late 1990s has seen acquisition activity smash all existing records, both in terms of the number of transactions and the size of those deals. Of the ten largest transactions, nine have occurred in the first six months of 1998 with annual global figures set to exceed $2 trillion for the first time in history, 50 per cent higher than 1989 (see Table 1.1) (*Financial Times*, 26 June 1998). The increasing globalization of multinational corporations, the dismantling of protectionist barriers, and an effort to consolidate along industrial lines horizontally bringing European and emerging market players more in line with US players in terms of both size and number, have all

Table 1.1 The ten largest acquisitions or mergers in history (by deal value)

Target	Activity	Bidder	Value £m	Value US$	Date Announced
Citicorp (US)	Banking/ Financial Services	Travelers Group (US)	49,699	82,500	April 1988
Ameritech Corporation (US)	Telecommunications	SBC Communications Inc. (US)	37,886	62,000	May 1998
NationsBank Corporation (US)	Banking/ Financial Services	BankAmerica Corporation (US)	35,943	60,000	April 1998
GTE Corporation (US)	Telecommunications	Bell Atlantic Corporation (US)	31,348	52,000	July 1998
Amoco Corporation (US)	Oil/Gas	British Petroleum Company plc (UK)	29,654	48,407	August 1998
Tele-Communications Inc. (US)	Cable Television Services	AT&T Corporation (US)	28,851	48,300	June 1998
Chrysler Corporation (US)	Motor Vehicles	Daimler-Benz AG (Germany)	24,010	40,000	May 1998
MCI Corporation (US)	Telecommunications	WorldCom Inc. (US)	23,041	37,000	October 1997
Monsanto Company (US)*	Chemicals/ Pharmaceuticals	American Home Products Corporation (US)	21,463	35,000	June 1998
Wells Fargo & Company (US)	Banking/ Financial Services	Norwest Corporation (US)	20,781	34,000	June 1998

* Bid later withdrawn

Source: IFR Securities Data (1 October 1998)

contributed to the frenetic merger activity. Buoyant and increasingly sophisticated stock markets and relatively low interest rates have only fuelled the drive to buy.

Europe is seeing a return of monopolistic acquisitions reminiscent of the US consolidation of 1900, albeit within the constraints of anti-trust legislation; examples include: Glaxo/Wellcome; Grand Metropolitan and Guinness; several banking acquisitions including SBC Warburg Dillon Read/Union Bank of Switzerland, ABN Amro/Générale de Banque* and Suez Lyonnaise des Eaux/Société Générale de Belgique; the German heavy manufacturing consolidation between Thyssen AG and Friedrich Krupp AG, and the cross-Scandinavian Enso/Stora Kopparbergs acquisition. The smallest of these transactions was almost $5 billion and the largest $25 billion.

These European examples highlight a growing global trend where attempts are made to consolidate and gain economies of scale within specific industries. If one takes a global view of markets, one could argue that this current acquisition wave is similar to the first US merger wave where the same occurred within the boundaries of the United States – the only difference is that now we are talking globally and, for the first time, markets are not defined by geographic boundaries. Indeed, global acquisition activity seems to be bearing this out with large-scale merger activity creating huge players in those industries which are truly global in scope (telecommunications, pharmaceuticals, defence, financial markets, automotive).

Activity in Asia and the emerging markets has also changed in context and scale during this last merger wave. While previous activity was supported primarily by Japanese businesses acquiring in Europe and the United States, this wave has seen an increase in intra-Asian as well as larger emerging market deals. This trend has continued with $1 billion-plus Asian deals becoming much more commonplace. Examples include: Pohang Iron and Steel acquiring Hanbo Group for $1.35 billion, San Miguel buying Coca-Cola Bottlers (Philippines) for $2.67 billion, and Barito Pacific Timber Group buying Construction and Supply House Ltd of Malaysia in a complicated $1 billion deal. In other emerging markets, buyers are taking advantage of increasing privatization of government holdings, including Spain's Nacionel de Electricidad taking a 29 per cent stake in Chile's Enersis for $1.5 billion and a Brazilian and American consortium buying Vale do Rio Doce, a Brazilian mining group, for $3.56 billion (*Acquisitions Monthly*, February 1998).

In terms of the number of companies undergoing an acquisition in the past decade, a US study estimated that 45 per cent of large American companies had undergone an acquisition either as acquirer or target between the years of 1984 and 1989 (Troy, 1992). The number of acquisitions in the

---

* Bid later withdrawn

UK is considered to be even higher with approximately two-thirds of large UK companies (with over 1000 employees) having had an acquisition or merger in their UK operation during the years between 1987 and 1992; with the current merger wave this figure is likely to be much higher (Hubbard and Purcell, 1993). Of UK companies which operate internationally, 95 per cent of those who expanded abroad during the late 1980s also did so via acquisition (ibid.).

Future acquisition trends

At the end of 1998, there appears to be no decrease in merger activity. A world-wide recession or depression, further financial woes in Asia, or perhaps a high-profile mega-merger disaster may prompt a rethink on their overall viability, but current thought is that the trend within those truly global industries is set to continue, as is European activity spurred on by massive institutional funds and buoyant stock markets. But I would like to interject a word of caution as the size of some organizations globally are reaching dangerous proportions. Mergers, joint ventures and strategic alliances are creating gigantic players with powers on a global scale which are reaching monopolistic levels. One only has to examine the telecommunications industry to see that three groups of alliances control the vast bulk of the world's telecommunications business. The worry is that unless there is a global merger regulator with some power, this trend to fewer, larger, and more powerful organizations will continue to the detriment of competition and ultimately the consumer.

ACQUISITION SUCCESS AND FAILURE: MEASURING SUCCESS

Several measurements have been used over the years to judge acquisition success and failure. These include using financial data such as stock market information, measuring the number of divestments of those companies pursuing a growth strategy and subjective measurements such as participant reaction and third-party assessments. Regardless of the measurement, the results are remarkably similar – roughly half of acquisitions fail to meet the objectives of the parties involved.

When using financial data to examine acquisition success and failure in financial terms, the research to date suggests that the only clear financial winners are those target company shareholders who received cash offers for their stake in the target company. As discussed above, a major reason for acquisition in the 1980s was a desire to maximize the acquiring company's shareholder value. Yet the majority of acquisitions fail to achieve any significant gain in value for acquiring company shareholders at all. In fact, many acquirers experienced negative abnormal returns on share prices, suggesting that stock market investors understand the difficulties post-acquisition with success not seen as automatically forthcoming – and the findings bear this out: several US studies found that the larger the target firm acquired, the greater the percentage loss in terms of market share after acquisition (Mueller, 1985; Fowler and Schmidt, 1989). One US study found this to be the case and added that overall success was related to the ability to implement the acquisition successfully (Ravenscraft and Scherer, 1987).

Porter (1987) chose a different means of assessing acquisition success and failure by measuring the number of divestments of organizations publicly pursuing acquisition growth strategies. He studied 33 of the largest US companies and found that over a five-year period between 1975 and 1980, they divested over 60 per cent of their related acquisitions and almost three-quarters of their unrelated acquisitions. As these companies were pursuing growth strategies, their divestments were deemed failures.

More subjective measures have also been used to determine acquisition success and failure including the opinions and reactions of the stakeholders involved. While this appears 'less scientific' in approach, the results are quite similar to the financially based findings.

The research results are consistent across four decades of research finding that poor acquisition performance is not driven by the type of transaction nor the reasoning behind it, as these, too, have changed over the decades. The percentage of acquisitions deemed failures runs the gamut across the research from a low of 50 per cent (Hunt et al., 1987; Porter, 1987; Coopers & Lybrand, 1992; KPMG, 1997), to 66 per cent (Magnet, 1984; Lubatkin, 1987), to 75 per cent (Kitching, 1967; Baker et al., 1981; Lefkoe, 1987). A recent pan-European KPMG study found that, contrary to their objectives, acquisitions systematically destroyed rather than created shareholder value (KPMG, 1997). A McKinsey study found that, over a ten-year period, only 23 per cent of acquisitions ended up recovering the cost incurred during the acquisition. The conclusion was that for 66 per cent of acquirers they would have earned a greater return in a bank savings account than by acquiring (Magnet, 1984).

REASONS WHY ACQUISITIONS FAIL: FIT AND PROCESS ISSUES

Over the years, research has found a variety of factors linked to acquisition success and failure which are discussed below. The reasons for acquisition failure can be sub-divided into two categories, fit and process issues. Fit issues are those which assess the juxtaposition of the acquirer and the target. For the most part the acquirer has little ability to influence these factors; some can be mitigated but remain largely out of the acquirer's control. Relative size of the target to the acquirer and age of the organizations are examples of these. The acquirer, however, has control over process issues, those issues surrounding the transaction and implementation process. These include the presence of pre-acquisition planning, implementation process and the tone of the negotiations.

Fit issues

1. **Size issues**. A mismatch in the size between acquirer and target has been found to lead to poor acquisition performance. Hunt et al. (1987) found a skewed effect on performance with those acquisitions having large differences in size being either very successful or highly unsuccessful as the acquirer either suffered 'acquisition indigestion' through buying too big, or failed to give the smaller acquisition the time and attention it required.

2. **Diversification**. Perhaps the demographic feature most mentioned when discussing acquisition failure is diversification. There is a large body of work which has found that acquisitions into related industries consistently outperform acquisitions into unrelated; this is reflected in the capital markets as diversified conglomerates have a lower base price/earnings ratio than almost any other industry sector. Unrelated diversification has been associated with lower financial performance, lower capital productivity, and a higher degree of variance in performance for a variety of reasons, including a lack of industry or geographic knowledge, a lack of focus as well as a perceived inability to gain meaningful synergies.

3. **Previous acquisition experience**. Results are mixed as to the role of previous acquisition experience and its bearing on future acquisitions. While previous acquisition experience is not necessarily a requirement for future acquisition success, very unsuccessful acquirers usually have little previous acquisition experience. Other factors related to this are likely to play a far more significant role in acquisition success, such as the organization's ability to learn from its previous acquisition mistakes and its willingness to take advice in order to maximize its chances of success. Those 'serial acquirers' who possess the 'in-house' skills necessary to promote acquisition success, such as a well-trained and

competent implementation team (see Chapter 5), are more likely to have honed their acquisition skills and find success; more so than those who have not.

4. **Organizational fit**. Organizational fit is described as the 'the match between administrative practices, cultural practices and personnel characteristics' of the target and acquirer (Jemison and Sitkin, 1986, p. 147). It influences the ease with which the two organizations can be integrated during implementation. Research has found that a suitable organizational fit exemplified by compatible management practices is a characteristic of successful acquisitions. Coopers & Lybrand (1992) found that target management attitude was a key determinant of acquisition success in the UK; this is somewhat misleading as the target's management attitude can be influenced to a greater or lesser extent by the acquirer. Organizational fit will be discussed in more detail in Chapter 3 when assessing whether or not to integrate organizational systems.

5. **Strategic fit**. An important element of acquisition success is the strategic fit of the parties, especially if the acquisition intent is to capitalize on mutual synergies. This includes those areas where the acquirer and target expect to gain organic growth via combining business units or less tangible working arrangements which require close co-operation between business units. Strategic fit can include the business philosophies of the two entities (return on investment versus market share), the timeframe for achieving these goals (short term versus long term) and the way in which assets are utilized (high capital investment or an asset stripping mentality).

6. **Cultural fit**. Although cultural fit is discussed here as a 'fit' issue, the relationship between cultural fit and acquisition implementation is highly related. As seen in the Global Products case study (Chapter 9), it is difficult, if not impossible, to undergo a successful implementation without adequately addressing the cultural fit issues. The findings of a recent European study concur; the 200 European Chief Executive Officers (CEOs) questioned said that in their experience, the ability to integrate the target company and its culture is a primary factor of overall acquisition success (Cartwright and Cooper, 1992). This is examined further in Chapter 3, as culture is one of seven areas requiring acquirer decisions regarding the implementation plan.

7. **Other demographic factors**. There are several other factors which have been associated with acquisition success: the healthy condition of seller, acquisition timing relative to the market cycle, the target's profitability just prior to acquisition, and the respective ages of the organizations.

Process issues

As will be seen, the issues which have the greatest impact on acquisition success and failure are those over which the acquirer has almost total control: the process issues. Yet acquirers continue to have roughly a 50 per cent success rate. This suggests a profound inability on the part of acquirers to understand and take control of the implementation process. It appears that few realize that when they do, they enhance the likelihood of their own acquisition success. It remains a missed opportunity.

1. **Negotiation issues**. The desire to complete the deal during its negotiation can lead to rushing into unsuitable alliances or overlooking key implementation areas. This can be exacerbated by the use of external advisors who get paid on the transaction's completion and not its success. There is some debate over the role of the tone of negotiations in acquisition success, with friendly or agreed acquisitions having a higher success rate. There could be a variety of reasons for this: a greater opportunity to conduct thorough due diligence, longer negotiations which could lead to greater understanding and trust between the parties, and a more positive management attitude towards the acquisition seen in the target management, for example.

2. **Inadequate pre-acquisition planning**. Research has found that roughly only half of acquirers had a pre-acquisition implementation plan (AMR, 1998), yet the majority of targets naturally assume their acquirer has a plan. This can create a host of mismatched expectations as the target employees look to the acquirer for direction and find none. The KPMG (1997) study found that the CEOs interviewed said that if they could do one thing better next time, it would be to have spent more time and effort in their pre-acquisition planning. It is also clear that it is impossible to communicate on 'Day One' and make implementation changes quickly without thorough and extensive pre-acquisition planning.

3. **Insufficient information gathering**. Adequate information gathering in the form of due diligence is critical in order to avoid 'any skeletons in the closet'. Yet the due diligence performed by many acquirers is almost solely based on issues which could 'scupper the deal', not sink the company after the deal is completed. As most due diligence conducted is financially based, it misses many key areas which could ultimately lead to implementation problems. An example of this is HR due diligence, where the KPMG study found less than 10 per cent of acquirers conduct a thorough human resource-related due diligence (ibid.). Yet as seen below, it is the source of many potential 'people problems' during the imple-

mentation process. In addition, most due diligence concentrates on 'fit' issues and rarely covers any of the process issues discussed, perhaps because these are under the control of the acquirer and, therefore, assumed to be of a standard to their liking. Problems then arise after the deal has been completed and not before.

4. **Price paid and method of payment for the target**. There is a debate over the importance of paying too much in acquisition failure. Some research has found that acquirers can simply pay too much for the target company. This can have repercussions if they then cannot follow through with the costs associated with an implementation plan or if it constrains the organization's resources. Similarly, paying by paper can create a debt mountain and, for many of the same reasons as paying too much, can have a lower success rate than those paid for in cash. Other researchers, however, have found price paid to be one of the least important reasons for acquisition failure.

5. **People problems**. How employees react to the management of the acquisition is deemed to be the cause of many acquisition failures, as 'employee reactions to change are a principle reason why over half of all mergers and acquisitions ultimately prove to be financial disappointments' (Marks and Cutcliffe, 1988, p. 30). A US survey found that 85 per cent of top executives believe personnel problems affect acquisition more than financial problems, compounded by the fact that these problems are not anticipated prior to the acquisition (Davy et al., 1988). Dealing successfully with stress issues relating to the acquisition and the ambiguity it creates is also seen to be a major component to overall success, as stress can cause a whole host of employee problems during acquisition.

6. **Implementation issues**. There have been countless studies highlighting the close relationship between implementation success and overall acquisition success. The Coopers & Lybrand (1992) study found a correlation between implementation success and overall acquisition success of 76 per cent. Hunt et al. (1987) found an 83 per cent correlation. KPMG's 1997 study found that implementation was the most important factor to overall acquisition success in acquisitions throughout Europe. My own research found that the greatest determinant of overall acquisition success was not a 'fit' issue but a carefully planned and executed implementation process.

7. **Communication**. One element of implementation highlighted as being crucial to the process and consequently acquisition in general is communication. Studies have found that effective communication during acquisition reduces ambiguity and employee stress thereby increasing

chances of success (Napier et al., 1989). I found communication to be a crucial step in overall acquisition success, although not in itself enough to guarantee success.

When examining the reasons for acquisition failure, many are highly interrelated and difficult to distinguish. If, for example, an acquirer pays too much for the target company, this can lead to the acquirer becoming cash strapped. This can lead to cost reductions which, in turn, could lead to people issues and implementation problems. Similarly, a poorly planned transaction can lead to poor due diligence and an inability to communicate and implement an effective plan, thus resulting in substantial people problems. Therefore, the ability to break down acquisition failure into neat categories is too simplistic a solution and impossible to do with any meaning. Instead, what is needed is a holistic approach to the acquisition process, its elements and outcomes.

My own research and personal experience is that one can take a deal which, on paper, looks doomed to failure and 'save it' by a well-planned and executed implementation process; conversely, it is very easy to take a perfect deal in terms of fit and strategy and destroy it by a faulty implementation. By a well-executed process, I mean one which is well-planned and thought out, is effectively communicated, implemented in a professional manner and monitored throughout. In psychological terms, it is the ability *to manage people's expectations* during the process of acquisition. This process will be outlined in the following chapter.

In taking this concept further, I will make a bold and contentious statement but one that I feel is very true. *Acquisition offers the acquirer an enormous opportunity like no other to shake and shape that organization, because people expect change.* My research and experience has found that employees will tolerate the most drastic actions after acquisition because of this. But there remains an important caveat: in order for it to be successful, the acquirer should follow the four simple steps outlined above – thorough planning, effective communication, professional implementation and sufficient monitoring. Thus, the acquirer has a window of approximately 100 days in which to make an important impact. The acquirer must seize the opportunity; how this can be done is discussed in Chapters 3–6.

2 The Psychology of Acquiring: Why Employees Act the Way They Do

INTRODUCTION

To fully understand the ramifications of why acquisitions create such stress and employee angst, it is important to explore how employees feel and think during the process: their concerns and reactions to events. In order to do so, I have used principally my own research into employee behaviour during acquisition as a basis for this chapter.

Organizational change including acquisition has been acknowledged to cause high levels of stress and uncertainty for affected employees. During acquisition, employees worry about a variety of issues, many of which have been likened to the most stressful events in one's life: divorce or separation, death of a loved one, moving house and job loss. The difference between acquisition and other forms of organizational change is considerable. Organizational change involves modification within an existing company where employees know the company, its culture and procedures as well as its leaders and their management style; as a result, there will already exist a mutual understanding between employees and the organization and possibly the existence of trust to some degree. In acquisitions, however, target employees are confronted with a new employer, procedures and culture, leaders and management styles with no previous history and no underlying trust. As a consequence, their concerns are magnified and more complex.

EMPLOYEE CONCERNS DURING ACQUISITION

My research discussed during the introduction of this book analysed employee concerns during acquisition. Employees reported having concerns in four main areas: their own job security, the well-being of their work groups and colleagues, changes in role, procedures and status, and finally concerns over changes in corporate culture. Employees reported that these concerns differed according to the employees' position in the organization as well as changed over the course of the acquisition. More importantly for the acquirer, however, is the finding that employee concerns differed according to how well the acquirer follow the acquisition process discussed throughout this book: having a plan, communicating the plan and implementing it in a fair and professional manner. This process ensured that acquirers managed employees' expectations and as a consequence those acquirers witnessed a drop in employee concerns over time. The five case studies found in greater detail in Chapters 7–11 are discussed below in order to illustrate these findings.

Employee concern differences by organizational position

Employee concerns differed dramatically according to the position they held within the organization. The vast majority of employees' primary concern was over their own job security. This makes sense – there is no point worrying about the company's procedures if you are no longer an employee. What differed to a large extent were employees' secondary concerns and those concerns they held after they were able to allay fears over their own job security. Senior employees (whom I term negotiators) were not particularly worried about colleagues but reported being worried about status, procedure and cultural issues. Non-managerial employees (recipients, as I call them) were almost as worried about their colleagues and work groups as they were about their own job security, while cultural and procedural concerns were of little interest to these employees. Enactors, those managers stuck in the middle, reported very complex concerns where they worried about everything – not only their own job security but also that of their colleagues, as well as procedural and cultural issues (see Table 2.1). Although their overall concerns were not necessarily higher than those of negotiators and recipients, they were more complex as they worried about all four areas of concerns during the acquisition process.

Table 2.1 Employees' reported primary and secondary concerns

Concerns	Individual job	Work group	Status and procedure	Cultural concerns
Negotiator	Primary	Minimal	Secondary	Secondary
Enactor	Primary	Secondary	Secondary	Secondary
Recipient	Primary	Secondary	Minimal	Minimal

These findings are important for acquirers to understand if they want to address (and hopefully reduce) employee concerns during acquisition. First, negotiators are those people who set the communication and lead the acquisition implementation process, yet they represent only a tiny fraction of an organization's total employees. If they base communication on their own personal concerns, they will be discussing issues which are of no interest to the vast majority of the workforce. In doing so, acquirers will fail to address the issues which are of the greatest concern to the workforce, namely work group issues. Second, if negotiators are unaware of the importance of colleagues on employees, they may not realize the impact of redundancies, relocations, and other detrimentally perceived changes on the remaining employees. If handled badly, these changes can create a host of bad feelings and negatively affect the perceptions of employees towards the acquiring organization, procedures, culture and management.

Concerns change over the course of the acquisition

Employees also reported that concerns changed over the course of the acquisition for a variety of reasons – more information became available, the implementation process gave rise to new concerns and, in some cases, the actions of the acquirer during this time reduced employee uncertainty. While negotiators, enactors and recipients all reported that their primary concern was job security, what differed was the extent to which this concern changed over the course of the acquisition and how other concerns came to the fore.

While all employees were concerned about job loss, directors' concerns in this area abated quickly as they received further information about their own job security (see Figure 2.1). With this concern out of the way, directors began worrying about what life would be like in the new organization in terms of procedures, status and culture. These concerns escalated during the implementation process as differences in ways of working came to light. These concerns fell greatly but did not abate during the stabilization period – perhaps as they decided whether or not to accept the changed environment or to leave the organization.

For acquirers, these findings suggest that more emphasis needs to be placed on understanding and communicating procedural and cultural differences between the acquirer and target if one wants the senior team to stay and be productive. While all changes may not be palatable, the shock of change is even greater if it remains misunderstood. The real issue is understanding the differences which abound through any means available in order for them

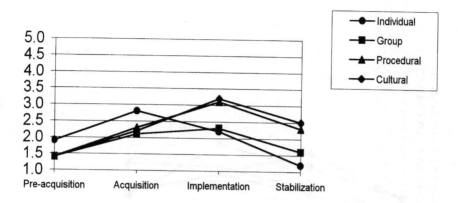

Fig. 2.1 *Senior employee (negotiator) concerns during acquisition*

to be addressed. Due diligence or post-acquisition management structure and culture audits (discussed in Chapters 3 and 5) are positive means of highlighting and dealing with any differences. It also means the acquirer must fully understand its own culture and structures, a feat the vast majority of acquirers have yet to master.

These findings also mean that if communication is based solely upon those senior employees' concerns, those communicating will feel other employees' concerns are waning when theirs are likely to be increasing. If their acquisition communication reflects this, it will be found lacking by the other employees.

Middle managers' concerns were the most complex of the employee groups over the course of the acquisition (see Figure 2.2). While they were not necessarily more concerned than the other types of employees, their concerns were more complex. In many enactors, each concern became a primary concern at a different stage of the acquisition: their own job at the announcement, the well-being of their colleagues during the implementation and procedural and cultural concerns during the aftermath. It will be seen in the case studies that how the acquirer handled the implementation process affected how greatly middle managers questioned differences in culture and procedure during the aftermath. In those cases where the implementation was perceived to be handled badly, procedural and cultural concerns rose; in the cases where it went well, these concerns fell during the course of the process.

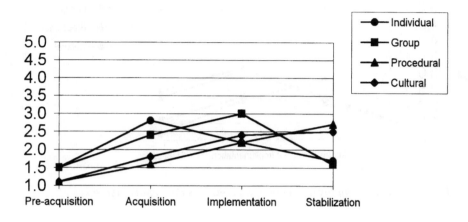

Fig. 2.2   *Middle manager (enactor) concerns*

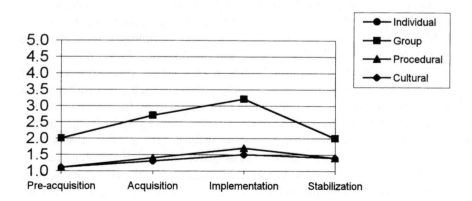

Fig. 2.3   *Non-managerial (recipient) employee concerns (note that Individual and Group data are the same)*

For acquirers, the ramifications are considerable. Middle managers are often considered to be the 'engine' of the organization – those individuals who serve as the link between the negotiators and the workforce. Many serve as opinion leaders and are crucial to the organization's success. As their concerns are often more complex than those of their bosses, they may remain misunderstood and, as a consequence, insufficiently addressed. If enactors' concerns remain unanswered, especially in terms of colleagues, it is likely that those employees who report to them will also remain dissatisfied. If middle managers are seen to be critical for the acquisition's success either because the top team is expected to leave or because the acquirer needs their expertise, special steps need to be taken in order to ensure middle managers' concerns are answered. This could include direct communication on those topics middle managers feel are important (colleagues during the implementation phase and career paths, for instance), involvement in joint integration groups, and in feedback mechanisms such as post-acquisition audits.

Non-managerial (recipient) staff concerns are the least complicated and easiest to address in that these employees are predominantly concerned with their own job security and that of their work groups (see Figure 2.3). Once these concerns have been addressed, recipients are relatively unconcerned about organizational issues such as procedures, careers, status and culture. Yet ironically recipients' concerns are often neglected often due to a lack of understanding of these concerns from the top (as they are not necessarily shared) and a shortage of time meaning that they are not seen as a priority.

If one is acquiring a highly participative workforce such as one which delivers 'zero quality defect' products or one which is highly customer facing, having their concerns addressed via managed expectations is a necessary element of a successful acquisition plan. Extensive direct communication needs to cover the two areas which these employees feel are important as the acquirer cannot rely on managers necessarily to cascade the information effectively down throughout the organization. Instead, both direct and cascaded communication can be used to ensure the acquirer's communication is received by all employees. In addition, in order to achieve the workforce's future co-operation, the implementation of the communicated plan also needs to be conducted in a 'fair' manner, an issue which is discussed in Chapter 5.

Concerns are affected by the acquirer's actions

If employee concerns were totally unrelated to the acquirer's actions, it would be pointless to devote so much time and energy into assembling and

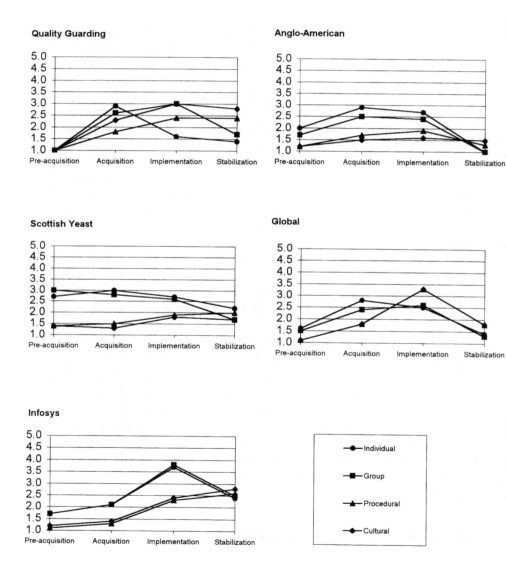

Fig. 2.4 *Employee concerns in the five cases studied*

implementing a cohesive acquisition plan. But this is not the case. *Employees' concerns are acutely related to the acquirer's actions and, more importantly, how the employees perceive those actions.* To illustrate this, employee concerns in the five case studies used later in the book are discussed (see Figure 2.4) . As will be seen, one (Anglo-American) was a very successful acquisition which essentially followed the process outlined in this book with another (Discovery) being successful in light of the adverse circumstances surrounding the deal. Global was very successful in managing only half of employee concerns, while the other two, Quality Guarding and Infosys, could have been handled better. When comparing employee concerns from these five acquisitions, it is interesting to note the relative differences especially during the implementation and stabilization phases. While all employees in the five case studies were almost equally concerned when the acquisition was announced, those where the implementation was 'successful' saw a plateau or even a drop in concerns from the time of the acquisition's announcement throughout the implementation; those which did not, had increasing concerns. This was seen very clearly in employees' procedural and cultural concerns. What is also apparent is that how the acquirer handles individual and group issues such as redundancies and relocations also affects employees' perceptions of the acquirer's culture and procedures. If the acquirer treats employees fairly and honestly, this sends a very different cultural signal to employees than acquirers who are seen to be ruthless or unjust.

THE PSYCHOLOGY OF EMPLOYEE CONCERNS DURING ACQUISITION

There are psychological reasons why these four areas are of major concern to employees during acquisition. Behind the obvious reasons such as job loss potentially causing hardship, there are more complex reasons as to why employees are concerned during acquisition.

Employees have pre-existing identities in both an individual ('me') and a collective group ('us') sense within the organization. As these are pre-existing, the acquirer plays no hand in their development but instead has to deal with these employee perceptions as they are at the time of the transaction. Areas of employee concerns can be shown in a two-by-two matrix which addresses both their individual and group concerns (see Figure 2.5).

On a personal level, affected employees will have concerns about their job in the new organization with job security being the top priority (Box 1). But it goes further than that – individuals will need to form a psychological contract with the new organization by re-evaluating and accepting their

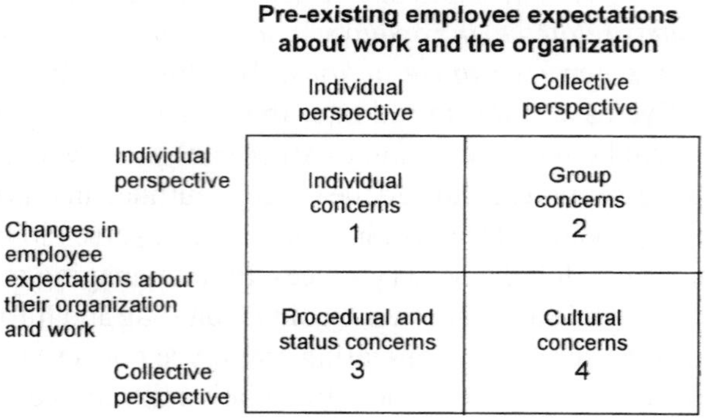

**Pre-existing employee expectations
about work and the organization**

	Individual perspective	Collective perspective
Individual perspective	Individual concerns 1	Group concerns 2
Collective perspective	Procedural and status concerns 3	Cultural concerns 4

(left axis label: Changes in employee expectations about their organization and work)

Fig. 2.5 *Dual expectations model*

positions in the new firm in light of any changes brought on by the acquisition and subsequent events.

The employees' group concerns focus on the new organization's policies concerning formal and informal employee groups (Box 2). Acquired employees will want to know about their colleagues' and their jobs' security, as concerns over colleagues will be as high as their own in certain employee groups. Individuals will also want information as to whether or not their groups will remain intact or change, especially in cases of full acquisition integration.

Employees will also have concerns about the wider issues of where they 'fit' in the new organization (Box 3). Employees are often concerned over any differences in the organizations vis-à-vis changes in procedures, careers or status which may affect them due to the acquisition; this can potentially affect both target and acquiring employees. Role ambiguity can become an issue, as can role conflict in some cases. This is potentially more acute in cases of full integration where layers of the organizational hierarchy (and employees) are affected by new corporate procedures and structures.

On an organizational level, some employees have concerns as to how the target company will 'fit' within the acquiring company and the effects of the acquisition on the combined company's culture (Box 4). Once again, it is likely that the degree of integration will influence the level of cultural concern, as the greater the integration, the greater the likelihood of cultural changes.

In order to fully understand employee behaviour, these four areas of concern will be discussed in some detail.

Individual concerns: the psychological contract

The psychological contract is the unspoken, unconscious yet mutually understood relationship between an employer and its employee which encompasses mutual expectations which have been built up over the course of the employment relationship. These include expectations of what is the employee's role and what behaviour is expected and rewarded in fulfilling that role. The relationship differs from employee to employee and is based on the communicated and inferred benefits that that relationship holds. Psychological contracts differ from expectations in that the psychological contract exists purely between the company and its employee and is not based on outside experiences of work and employment but on that specific job in that company (Robinson, 1996).

If the psychological contract is altered in any way it must be renegotiated. This includes changes brought on either by being acquired or by existing employees being affected by a new acquisition. The greater the changes, the more time is needed to fully understand them, the perspectives of the employee, and organization and come to a mutually acceptable arrangement. This requires two main elements: trust and effective communication. This renegotiation relies heavily on trust – trust that neither party will take advantage of the other. It is highly unlikely that this degree of trust will exist in target employees after acquisition for some time *even if* the implementation process goes well. What a smooth implementation process does give the acquirer is time in which to develop an atmosphere where employees are willing to undergo the new socialization process, the outcome of which is the new psychological contract.

The other element necessary for a new psychological contract is effective communication to each employee. A problem for the acquirer is that each acquired employee's psychological contract with the target differs as each employee expects different things. The acquirer is not aware of each individual contract, and in most cases has neither the time nor the inclination to find out, except for those truly indispensable employees. Similarly, as the psychological contract is not a conscious agreement, employees themselves are not aware of its existence, that is, until it is broken. As employees' psychological contracts will have similar components, general communication about the four areas of concern outlined above will address much of the information required to begin the renegotiation process. But as each psychological contract differs, effective individually based two-way communication is also needed, at least in part.

Group concerns: group and socialization issues

All organizations are composed of both formal and informal work groups. The latter allow employees to operate more effectively within a company, and include informal task groups and communication groups which pass on relevant information, friendship groups. During acquisition, the combination of the situation's uncertainty as well as scarce information from formal sources can lead to informal sources becoming the most powerful channels of information available to group members. These informal groups can be far more powerful and cohesive than their formal counterparts and, as such, can either help or hinder the organization in working towards its goals and objectives. Yet the informal group nuances are the hardest for the acquirer to understand and anticipate as they do not conform to reporting lines or structures.

When an employee enters an organization, whether or not via acquisition, he or she undergoes a socialization process which includes becoming familiar with the organization's procedures and culture. While employees are undergoing this process, their productivity is naturally low and their stress levels higher as they try to learn as quickly as possible how to 'get around' the company. The success of the socialization process depends on both the employee and the organization: how motivated the employee is to comply with the process, and the extent to which the organization will use inducements to keep the individual from leaving the organization during the process. Thus, during this time, the acquirer must make it worth the employee's while to remain with the company in terms of encouragement or inducements. The latter can include pay, training to help them get through the socialization process more quickly or a commitment to understanding and fair behaviour; this in turn can lead employees to more readily accept the new psychological contract and company culture. This is discussed further in Chapter 5.

When joining a company, it can be assumed that employees have done so willingly, thereby suggesting that they are receptive to the organization. Employees in acquired firms can find themselves in the difficult position of being members of an organization into which they never agreed to enter. While they may have been amenable to their original employers, they may not like the acquiring organization or its way of conducting business. Consequently, they may not be willing to undergo the acquirer's socialization process which would normally culminate in an acceptance of the new psychological contract.

Most acquirers overlook the importance of the group on the individual employee. As seen above, the vast majority of employees are highly concerned about the well-being of their group members, both formal and informal. Employees will very carefully assess how the acquirer treats their fellow employees. Callous or unfair treatment, especially during redundancy, can send shockwaves through the entire group in a very negative manner by turning those not directly affected against the acquirer. Word can spread very quickly via the existing informal information channels and may be embellished along the way. The outcome can be a mass psychological revolt against the perpetrator (the acquirer) resulting in many of the wide-scale problems discussed above. This includes an unwillingness to fully undergo the resocialization process as the inducement of understanding and fair behaviour is gone. This is seen very clearly in the Quality Guarding case study discussed in Chapter 8 where a faulty implementation process led to many key middle managers deciding to leave the company. One manager said, 'Many of us will leave just for the sake of that scalpel cut being a touch too deep.'

The level of group upheaval may be dictated, to some extent, by the degree of integration between the target and acquiring firm – the greater the integration the more likely that both formal and informal work groups will be altered or affected by redundancy. These changes include not only those affecting groups of colleagues but also those affecting the manager–subordinate relationship.

Status and procedural concerns: role ambiguity and conflict

After acquisition, some employees will be concerned over what their role will be in the new organization. Areas of concern can include changes in job roles and assignments, in career path, power, status and prestige. As a result they will seek guidance in what to expect regarding how to perform their jobs and what elements of job performance are important in the new organization. If they are unable to determine these factors, role ambiguity can develop. Role ambiguity can be defined as a lack of clarity in performing one's corporate duties which leads to employees not knowing what behaviour is appropriate and, therefore, what behaviour will be rewarded. Research has found that role ambiguity after acquisition is a major employee issue, yet it is likely to be overlooked during implementation, causing major problems for the acquirer. Middle managers are most susceptible to role changes as usually they have had little influence in their job definition and yet have most to lose in terms of career path and job assignments.

Many acquisitions occur for synergy, asset potential and economies of scale, all of which generally require the role of some employees changing. In many cases, affected employees are having to work in new groups and with different tasks and potentially with fewer colleagues. In those cases where cost savings are the acquirer's primary objective, managers may be forced to take on the roles of redundant colleagues which also changes their existing roles. All of this occurs within the backdrop of new organizational procedures and rules which can add greatly to the affected managers' confusion.

After acquisition, role ambiguity may also arise from employees not receiving immediate feedback on what is appropriate behaviour. The first few weeks after an employee enters a new job are spent trying to determine what is the appropriate behaviour in terms of tasks, priorities in their performance and how they are rewarded. The more realistic the job expectation, the easier it is to define one's job and perform it. Employees who have incomplete or incorrect information will have greater difficulty in discovering what their roles should be, thereby increasing the likelihood of role ambiguity. Unfortunately, it is often during this time that newly acquired employees are being assessed as to their ability, yet they do not necessarily understand the structure in which they are being asked to work. This is seen very clearly in Chapter 9 in the Global Products case study.

The importance of changes in role is also linked to cultural issues, as one's role in the company is, in many senses, the manifestation of its culture. In some cases role issues become a major source of contention, such as in those companies with distinct company cultures. This is seen very clearly in the case of Global's acquisitions, where employees' role concerns increased dramatically as it became clear that they were expected to operate within an environment which they did not understand and with which they were given no assistance. But role ambiguity can be just as damaging and harder to expect in those cases where the changes are more subtle. Changes in role at Anglo-American were subtle, with middle managers taking on more personal responsibility, but the changes were anticipated and openly discussed, thereby limiting any role ambiguity (see Chapter 7). One affected manager said, 'I was very nervous (of being promoted) but Gas Appliances were very good and they all helped me, once I made the move it was quite good and I surprised myself that I could do what they thought I could do.' In Quality Guarding, however, the changes in role for middle managers were not any greater but, as they were not anticipated, they were not sufficiently addressed and as a consequence became an ongoing issue until resolved.

Role ambiguity has been associated with inadequate communication and feedback, a common characteristic of the post-acquisition period. This can lead to increased stress, a drop in self-confidence and job performance and can result in an increased sense of futility. Conversely, the lowering of role ambiguity is associated with the formalization of working practices, goal consensus and clarity as well as a change in employee expectations, none of which are typical of the post-acquisition phase.

Research has found that supervisors can play a significant role in the lowering of role ambiguity. Where supervisors were perceived to manage effectively by setting goals and job parameters, helping with problem solving, providing support and feedback on job performance, their subordinates experienced greater role clarity. During acquisition, however, supervisors may not be in a position to provide clear information due to a shortage of time, information and introversion due to their own concerns, thereby inhibiting their ability to manage other employees effectively.

Role conflict occurs when an employee is 'caught in the crossfire of incompatible orders or incompatible expectations' (Rizzo et al. 1970, p. 150). This can have the same outcome as role ambiguity but can actually be more detrimental to the organization by causing employees to feel increased hostility and passive resistance. In the end the employee either overcomes the negative feelings and adjusts his or her expectations of work or rejects the organization entirely and leaves. The turmoil caused by role conflict was seen at Quality Guarding (see Chapter 8) which resulted in some employees rejecting the new organization entirely.

Cultural concerns: the organization's new culture

An organization's culture can be defined as 'tradition and the nature of shared beliefs and expectations about organizational life' (Buono et al., 1985, p. 482). Each organization's culture is unique as it builds up its own history and way of conducting business, and it can become a powerful determinant of employee behaviour as employees share a common belief of how things should be done around the company. Because of the implicitly historical nature of cultural evolution, it is near to impossible to replicate it entirely and it is arguable whether it is possible to maintain it during times of change.

Employees will gravitate towards organizations whose culture has similar beliefs to their own if at all possible within the constraints of the labour market; organizations also recruit individuals whom they feel will 'fit' in the company's culture. What can develop is a distinct and constant way of conducting business as the shared psychological contract operates within the parameters of the organizational culture. This cycle continues as new employees are recruited willingly into the existing culture and perpetuate it.

When acquiring, the two organization's cultures can actually be very dissimilar. These differing beliefs can lead to potential conflicts manifest in differing procedures, schedules, management styles, accepted behaviour, role fulfilment and ultimately the acceptance of the psychological contract. Cultural issues can be a major source of concern during acquisition, especially for managerial employees. What makes the differences even more problematic is that employees tacitly understand their own culture (having unconsciously undergone the socialization process) but often cannot explain it to their new colleagues. Thus, learning the unwritten ways of doing business in a new company is usually discovered via a painstaking process of trial and error which can be disturbing for those employees experiencing acquisition in companies with highly different cultures where the gulf of understanding is great. The greater the cultural differences and the higher the degree of integration chosen by the acquirer, the more employees will be affected by cultural changes and the greater cultural diversity will be; therefore, the greater the potential for problems will be. The issue of culture is dealt with in more detail in Chapter 5, 'The Implementation Process'.

The manifestation of employee concerns during acquisition

Any acquisition, whether or not it is well managed, creates a great deal of uncertainty as employees worry about any changes the process may bring. But importantly, it is the perceived threat of change which causes the large measure of stress; it is often far more stressful than the actual outcome. As a result, any acquisition brings with it drastic changes in employee behaviour. Employee productivity can drop by as much as 50 per cent during the first few months of acquisition with this destabilizing influence taking up to two years to be rectified (Wishard, 1985). Employees can also lose up to two hours of productive work time every day through gossiping about the acquisition (Carbrera, 1971).

The ambiguity and uncertainty of acquisitions manifests itself in both physical and emotional problems. Falling morale and undesirable power struggles can occur during acquisition, both of which further hinder the organization's day-to-day functioning and its ability to cope with the implementation process. Decreases in job satisfaction, organizational commitment, job involvement, morale, performance, perceived organizational and management trustworthiness, and motivation during acquisition, can result in negative physical reactions, emotional distress, increases in absenteeism, intentions to leave and staff turnover. Increases in organization-wide stress, perceived uncertainty and tangible measurements such as absenteeism, acts of sabotage and petty theft, increased employee turnover and intention to quit, and accident rates, occur after acquisition. These traits can occur in both the target and the acquirer; the degree to which they occur in both will depend on the intended degree of integration and amount of personal change as perceived by those affected and not necessarily by the change itself. Employees at all levels from senior management to the shopfloor can feel very threatened even by a friendly, agreed acquisition.

While all of these elements are present in any acquisition to a greater or lesser extent, it is how the acquirer handles the acquisition process which greatly influences the intensity of perceptions in those affected. In effect, any of the negative feelings associated with acquisition are greatly exacerbated by a poorly managed implementation process. Likewise, an acquisition process which is well handled can positively enhance the perceptions of employees discussed above, with higher trustworthiness, management and organizational credibility, belief of communication and intention to stay with the employer all being positive outcomes of a well-managed acquisition implementation.

Behaviour during acquisition: what to expect from employees

Because of the high concerns and emotions discussed above, it is not surprising that after acquisition, employees in both the acquirer and target companies generally behave in a different manner than they do normally. There are certain behavioural characteristics which are often seen after acquisition in both the target employees and the acquiring employees. First, as discussed above, concerns regarding job security, roles, friends, one's status and the company culture run high during acquisition. Another trait which arises is the usage of a 'them and us' comparison at any opportunity pointing out any marked differences between the target and the acquirer, their employees, procedures and culture. One manager acquired by Global (Chapter 9) described this behaviour:

> My boss was tremendously supportive but there were people I worked with who for the first eighteen months, and when it suited them and they thought they could get away with it, would have no hesitation in saying I didn't know this or wasn't doing it right because I wasn't 'one of them'. I saw colleagues who were really crushed by it; I watched them wilt. It was such a shame because they were not untalented people.

There is also a general reminiscing of the past and the 'good old days' which is usually unrealistic. Instead of the reality of corporate life pre-acquisition, employees tend to remember it through 'rose-tinted glasses' forgetting many of the negative aspects. Finally, employees tend to be more lax in their dealings with their fellow employees during acquisition; performance reviews, procedures and general discipline tend to be less stringent during acquisition as employees want to 'go easy' on colleagues during such a difficult time. This tendency towards kindness is fine during acquisition but can create problems after the implementation's completion when life returns to normal.

Behaviour to expect from target employees

Target employees often experience high emotions whether or not there are to be massive changes. As a consequence, the acquirer is often met with strong emotions from these employees including a high degree of fear, wariness and even outright hostility in some cases. Target employees often believe that any action the acquirer takes will include 'hidden agendas' which is a symptom of the low-trust environment existing after acquisition. In addition, most acquired employees believe in a 'worst-case scenario'. For example, if 5 per cent of the workforce is to be made redundant post-acquisition, employees will often believe that 5 per cent is actually 50 per cent and that it automatically includes them.

Perhaps to mask the high levels of fear and to counterbalance arrogant acquirer behaviour, several traits are often seen in target employees. A common characteristic which emerges is a high degree of 'defensive superiority'. This has been described as the employees focusing on those issues or areas where the target feels it is better in performing than the acquirer. Comments such as, 'They bought us because we are good (or better than they are)', are common manifestations of defensive superiority. Another example was seen in the comments of an Infosys manager about his new TeleCable Group colleagues:

> I look across at TeleCom Group colleagues with anger, envy, bewilderment on why they are in their positions: politics and playing games. I am no good at playing games. They just don't hold a candle to us, we get things wrong here at Infosys but we are ten times more professional.

Another trait which is often prevalent post-acquisition is the presence of political behaviour as acquired employees try to find their way around the new organization in a manner which they think will ensure their survival. The combination of employee concerns and failure to be fully socialized in the new company can lead to some target employees saying what they think the acquiring management wants to hear rather than the truth.

Related to this is the common target employee reaction of ceasing to work after acquisition. Because of the lack of clarity which usually follows acquisition in terms of employees' roles and the corporate direction, many employees simply stop working because they are uncertain if their actions will be favourably received by the new owner. The result can be corporate paralysis unless employees are told that the 'old style' behaviour is appropriate until told otherwise or they are given new guidelines to follow.

Finally, more often than not there is large-scale rumour spreading which substantiates any of the negative points above; hidden agendas, political behaviour, lies, 'them and us' mentality, worst-case scenarios, and adverse acquisition-based behaviour are all open for discussion. Generally during acquisition, nobody wants to be the bearer of good news in the target – during times of adversity it is much more popular amongst one's peer group to tell negative stories rather than pleasant ones, thereby feeding on the already existing levels of distrust. This often means the distortion of facts in order to make the story fit the bill.

The most effective means for minimizing the negative aspects of target employee behaviour following acquisition is to sufficiently manage employee expectations in the manner discussed below with the seven factors being crucial for keeping negative behaviour at bay. This includes consistent communication using more than one channel if possible in order to reinforce the central messages, thereby reducing rumour and negativism. In addition, the publishing of the philosophy used during the acquisition and an accepted behaviour, quashing any negative behaviour, rewarding good behaviour, and leading by example are all means of further minimizing negativism after the deal. This is discussed in more detail in Chapter 5.

Behaviour to expect from acquiring employees

Target company employees are not unique in behaving out of character during acquisition – acquiring employees are also prone to certain behavioural anomalies. There is almost always a feeling of 'conqueror's syndrome', whereby the acquiring employees feel that solely because they are the acquirers, that their systems and people are automatically better than those of the target. As one director whose company was bought by Global (see Chapter 9) said:

Companies which are bought are seen by acquiring management as failures. It doesn't matter how good they are, the sheer fact that they were bought makes them failures. So there is that uncertainty about anyone who has been bought, particularly if they were middle or senior management and they were leading that company.

The outcome of this can be a great deal of unconscious arrogance displayed by acquiring employees vis-à-vis their target company colleagues, often without them even realizing that they are doing it. In light of the defensive behaviour seen in most target employees, the effect of this arrogant behaviour is amplified. In addition, acquiring employees generally feel in control of the process with the tacit assumption that as they are the acquirers, decisions will automatically favour them and not the target. On those occasions where decisions 'go the other way', acquiring employees are usually shocked and filled with disbelief. This is especially acute in cases of redundancies being felt on both sides. If acquiring employees' expectations are not managed prior to this happening, when it does occur the shock effect is far greater.

Finally, there is always an assumption on the part of acquirers that the systems and procedures being adopted are those of the acquirer and that those systems are fully understood by those being acquired. There is usually little need felt to explain the underlying procedures or culture within the acquirer or the new entity, but rather it is assumed that target employees will automatically and quickly pick up the ways of doing business. As a result, it is common for acquiring employees to judge newly acquired employees without the latter fully understanding the company and with the former not understanding the ramifications of their actions. Because this fact is also often overlooked by acquiring employees, the result can be an over-critical and inaccurate judgement of target employees.

ADDRESSING EMPLOYEE CONCERNS: THE IMPORTANCE OF MANAGING EMPLOYEE EXPECTATIONS

As discussed earlier, employees' concerns are greatly affected by the acquirer's actions during the implementation process. Contrary to what many believe, it is not what you do to employees after acquisition which causes the stress, uncertainty and concern, but rather how you do it. Countless studies conducted throughout the US and Europe suggest that employees find the uncertainty related to acquisition hard to bear; in fact, the uncertainty associated with acquisition is what causes much of the stress, not the events themselves. *Employees will accept almost all outcomes after acquisition, including negative ones, if they are psychologically prepared for them prior to their occurrence and are treated fairly during the process of implementation.* The business world has changed – the vast majority of employees accept that they no longer have jobs for life. What has not changed, however, is the average employee's desire to be treated justly, and this includes prior warning of fundamental changes to one's working environment. As discussed in the Introduction and Chapter 1, this amounts to the process of managing employee expectations, including:

1. the pre-acquisition planning phase
2. communication of the post-acquisition plan
3. implementation of the post-acquisition plan including managing discrepancies between communicated and enacted plans via feedback procedures
4. stabilization and assessment period.

   The process of managing employee expectations via an acquisition plan is outlined in the next four chapters with each discussing in more detail the four stages of the process. The psychological reasons as to why it is important, however, will be discussed below.

Managing employee expectations: a definition

Expectations in a work context can be defined as the beliefs employees hold about which actions and behaviours lead to what outcomes within an organization. Expectations differ from psychological contracts in that the latter is a relationship between the specific organization and its employees; expectations are developed not only within the context of the present employer but over a lifetime of previous work experiences. Yet expectations are constantly being modified in light of the current environment, communication and employee interactions. If any of these elements are either ambiguous or conflicting, the ability to manage expectations is lessened. Employees can also become disillusioned if their organizational expectations are not reinforced by subsequent actions on the part of the organization.

   Unmet expectations are the 'discrepancy between what a person encounters on the job in the way of positive and negative experiences and what he or she expected to encounter' (Porter and Steers, 1973, p. 152). When expectations are not met, employees experience a feeling I call 'expectation dissonance' where they must try to reconcile themselves to what actually happened, rather than what they expected to happen. Employees describe the feelings as unexpected alarm and surprise as they try to rationalize the stated communication or behaviour with the preconceived expectation of what they thought would occur. If further information is provided to explain any changes in stated plan, the dissonance is greatly reduced. Only once this balance has been internally redressed and rationalized do the warning bells cease. For the reconciliation to occur, a new explanation needs to be internalized either supporting the old preconceptions or developing new ones.

From the employees' point of view, the process they undergo is threefold regarding their expectations in response to the acquirer's actions. Thus it is inherently reactive rather than proactive in assessing information as it becomes available from the acquirer and a variety of other sources. The process includes:

- **expectation setting** – the employees' search for information and setting of expectations
- **expectation appraisal** – the assessment of their expectations vis-à-vis the events which occur
- **expectation outcome** – their reconciliation of the expectations and events.

It is very difficult to alter employees' first impressions as these serve as the basis for their existing and internalized attitudes. Thus employees will generally attempt to reconcile themselves to any differences during the expectation outcome within the boundaries of their set expectations. When this happens, their expectations are met; if not, they are redefined in light of the dissonance experienced.

When employees' expectations are met, employees experience an increase in organizational commitment, job satisfaction, management and communication source credibility, and feelings of fairness. Conversely, there has been found a negative relationship between met expectations and employee turnover, intention to quit, and damaged trustworthiness of the organization.

During acquisition, the expectation setting stage between the organization and employee is often hindered by the acquisition process itself: through potentially unwilling acquired employees, the absence of a clear post-acquisition plan by the acquirer, a faulty implementation process, or a combination of these. If the new organizational vision, processes or culture are not discussed openly after a merger or acquisition, the organization cannot expect the new target company employees' expectations or behaviour to necessarily fall in line with the acquiring organization's expectations. Rather, the employees' expectation of work has been developed by previous employers and will most likely remain in that format until new behaviour can be accepted and learned. Employees who are acquired need to undergo much of the same socialization process that new recruits undergo when joining an organization. The amount of change related to the acquisition and, hence, the amount of organization learning required by target employees, will depend on numerous factors including cultural diversity between the two companies, the degree of integration pursued and the changes new employees will experience in terms of job performance, work groups and procedures.

Of the five companies studied, only one – Anglo-American – adequately addressed all the issues of expectation management, and even they were criticized by some shopfloor employees as not going far enough. The ability to manage expectations by the other four cases ranged from managing only part of the process (Global) to total mismanagement of employee expectations (Infosys). Acquisition success was related to the ability of the acquirer to manage employee expectations and not the degree of change inflicted upon the target. As acquirers rarely follow the process of acquisition described above, it is not surprising that few acquirers can satisfactorily manage employee expectations throughout implementation; those who do are successful, those who do not are met with varying degrees of success and failure.

Factors influencing the ability to manage employee expectations

When assessing the acquirer's ability to manage employee expectations, seven factors are highly relevant: communication, honesty of communication, consistency of communication with subsequent action, fairness of action, logic of action, trustworthiness of the organization and its management, and management credibility. Not only were these found to be key to managing employee expectations in my research, they were found to be important in retaining staff and overall acquisition success.

They will be discussed in turn.

1. **Communication** is the cornerstone of managing expectations – the acquirer's management can have the most sophisticated acquisition plan but if its intent is not communicated to affected employees, the bulk of the positive effect associated with extensive planning is lost. Communication is also crucial as its form and substance play such a critical role in two other factors, honesty of communication and consistency. Without it, there is no expectation to judge; with uncommunicated intent, employees will form their own expectations without the acquirer's input. In these circumstances, it is likely that their expectations will be wrong.

2. **Honesty of communication** is also crucial for managing expectations in that those sources of communication which are perceived to be honest are ones which employees will trust in the future. Those communication channels which disseminate incorrect information are never seen as fully trustworthy again. This is seen quite often in the internal and external communication surrounding the implications of acquisition. In some cases, acquirers will publicly announce to shareholders, the City or analysts, major structural changes to the organization including job losses or relocations, yet internally promote the idea of no changes occurring. When change does inevitably occur, management's credibility as a source of honest communication is shattered. Instead, the source which has proven correct in the past is relied upon in the future. This is discussed further in Chapter 4 and seen in the Quality Guarding case (Chapter 8).

Research has consistently shown that employees would rather know the truth via honest communication even if it is bad news, than be told platitudes which ultimately turn out to be incorrect. In fact, the sense of betrayal in feeling misled far outweighs the short-lived relief of business as usual. At the time of acquisition, if honest answers about the future cannot be given, then those affected react best to an honest, 'I don't know the answer but I will find out for you by next week' (and then the appropriate follow-through) rather than a misleading lie. Employees will also accept that they are not privy to all commercially sensitive information and that in some cases they cannot be told certain details – rather than be misled, an honest reply to this effect is a far greater winner of respect, thereby enhancing management's credibility.

3. **Consistency of communication and subsequent action** is the initial action from which employees assess whether or not an employer managed their expectations. If a message is communicated by the employer and then unfulfilled, expectational dissonance will occur; if met, both credibility and belief in the communication source are enhanced. If a message is communicated and then not fulfilled and an adequate explanation is given detailing the reasons why it did not happen, management credibility can be restored to a greater extent (depending on the believability and logic of the explanation). A Quality Guarding employee explained:

> If your mate invites you over for dinner and asks, 'What is your favourite dessert?', to which you reply 'Apple pie', this leads you to expect that you will be served apple pie when you go to their house. When you are then served chocolate cake, it leaves you disappointed, when if he hadn't said anything, you wouldn't be. If he turned around

and said, 'My wife tried to make an apple pie but burnt it in the oven so we had to go out and buy the chocolate cake', then it is all right again. But they need to tell you in order for it to be okay.

This example also demonstrates that communication is not necessarily spoken but that expectations can be formed on the basis of inference, and, in many cases, they are. Thus communication is more than what is just spoken; therefore, the greater the number of channels giving a single message followed by specific and visible actions, the less likelihood of misunderstanding occurring.

4. **Fairness of action** was one of the factors in my research that was mentioned most often in those acquisitions in which the implementation process did not go well – Quality Guarding and Infosys. As mentioned above, as long as employees were aware of future events via honest communication and then were treated fairly during the implementation process, the vast majority accepted the outcome – whether positive or negative. How employees were treated became fundamental to this. In those cases where employees were treated unfairly, they began to question not only management credibility and their perceived trustworthiness, but also the processes behind the decisions and the organization as a whole, including its culture. This concept is explored further in Chapter 5 as a key element of procedural justice theory.

    The other element of fairness is the relativity of actions between one function or site and the others. In the case of Quality Guarding, the fact that head office survived relatively unscathed while the operating units suffered redundancies, caused further resentment. One operational manager commented:

    > It is just par for the course that they [Group] stayed intact while they decimated the regions; I remember speaking to a secretary at Group, subsequently they have had to move offices but at the time they were still at [the stately home] and she said, 'Oh it is fine, isn't it? Not that big a change.' It made my blood boil. I know Group is isolated from us but that was ridiculous.

5. **Logic of action** is an often overlooked element of acquisition as many managers assume that employees will automatically see the logic behind decisions. This includes the rationale behind the original purchase of a target. As in expectation formulation, if there is no logic surrounding a particular action which is communicated or totally evident, employees will draw their own conclusions. As discussed earlier, target employees

will usually assume the worst; this also holds true when decisions are not perceived as logical. In cases where the logic is not seen or what is communicated is not believed, claims of 'hidden agendas' will be made and believed. This is seen most clearly in Chapter 11, regarding Infosys, where illogical implementation decisions led to employees believing other issues played a major role in their determination. One Infosys director commented:

> It seems to us that a lot of the decisions being taken are being taken on political rather than business rational reasons; I am aware of a number of cases where the commercial arguments seem to me and everyone else I talk to here, glaringly obvious to us. From our point of view they can only be raised for political or personal reasons.

The logic of the acquisition, while obvious to senior employees, is also not necessarily apparent to all other employees. Using the acquisition process outlined in Chapter 3, employees will find using an acquisition overview a useful step in clarifying what can be rather nebulous or generalized reasons for buying a company.

6. **Trustworthiness of the organization and management** is fast becoming considered a source of competitive advantage. It is also crucial for the acceptance of any changes to the employee–employer relationship, such as in redefining psychological contracts. Yet trust or its precursors, believability and trustworthiness, require time to develop and, as a result, are not usually present after acquisition. The process for developing it is long and arduous. Yet even during downsizing the foundations of trust can be laid via managing employee expectations. In the case of Anglo-American, employees repeatedly said that while they did not necessarily like their new owners, they believed them and found them trustworthy because they said what they were going to do prior to doing it. When they did so, they did it professionally. The quickest way an acquirer can destroy the opportunity for building trust is to mislead acquired employees or fail to deliver on timescales or outcomes.

    After acquisition, acquiring employees can also experience changes in trust with the acquirer, especially if they feel misled during the process. If they undergo redundancies or a 'reverse takeover' when it is not expected, employers can find even long-serving employees' trust greatly damaged. This is seen at Quality Guarding in Chapter 8 in which the unfair perceptions of the implementation process led to damaged trust and a wholesale questioning of the new organization's culture by many shaken employees who had previously wholeheartedly trusted their employer. One such manager of 18 years' service commented:

> It has been handled atrociously and the whole thing has been an unmitigated disaster for the last six months. The company has lost its way, a lot of people are gone and we are starting to see people go by their own choice, it is not the same company.

7. **Management credibility**, like trust, not only aids in delivering a successful acquisition implementation process, but is also a direct beneficiary if the process has gone well. When the process is seen as being handled professionally, management credibility increases; if the obverse occurs, it suffers. In those cases where the acquirer has a charismatic leader, it is to their benefit to ensure he or she meets as many acquired employees as possible. As discussed above, acquired employees will tend to view events in a negative light – if a powerful leader is visible in the acquirer, this can go a long way towards quieting concerns as employees experience his or her leadership first-hand. In both Gas Appliances and TeleCable Group, two very different but equally accomplished leaders positively influenced target employees – the former by virtue of his knowledge and delivery and the latter due to his honesty and integrity. Each leader's positive perception lent credence to the acquiring organization and its implementation plan.

Interestingly, the role of management credibility and trust were twofold: not only do they positively affect perceptions of the implementation process, but also they were seen as outcomes; in those cases where the acquirer managed employee expectations sufficiently, management credibility and trust were enhanced in the affected employees' eyes. Likewise, in those cases where management credibility and trust were present, they served to facilitate the expectation management process. The seven factors also seemed heavily interdependent on each other in that if one is mismanaged during the acquisition process, it affects the other factors – almost a 'domino effect'. For example, logic of action enhanced management credibility while the quality of communication influenced perceptions of consistency of communication and action as well as the believability of communication (see Figure 2.6). The end result is a three-part process with communication serving as the foundation, trust and management credibility becoming outcomes and the other factors facilitating the development of the outcomes.

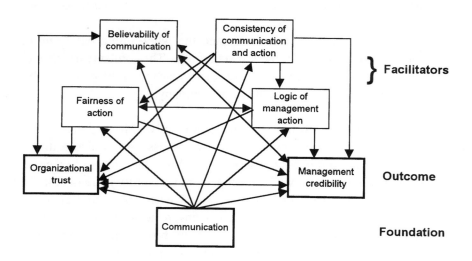

Fig. 2.6 *Relationship between acquisition factors*

Relationship between managing expectations and intention to quit the organization

In my research, the employees interviewed were asked to answer 'Yes' or 'No' to certain questions, the results of which are discussed below.[1] The first of these questions was, 'Did the acquirer manage your expectations during the acquisition?' (see Table 2.2). As will be seen in the case studies, the five acquirers varied quite widely in how successfully they managed employee expectations. At one end of the spectrum, Anglo-American managed employee expectations for the wide majority of employees. At the other end, TeleCable Group did not. It should come as no surprise, therefore, that Anglo-American's acquisition of Gas Appliances was the 'most successful' acquisition with employees accepting the changes and results showing most quickly. TeleCable Group's acquisition of Infosys was the least successful acquisition with highly dissatisfied employees and a great deal of upheaval made all the more unfortunate by its strategically good fit and potential.

1. The number of responses was 154 for all except Table 2.1, where it was 151.

In terms of relating expectation management and acquisition success, a good indicator of success is an employee's intention to quit the organization. Using the actual number of resignations is not good representation of employee disenchantment due to economic and other factors which may prevail at the time. Instead, in the study discussed above, employees were asked if they would leave their current organization for a job with similar pay, career prospects and location (see Table 2.3).

Table 2.2   Did the acquirer manage employee expectations during the acquisition process?

Company	Yes, they did (%)	No, they did not (%)
Anglo-American/Gas Appliances	74	26
Service Conglomerate/Quality Guarding	25	75
Discovery/Scottish Yeast	48	52
Global	50	50
TeleCable Group/Infosys	3	97

Table 2.3   Is it your intention to leave the organization (by case study)?

Company	Yes, it is (%)	No, it is not (%)
Anglo-American/Gas Appliances	0	100
Service Conglomerate/Quality Guarding	41	59
Discovery/Scottish Yeast	17	83
Global	7	93
TeleCable Group/Infosys	55	45

The mismanagement of expectations did not necessarily lead to employees intending to leave the organization, yet the successful management of expectation factors and outcomes seemed related to a willingness on the part of employees to remain with the organization. This sense of 'goodwill' was not necessarily present in those employees who felt their expectations had not been managed; it was almost as if they didn't expect to have them managed. Thus those acquirers who do not manage employee expectations in totality may not experience a mass exodus of employees, but those who do manage employee expectations may find themselves overcoming any acquisition difficulties far more quickly and easily than those who do not.

Table 2.4 is an amalgamation of the five studies' findings based on employees' positions in the organization; those who reported being the most vulnerable in terms of leaving the organization were middle managers (enactors). It is interesting to note that while all employees were equally concerned during much of the acquisition, negotiators reported the lowest intention to leave the organization by the time the interviews took place. An explanation for this is that at the end of the implementation process, the negotiators who remain are back in a controlling position of their future roles and concerns and this created a willingness to stay within the organization. As discussed earlier, however, enactors had the most complex concerns and ones which generally were not totally managed. These unanswered questions seem to have resulted in a higher level of 'expectational dissonance' and a greater desire to leave the organization. As these managers probably have a greater opportunity to leave the organization, the threat to the acquirer of a mass exodus of talent is very real.

Table 2.4   Is it your intention to leave the organization (by organization position)?

Employee position	Yes, it is (%)	No, it is not (%)
Director (Negotiator)	13	87
Middle manager (Enactor)	43	57
Workforce (Recipient)	27	73

There are implications for acquirers. First, if the acquirer has few spare resources and needs the acquired employees to remain with the target and motivated, then managing their expectations is a crucial element to the acquisition implementation process. Likewise, if any employees (such as middle managers) are seen as key to the organization's success, they need to have their concerns adequately addressed if they are to stay and be productive in the new organization. Second, enactors or middle managers are often key to the implementation success, yet their expectations are usually mismanaged and they are the most likely to leave the organization. If an acquirer feels these employees are key to the deal's success by virtue of their link to the shopfloor, their expertise in case of board dismissal or in acquisition implementation, it is crucial to ensure adequate care is taken in managing these employees during the implementation period. Finally, while mismanaging employee expectations may not necessarily lead to a mass exodus of employees, by doing it right, the acquirer creates a feeling of goodwill with acquired employees that can serve as a very real employee motivator, even during times of organizational upheaval and change.

3   The Process of Pre-acquisition Planning: The Foundation for Acquiring Success

INTRODUCTION

Although the pre-acquisition phase is the most complicated stage of acquisition, it remains an essential element, for it serves as the foundation for the process that follows. The difficulty comes with making the decisions that underpin the process, not with developing a workable plan. Outlined below is a process for pre-acquisition planning and several key decisions an acquirer must make prior to buying the target:

- the objectives of the transaction
- the degree of integration which is most effective
- how to choose your advisors
- speed of implementation
- the levels of employee participation
- the role of target management in the new company
- integrating systems and employees
- addressing cultural differences.

The culmination of these decisions is the amalgamation of the post-acquisition implementation plan and an acquirer prepared for 'Day One' of the acquisition. The difficult element of this process is making the decisions which form the basis of the plan, not actually drawing up the plan. What is found lacking in many pre-acquisition plans is the thought behind the decisions. Ironically, the more thought and preparation that go into planning, the easier it is to design and implement the plan.

THE PROCESS OF PRE-ACQUISITION PLANNING

Pre-acquisition planning is a grossly undervalued yet fundamental element of acquisition success. In fact, the nature of its importance lies in the fact

that it serves as the foundation for acquisition communication and implementation. Its success is important for several reasons:

1. Pre-acquisition planning can greatly simplify the communication and
    post-acquisition implementation process. In fact, the last stage of pre-
    acquisition planning, the acquisition blueprint, serves as the
    post-acquisition plan.
2. To communicate effectively on 'Day One' of the acquisition, adequate
    prior planning must have occurred in order to write, prepare, co-ordinate
    and distribute the communication information pack.
3. If one is acquiring and planning to introduce significant changes during
    the early stages of the implementation process, the decisions underlying
    these changes need to be addressed prior to the deal's completion during
    the planning stages in order for them to be communicated effectively
    and planned with enough lead time to ensure that it is done professionally.
4. During acquisition, the acquirer and its personnel have one opportunity
    to make a first impression, with all subsequent interactions being
    modifications of that opinion. With sufficient planning it is easier to make
    a first impression of a knowledgeable and professional management who
    is in control of a planned process. If one has not done adequate planning,
    it is unlikely that this will be the impression given.

In spite of the benefits of pre-acquisition planning, less than one in five
acquirers actually do what they consider to be adequate pre-acquisition
planning prior to the deal. There is the potential for a great mismatch of
expectations as most acquired employees assume that their acquirers have
done pre-acquisition planning. Many target employees therefore look to the
acquirer with great expectations of what would be said and done only to
find that these expectations are not met, with the likely result of a poor first
impression. KPMG's recent pan-European study found that of the CEOs
interviewed, the most commonly cited 'lesson learned' was not having
done adequate pre-acquisition planning and not allowing enough time for
it (KPMG, 1997).

When looking at the four-part process of acquiring – pre-acquisition
planning, communication, implementation and stabilization, as described
in the Introduction – the process of pre-acquisition can be broken down into
five further elements (see Figure 3.1). These five elements of pre-acquisition
planning will be discussed in turn and examples given as to their application.
But before beginning one's pre-acquisition planning, one must choose
which advisors are going to play a key role in the process.

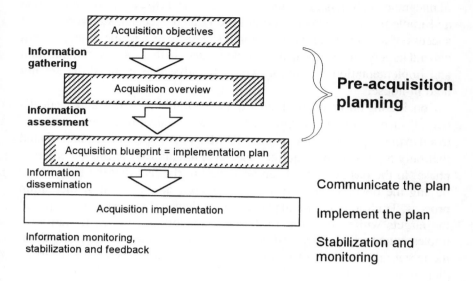

Fig. 3.1 *Pre-acquisition planning phase of acquisition*

Choosing your advisors

One of the biggest dilemmas faced by first-time acquirers is the choice of advisors: strategic consultants, lawyers, accountants, bankers, stockbrokers, various due diligence experts, market research providers, communication companies for internal and external communication and consultants to help with the implementation process. There are two key decisions which must be made prior to selecting who will advise you: which services are important to you in assuring not only that you secure the target but also ensuring that the acquisition is a success, and who do you choose to help guide you through the process?

Certain services are mandatory during acquisition, such as legal advice and due diligence indemnification. Increasingly, other skills, such as corporate finance advice, communication advice and implementation services, are being brought in-house thereby negating the need for outside help. These are likely, however, to be skills held by more seasoned acquirers rather than novices. A rule of thumb for hiring external advisors is to determine which services you feel are important for the deal's success and getting advice in those areas. These will differ from deal to deal. In some acquisitions there is little attempt at synergies or there exists a low degree of integration between the acquirer and target – in these cases, communication and implementation experts are not likely to be needed. Conversely, the success of a full merger with economies of scale as a prime objective will depend largely on how the deal is implemented; in this case, communication and implementation consulting would be advisable if the skills are not held in-house.

Considering how closely allied acquisition implementation and the deal's overall success are, it is surprising how few organizations hire consultants to aid in the implementation process. KPMG's 1997 study of acquirers found that only 5 per cent of acquirers used consultants for the implementation phase. In the past, this has been attributed to the fact that the individuals buying the business are not the individuals leading the implementation process. Traditionally, the managing and finance directors have acquired the targets while operationally based managers have been tasked with implementing any changes post-deal; new managers must learn quickly about the target and the deal, often losing continuity. One way to alleviate this dichotomy is to employ one group of advisors which spans the acquisition process from pre-acquisition planning or due diligence right through to involvement in the implementation process; another is for the person charged with the implementation also to sit on the negotiating team.

Once an acquirer determines which advisors are needed for the acquisition, it must then decide who best serves its specific needs. In some cases, advisors are either long-standing or pre-selected for a variety of reasons (for example, a merchant bank bringing a target to the attention of the acquirer). In many cases, however, the acquirer must choose its advisors. This choice can be based on many factors; for example, size, reputation, expertise in a specific industry or geography, or personal relationship.

In choosing an investment bank, for instance, one must decide whether to go with a large name or a smaller niche player. Both have their strengths and weaknesses. Large banks such as some of the American houses bring with them stellar reputations and huge placing power. If one is reliant on placing paper to buy the target this may be the preferred option. Similarly, if one is a first-time acquirer and needs to impress the target or financial institutions, then choosing a prestigious partner may be the best way forward. But this comes at a price. One large American house has said recently 'off the record' that it will not consider a deal which does not generate at least $5 million in fees; due to the current merger wave, this selectivity may not be uncommon. Second, a new or smaller client will not take the priority position that say, a Shell, General Motors or Unilever would with these institutions.

In some cases it is preferable to go with a boutique or niche player. In many cases they can offer greater expertise in a specific industry such as financial services or biotechnology or in a geographic location. Second, they can offer much the same level of expertise and professionalism as the larger players, but at a lower cost. Finally, as a client, you may find that your business is more important to them relative to the larger houses. But you may find that they don't have the placing power of their larger counterparts.

What every acquirer desires is an advisor who is looking out for the acquirer's best interests and who is not just interested in getting a deal done in order to earn a fee. One investment banker told me that he has earned more business in the long run by telling his clients not to do a deal when appropriate rather than doing a bad deal, although this attitude is not necessarily the longer-term perspective prevalent in the major financial centres. In order to find advisors who are looking out for your interests, there are several routes to take.

The most reliable way to ensure advisors are working for you and not for their own fee generation is to find key advisors and, over time, build personal relationships with them. In this way they will understand your business and long-term strategy. To find individual advisors who have expertise and integrity, ask people's opinions: ask colleagues, trade organizations, friends, suppliers and customers whom they have used or recommend. Take the time to meet the advisor and get references from previous clients to understand exactly what their role was and how well they performed. As this is a time-consuming process, it is worth doing prior to the beginning of a transaction in order to build a working relationship while not under the stress of a deal.

Another issue which arises when assessing advisors is their fee structure. Success-based fees inherently create an urge on the part of the advisor to get the deal done at any price, while retainers are costly. Some acquirers use a combination of both to mitigate the 'drive for the deal'. Advisors getting paid a percentage of the transaction is also a source of contention; it is ironic that advisors get paid more if they get the acquirer to pay more for the target. Some acquirers get around this by offering advisors an incentive for coming in below a given price; for instance, by giving advisors their ceiling price that they are willing to pay for the target, with any savings under that price resulting in a percentage bonus for the advisors.

Acquisition objectives

When a company first decides to acquire, they should be aware of the risks involved. Roughly half of acquisitions fail to deliver what was intended. Even with expert advice, the transaction can be a failure. Bearing this in mind, it is worth the acquirer considering exactly what they are hoping to achieve by acquiring.

Other options

If one is acquiring with a strategic intent in mind, it is surprising how few acquirers explore other options open to them before taking the plunge of a full merger or acquisition. Because of acquisitions' risky nature, other options should be considered to see if they can meet the acquirer's strategic needs without the associated risk. Other potential options can include joint ventures, strategic alliances, or long-term customer or supplier relationships (discussed below).

A **joint venture** is a newly established entity with at least two owners and ownership split in some manner between the parties. It enables the two companies to work together on a neutral basis while protecting their existing businesses in a way in which acquisition does not. It is also commonly used in Asia and the Middle East where some nations require foreign companies to form joint venture arrangements in order to trade or manufacture in that country. The incoming company often provides new technology and manufacturing prowess while the host joint venture partner supplies local culture and political knowledge and assistance and, in many cases, the workforce. It is vital not to underestimate the importance of the local partner's role in this type of joint venture agreement as their insight into local customs – and especially governments – can be crucial to the venture's success. In these circumstances two points are important to ensure success: finding the right partner and negotiating the best ownership split. In terms of the latter, it is a mistake to believe that the widely acknowledged figures of foreign allowed ownership are etched in stone; rather, they depend on the attractiveness of the inward investment in terms of technology and capital and are open to negotiation. Thus it is important for the incoming partner to negotiate the most advantageous position possible when investing.

Strategic alliances can also be used instead of acquisition or as a first step towards a merger or acquisition process between the parties. Alliances have been seen most commonly in industries where government interests or size have precluded the ability to merge, such as the airline and telecommunications industry, but is being seen more often now as a 'testing of the water' rather than a headlong plunge into merger (for example, Industrial Bank of Japan and Nomura Securities). Alliances can run the gamut from a casual cross-referral of business between two companies all the way to a complex cross-holding of shares and ownership between those parties involved. An alliance offers the parties the opportunity to get to know each other by working closely together but without the risk associated with acquisition or merger. This closer knowledge of the parties prior to merger can lead to greater trust and mutual understanding between the parties and, therefore, a lower risk of misunderstanding if merger is to occur down the road.

Long-term customer and supplier agreements can derive much of the benefit associated with acquiring vertically up or down a supply or distribution chain, but again, without the risk of acquisition attached. It is common, most notably in the automobile industry, for these relationships to include customer or supplier involvement in new product development and in improving manufacturing delivery capabilities. These can also serve as the foundation for a future acquisition or merger while allowing both parties to work together before such a drastic step is taken.

While acquisition may be the logical or preferred route to achieving the organization's long-term objectives, it is always worth considering the other options. If the due diligence process uncovers cultural or management structure problems which may negatively impact the deal's overall success, it is worth the acquirer exploring other options which could perhaps achieve the organization's goals. It is best for acquirers to keep as many options open as possible, as information may become available which could affect the deal and its overall success.

Acquisition objectives and the reasons for acquiring

If one decides that the best route for achieving one's corporate goals in the allocated timeframe is acquisition, then the acquirer can begin tracking and securing a target. During this process what should remain foremost in the mind of the acquirer is the reason for buying the business. This is the first step of pre-acquisition planning (see Figure 3.2).

If one is buying for, say, market share, a list of potential candidates which fit the criteria may be drawn up, assessed and tracked. This may be done internally or externally with the help of advisors. In either case it may be worth tracking key targets for a specific business or geography with the hopes that they will some day become available. A more proactive approach is to approach the owner of the target and ask if it is for sale or whether or not its sale is anticipated in the future. Two clear benefits are that this approach may preclude an 'auction' with other bidders which could potentially drive up the purchase price, and it also allows the sale to be conducted in some degree of privacy away from the public gaze. More often than not, however, the ability to buy a business presents itself as a fleeting opportunity; therefore, deadlines are tight. It is very difficult to operate in this environment and ensure that adequate due diligence and planning have taken place. In

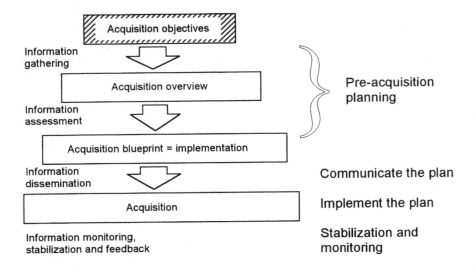

Fig. 3.2 *Acquisition objectives: the first step of pre-acquisition planning*

these cases, it is an advantage to bring in external resources to aid in the process.

There are many reasons for acquiring, both personal and strategic. A UK study asked acquirers why they acquired and found a whole host of reasons for acquiring, including to 'sort out another problem' and to 'retrieve "face" ', along with the more traditional responses (Hunt et al., 1987). In fact, 31 per cent said the major motivation for their last acquisition was not strategic but personal or political (see Table 3.1) (ibid.). The most commonly mentioned reasons (both strategic and personal) for acquisition were related to market share, acquiring new assets in terms of technology or skills, the improvement of financial indicators and sending the right messages to the financial institutions.

When examining the reasons given for acquiring, two issues stand out. First, several objectives are related; defending markets and acquiring for market share enable an organization to strengthen its position vis-à-vis its customers in an existing market. Earnings per share (EPS) and return on investment (ROI) enhancement are related to the acquirer's ability to manage the target's assets upon completion. Second, any personal or political motivation is achieved upon completion of the deal and does not depend on whether or not the transaction is successful in the long term.

Table 3.1　Motivation for acquisition

Political/personal reason for acquisition	Dominant or primary motivation (%)	Mentioned motivation (%)
Sending the right signals to the 'City'*	20	40
Chairman's insistence	8	35
Retrieve 'face'	5	18
Rise in technology league	–	15
Impress competition	3	8
Buying a tradition	–	8
Cash cow for other bids	3	5
Sort out another problem	–	3
Financial or strategic reason for acquisition	**Dominant or primary motivation (%)**	**Mentioned motivation (%)**
Return on investment improvement	10	33
Earnings per share improvement	3	3
Assets improvement	–	15
Market share	33	100
Technical capacity	10	35
Management capability	–	33
Synergy/economies of scale	8	25
Defending markets	5	18

* The capital markets for the UK, based in the City of London, with Wall Street being the equivalent in the US.

Source:　Reproduced with permission from J.W. Hunt et al., Acquisition: The Human Factor, London: London Business School–EZI, p. 27. © 1987, London Business School and Egon Zendher International.

Strategic reasons for acquisition

When one buys a business for personal reasons, it has no impact on subsequent implementation-based decisions. In other words, it is not related to the degree of integration chosen by the acquirer nor the implementation of an acquisition plan, because the sheer act of buying the target means that you have achieved your objective. Thus I discount personal reasons for buying a company as a sound business decision. If the reasons for the transaction cannot be placed on the front page of the *Financial Times* or *Wall Street Journal* (which they may be!), the deal is not worth considering. Thus only strategic objectives are discussed further in this book. With this in mind, the strategic objectives for acquisition can be grouped into six reasons:

1. **Market penetration**, where an organization acquires for market power. This can be via customer-base similarities, the strengthening of power vis-à-vis the customer base, increased market share, market share protection or expanding on a geographic basis.
2. **Vertical expansion**, in which organizations attempt to gain greater control over the procurement of resources, distribution channels or technology via vertical or related acquisition.
3. **Financial synergies**, where organizations acquire in order to achieve earnings enhancement via accounting modifications, tax breaks or more attractive financing terms and facilities.
4. **Market entry**, where organizations acquire to enter new markets, in related or unrelated markets (diversification strategy), or to enter new geographic regions, such as in cross-border acquisition, or to enter into a new but unrelated industry.
5. **Asset potential or synergy**, where organizations acquire because their management believes they can better use the target company's assets. This can be via more effective or aggressive management, transfer of technology or knowledge, increased use of synergies with the acquiring organization or by a change in control systems.
6. **Economies of scale**, involving the integration of parts or the whole of the target and acquiring organizations. This streamlining can take the form of combining operating sites, administrative departments, functions and/or counter-cyclical business lines in order to achieve cost savings via rationalization.

How far do you integrate the target and acquirer?

When acquiring, there is the delicate balance of trying to achieve the acquirer's goals in the quickest time possible yet without disrupting the target's structure from which the skills originate to the point where the benefits are not realized. A large element of this debate is how far one integrates the target into the acquirer (or in some cases, vice versa). There is a wide spectrum of options open to the acquirer, ranging from a laissez-faire approach with little contact between target and acquirer, to a full integration or merger of both entities. Full integration is defined as the 'generalized adaptation of the acquiring organization's operating, control and planning systems and procedures, and complete structural and cultural absorption of the acquired firms' (Pablo, 1994, p. 807).

While an acquirer can sit anywhere along the spectrum of integration, I have found that generally there are four stages of integration open to the acquirer with regard to the degree of integration its management chooses:

1. **'Total autonomy' policy**, in which the target company does not have a physical integration with the acquirer but instead is controlled entirely via financial controls. The target is left in a stand-alone capacity to operate as it did prior to the acquisition. Examples of this can include the purchase of a company in order to secure a quality component needed for production, to gain entry into a new geographic location or to achieve financial synergies. This approach is generally uncommon in situations other than those mentioned above.

2. **Restructuring followed by financial controls**, where a target company is acquired, modified to some extent by the acquiring company, and then left to operate in a stand-alone capacity with little interaction with other business units. Financial controls are implemented to ensure that the business unit complies with head office strategies and objectives. Examples of this could include the introduction of new technology or more efficient working practices, the replacement of existing management with new managers supplied by the acquiring company, or making the target's assets work more efficiently.

3. **Centralization or integration of key functions**, involving the combining of one or more key functions or departments with the intention of achieving cost savings via economies of scale. This could include the merging of marketing or administrative departments or centralizing of functions at a head office location.

4. **Full integration**, occuring when, after acquisition, the target and acquiring companies merge the operations ostensibly into one for the intended achievement of economies of scale, substantial cost savings and the fulfilment of operational synergies.

There are several issues which should be considered when deciding how far to integrate the target and acquirer. First, the degree of autonomy given to the target company can be a major concern to employees, especially at senior levels as it is often related to certain outcomes. Fuller integration is often associated with job losses and a loss of power on the part of the target and, as such, it is seen to be a determining factor for some employees as to whether or not they remain with the company. What seems to be critical is not the actual degree of autonomy granted to employees post-acquisition but what they perceive to be their level of autonomy within the constraints of financial and other controls. Senior employees who are used to autonomous working may perceive the changes post-acquisition to be a drop in status or role and, therefore, leave the company. Supporting this, research has found that the greater the degree of integration, the greater the likelihood of senior target employees leaving the company voluntarily.

In addition, the further an acquirer integrates the target into an existing operation (or vice versa), the greater the complexity of the implementation process. The number of employees affected increases, potentially spanning the length of the organizational hierarchy from director to shopfloor and including employees from both the target and the acquirer. The relative number of affected business units increases. Employees from both the target and acquirer may also face major changes including job losses, relocations, new working groups, and new terms and conditions, as well as more intangible issues such as role and cultural changes.

Finally, acquisition implementation brings with it a degree of upheaval for affected employees as they are reorganized, downsized, relocated and/or given new roles. If one is acquiring with some regularity and integrating targets and the acquirer is thereby affecting both groups of employees, this means a continual state of disruption for affected employees. It is possible to integrate target employees into an existing acquired company environment including its culture and procedures (see Chapter 9, the Global case study) which mitigates the disruption to acquiring employees to a greater extent. But it is important to note that it is likely that you will lose many target employees, some of whom may or may not be key to that business's previous and future success.

Relationship between reasons for acquisition and degree of integration

Until recently, there hasn't been a great deal of exploration into the reasons for buying businesses and the subsequent degree of integration an acquirer may choose with that target. Some reasons for buying a company automatically exclude certain degrees of integration if the objective is to be achieved. For example, an objective such as market penetration leaves all degrees of integration options open to the acquirer as the act of buying the target automatically increases market share. Other options, such as economies of scale, necessitate integrating the businesses in some form in order to achieve the inherent cost savings. Thus, I have developed a model which outlines the relationship between the reasons for acquisition and the subsequent degrees of integration from which organizations may achieve their acquisition objectives (Figure 3.3).

It is unlikely that acquirers purchase a target solely for just one reason – in reality, their intentions are a more complex arrangement of reasons with a predominant and supporting objectives. What Figure 3.3 highlights is the number of options open to the average acquirer in pursuing the achievement of those objectives. Take, for example, an acquirer who buys a target for market share as its primary objective and economies of scale as a secondary

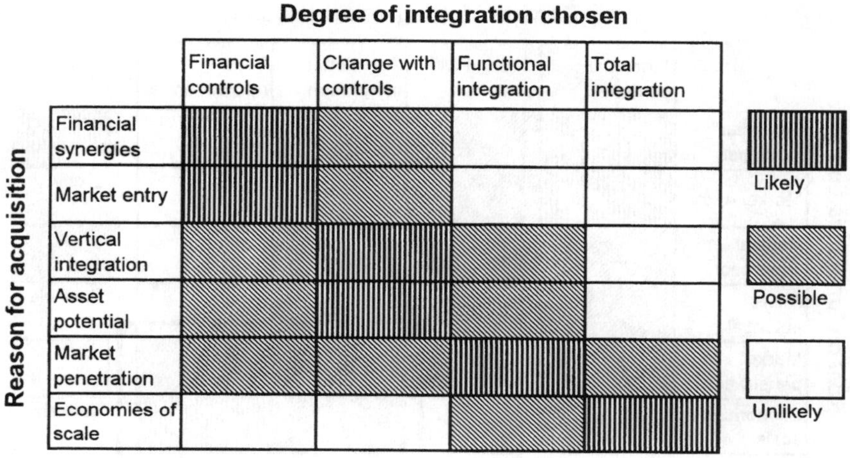

Degree of integration chosen

Reason for acquisition \ Degree of integration	Financial controls	Change with controls	Functional integration	Total integration
Financial synergies	Likely	Possible		
Market entry	Likely	Possible		
Vertical integration	Possible	Likely	Possible	
Asset potential	Possible	Likely		
Market penetration	Possible	Possible	Likely	Possible
Economies of scale			Possible	Likely

Legend: Likely, Possible, Unlikely

Fig. 3.3 *Acquisition objective and required degree of integration*

objective. That acquirer has two options – a strategy of functional or total integration, either of which still achieves both the intended objectives. The acquirer thus gains increased flexibility where various options allow for the meeting of acquisition objectives. Which route is the best to take in terms of the degree of integration will depend on several factors, including the post-implementation cost, available budget, manpower availability, time, organizational and systems constraints. These are discussed below ('Information assessment').

Example: Advent and Zenith building societies

Throughout this book I will use a fictitious acquisition in order to illustrate many of the points in a more practical manner. The example used is a building society called Advent Building Society which buys another called Zenith Building Society. Advent and Zenith have complementary businesses as both are medium-sized building societies. They are located in adjacent regions of Britain with a small degree of overlap between them affecting roughly 10 per cent of their combined branches. The objectives of the acquisition are relatively straightforward: a primary objective is market penetration and a secondary objective is economies of scale (see Figure 3.4).

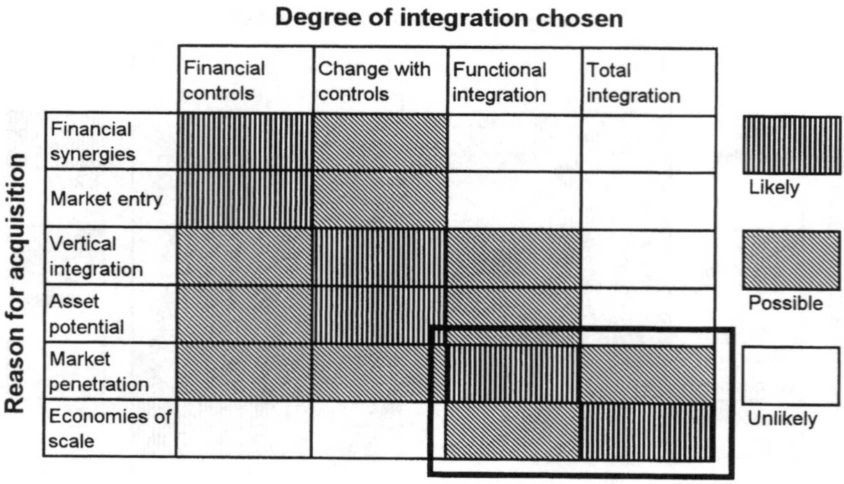

Acquisition

Degree of integration chosen

	Financial controls	Change with controls	Functional integration	Total integration
Financial synergies	Likely	Possible		
Market entry	Likely	Possible		
Vertical integration	Possible	Likely	Possible	
Asset potential	Possible	Likely	Possible	
Market penetration	Possible	Possible	Likely	Possible
Economies of scale			Possible	Likely

Reason for acquisition

Legend: ▨ Likely ▨ Possible ▫ Unlikely

Fig. 3.4 *Acquisition objective and degree of integration for Advent and Zenith building societies*

Because of this, Advent could choose to integrate only some of the functions of the businesses such as administration, accounts, and customer services, or merge the two businesses fully together; either action would achieve both objectives.

Information gathering

Once the acquisition objectives have been established, the next step of pre-acquisition planning is the information gathering phase (see Figure 3.5). In actuality, this phase often begins far in advance of the deal being tabled and is the key to enabling the acquirer to approach the appropriate target company in the first place. The primary source of information gathering is usually due diligence, but if an acquirer relies solely on externally provided due diligence for its information, it is both missing an opportunity and taking a very serious risk that it is not in possession of all the available facts.

Difficulties encountered during due diligence

Gathering due diligence on an acquisition target is not necessarily a straight-forward exercise. In some cases, such public bids or those involving direct

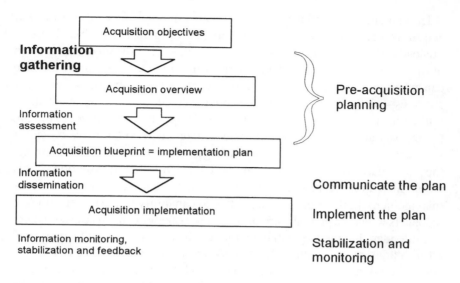

Fig. 3.5 *Information gathering as part of the acquisition process*

competitors, the target may limit the amount of information available to the acquirer. This can be done by limiting access or by imposing strict time constraints during which data can be collected. In these cases, the acquirer may find itself having to rely more on alternative sources of information rather than those provided by the target. In those cases where an acquirer purchases a direct competitor and finds target provided information is less forthcoming, at least it has in-depth industry knowledge which may assuage some of the information insufficiencies.

Another major problem of due diligence which occupies the other end of the information spectrum can be the sheer volume of material available during the process, leading to useful information becoming concealed in irrelevant or unfocused data. Bearing in mind the reasons for acquisition, the due diligence process is most effective if it concentrates on those areas for which the deal is occurring. For instance, if market share is the main objective for the acquisition, then a thorough marketing and client audit should occur. Likewise, if the deal is providing market entry into a new geographic location, a full environmental due diligence would be recommended, including a complete analysis of local demographics, politics and working practices. If economies of scale are the reason for the acquisition, then a full fit analysis should occur, including management, strategic and cultural fits, in order to ensure that the merging of departments can be successfully achieved.

Human due diligence is an interesting area in point. Around one-third of acquirers performed a cursory human due diligence, but this figure is misleadingly high as it usually entails a quick look at the most senior team of directors and does not extend much further than that. HR due diligence can provide a valuable insight into the target by analysing several key areas, especially if the acquirer does not have adequate management skills (either due to manpower deficiencies or incompatible skills base) to run the target. An audit of the target's middle management could prove crucial if it is likely or possible that the target management may leave (if, for example, they are made financially independent following the transaction). This would also apply if the acquirer is intending to remove the target's senior management. In these cases, the depth and capability of the target's middle managers would be good information to have. Likewise, in those cases where it is intended that the target management will continue to run the operation, a full human resource due diligence should also occur which assesses the skills and talents that team brings to the deal. Second, the industrial action and tribunal record of the target provides insight into the relationship between management and the workforce. If there is a mismatch between the styles in which the respective managements deal with employees (co-operative versus combative), cultural issues may make the merging of acquiring and target employees problematic. Finally, an analysis of employee terms and conditions is critical in those cases where integration of some description is to occur. Harmonizing terms and conditions for employees working in merged departments is inevitable; without understanding the relative employment costs, unanticipated increases in wage bills may occur after integration and harmonization takes place.

What due diligence should provide

In many cases, due diligence is used to provide the acquirer with professional indemnification against the accuracy of the financial information provided and the target business's state of health. But due diligence can and should provide much more; it should not only give insight as to whether or not the deal should go ahead but also point out the risks involved with doing the transaction and bringing the target and acquirer together. Thus due diligence should be holistic in approach and not only address the financial indemnification of the target but also look at areas which could cause the deal to fail in the long run. These could include:

- financial information
- cultural fit

- strategic fit
- synergy potential
- management fit in terms of philosophy and attitude
- management talent
- corporate demographics (relative sizes of parties, histories of companies, track records, and so on)
- structural fit
- industry and geographic demographics
- a wide-reaching competitor analysis.

Due diligence should, however, assess not only fit issues but also the process issues surrounding the deal. As seen in Chapter 1, process issues account for the vast majority of acquisition failures, yet due diligence rarely addresses these areas. Has the acquiring management carried out sufficient pre-acquisition planning? Does the acquirer have an adequate communication and implementation plan? Is it prepared to walk away from the deal or is it so emotionally involved that it will buy at any price? Has the acquirer explored all the consequences of its plan, its implementation and its effect on the industry and competitors? Where does this transaction fit into the overall strategic and business plan of the acquirer? These are the kinds of questions traditional due diligence should address and, in most cases, does not. In essence, holistic due diligence is needed to guarantee not only transaction success but also acquisition success.

Sources of information

There are many more sources of information available to the acquirer which can supplement financial due diligence. Access to those discussed below will vary according to whether the deal is agreed or contested, public or private, and into a related industry or a diversification (market entry) purchase.

1. **Due diligence** should include more than just financial indemnification and be used to target areas which are seen as critical in the deal as discussed above.
2. **Personal experience** can provide insight especially in those acquisitions where one is acquiring in the related industry. In many cases, management in the acquirer and target will know each other or have come into contact in the past. Employees in the acquirer may have worked for the target in the past and may be able to add to the intelligence available on the target, its culture and systems, as well as its personnel.

3. **Market knowledge** again is most relevant in related industry acquisitions, especially when buying a competitor. Similarly, if one is acquiring into a foreign market, there may be other business units of the acquirer operating in that arena which may be able to provide useful insights.
4. The **media** can provide a large scope of information all of which is in the public domain. With the advent of online information systems, it is possible to paint a reasonably accurate picture of many organizations simply by accessing available data. This can be especially helpful in assessing senior management, their management style, the organization's culture and strategic focus and, consequently, many 'fit' issues.
5. In some cases, the **negotiation process** can provide a first-hand opportunity to see target senior management in action and to assess their capabilities and management styles. This assumes that senior management is negotiating on behalf of the target's sale; in some cases, especially subsidiary sales, the negotiations may take place at a divisional or head office level and not directly involve the target's senior management.
6. **Industry contacts**, like market knowledge, give the acquirer first-hand knowledge of those within the industry who may be able to provide information on the target (within the legal constraints of inside information and public bids). This may provide information for cross-border acquiring or allow the acquirer to speak to the target's client base to gain a feel for its position in the industry.
7. **Pre-acquisition interviews** are still unusual but provide the greatest form of first-hand information on a target. In agreed bids, it is sometimes possible for the acquirer to commission an external consultant to conduct a series of interviews with key employees after heads of agreement have been reached and prior to the deal's completion. The consultant can assess management talent and gain a good understanding of the target's culture, management style, organizational structure and some of the issues which may arise from the acquisition. In terms of acquisition success, the ability to access this kind of information prior to the deal's completion should enable the acquirer to make informed choices as to the degree of integration pursued and to avoid 'skeletons in the closet' which cause a significant number of acquisition failures.

Acquisition overview

Definition

The step following due diligence in the acquisition process is called the acquisition overview (see Figure 3.6). This step acts as the bridge between the acquisition objective and the blueprint, or operational plan. The overview clarifies how the acquisition objectives, which are general and not specific, can be met by the acquisition at hand. It helps employees better understand the link between the nebulous acquisition objectives and the specific acquisition.

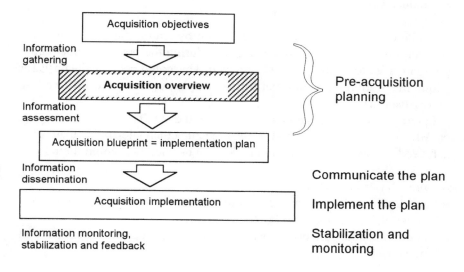

Fig. 3.6 *Acquisition overview as part of the acquisition process*

A major problem of acquisition is the inability of the acquiring management to make the linkage between the general objective and tangible outcomes, for example the mental jump between buying for market penetration and the project management of a product overview and profitability review. An acquisition overview assists this process by serving as a practical reminder of the acquisition objectives thereby ensuring that these objectives remain at the fore during the acquisition implementation process. It also serves as the foundation of the project management element of the implementation process.

Example

The best way to understand an acquisition overview is to use the example discussed earlier. If Advent Building Society were to acquire Zenith Building Society, the acquisition objectives would be market penetration and economies of scale. If these are the two objectives, there are several overview steps which would help in achieving both objectives. For market penetration, the following could be sub-objectives met by pursuing the acquisition:

- cross-sell or broadening of product lines
- consolidate the position within the market place
- reduce competition.

While the last two of these are achieved by simply buying Zenith, the first requires some action by the acquirer during the post-implementation phase in order to be successfully achieved. This could become the basis for a joint integration group or other form of implementation decision making body (discussed in Chapter 5).

In terms of achieving economies of scale, the results are far more reliant on Advent's handling of the post-acquisition implementation rather than being achieved just by consummating the deal. Sub-objectives could include:

- branch rationalization
- head office closure (based on information such as leases and space constraints, it is likely to be Zenith's)
- combine some functions such as back office, support functions, and marketing.

Unlike end user enhancement, none of the sub-objectives outlined above are achieved simply by doing the deal; they must be implemented in order to be successful. Thus, these sub-objectives can serve as the basis for post-acquisition working groups or as unilaterally imposed acquirer-led decisions. If the latter is chosen, far-reaching pre-acquisition planning is critical for their successful implementation.

Information assessment

Once the overview has been determined, there are seven main decisions which have to be made by this stage of the acquisition process to ensure the overall acquisition objectives are met:

1. Degree of integration chosen and resource considerations
2. The degree of cultural relatedness and its ramifications
3. The level of employee participation in decision making
4. The speed of the post-acquisition plan changes
5. Whether or not to integrate systems

6. The role of the target's senior management
7. Degree of integration of employees.

These decisions form the basis for the post-acquisition plan and how it is to be communicated. Based on these decisions, the degree of integration chosen can then be reassessed in order to ensure it is the one most appropriate in light of the decisions taken. In addition, as these decisions form the basis for the communication and implementation plan, they need to be agreed before either can be constructed. The seven key areas will be discussed in turn.

Decision One: degree of integration chosen and the ramifications for further actions

When choosing the degree of integration which is most appropriate for the acquisition, there are two variables which should be considered: achieving the objectives and the resource considerations in doing so.

In achieving the objectives, it is important to know which is the primary objective and whether or not completing the transaction is enough to make the deal a 'success' in the eyes of the acquirer. Second, are there secondary objectives and are they also crucial to the deal's success? If they are, they will tend to limit the options open to the acquirer vis-à-vis the ideal degree of integration chosen. Third, is it realistic that the objectives can be achieved in tandem, or are they incompatible? An example of this would be to acquire for market entry and economies of scale; if a clothing manufacturer diversified into food distribution and hoped to gain economies of scale as well as market entry, it is unlikely that these objectives would both be met on a realistic scale.

There are some advantages for pursuing a low degree of integration between the acquirer and target. Research has found that 'clarity of purpose' is an important critical factor in acquisition success; low levels of integration ensure that the set objectives remain the central focus in the target company. Second, as seen below, cultural issues affect fewer employees in lower integration acquisitions. Third, you are more likely to voluntarily retain senior staff in low integration acquisitions when compared to higher integration mergers. Generally, they are easier to manage and less traumatic as the overall interface between acquirer and target is greatly reduced to only the most senior employees.

Resource considerations should affect the degree of integration chosen by the acquirer. Resource considerations can be broken into three areas: the 'one-off' financial costs associated with the deal, the human resource costs, and the continuing financial costs. 'One-off' financial costs include not only those costs relating to the purchase, such as advisors' fees, but also to implementation costs. These include redundancy expenses especially if one is acquiring for economies of scale, capital expenditure usually associated with asset potential and synergy acquisitions, and system harmonization costs. These additional costs should not be underestimated and their realistic budgeting in the acquisition plan gives a better indication of the overall costs associated with the acquisition.

Also related is the human resource costs needed to implement the acquisition. This includes not only the time needed to execute the acquisition plan, but also the expertise required for any changes to be instituted. The amount of time needed to properly implement a post-acquisition plan often prevents key managers from pursuing other projects deemed to be important for the organization; others see this as a time when 'the eye is taken off the ball', often viewed by competitors with an opportunistic glee. In addition, if the expertise for change is not held in-house, it needs to be imported and the cost of this included in any cost-benefit analysis in terms of doing the acquisition.

Perhaps the most overlooked financial cost associated with acquisition is the long-term costing related to the harmonization of employee terms and conditions in those cases where some degree of integration occurs. Whereas the previous costs are budgeted 'one-off' costs, the increased wage bill often associated with merging working groups is a continual financial cost which needs to be borne by the acquirer on an annual basis. The greater the degree of integration, the higher the number of employees affected by harmonized terms and conditions. With harmonized wage bills rarely decreasing, the cost in cases of full merger can be significant.

These three areas of costs should affect the degree of integration chosen by the acquirer. If, for example, the acquirer does not have the human capital or financial resources to fully integrate the target, a strategy of functional merger may be the safest alternative, achieving some of the acquisition's objectives without endangering the businesses' overall success. Further integration could occur at a later time when those resources became available. If this route is chosen, careful planning and communication of the plan to affected employees becomes crucial to keep them from jumping to conclusions or leaving prematurely.

Decision Two: dealing with cultural differences between the acquirer and target

There are three types of cultural differences which employees can experience at acquisition: cross-national, intercompany and across business units or functions. The cultural implications can be manifest, in different:

- work legislation
- language
- working practices
- company procedures
- management styles and philosophies
- employee attitudes and behaviours.

CROSS-NATIONAL CULTURAL DIFFERENCES

Cross-national cultural differences are often acknowledged when the acquirer and target speak different languages. The use of translators always brings with it a risk that what you are saying is not being translated in the tone you desire. If possible, have at least one member of your team speak the language of the target, but, at the very least, have an advisor who speaks that language fluently.

However, cultural differences go much further than a language barrier. Americans who very commonly use first names when addressing colleagues they have just met will find it very strange that Swiss colleagues often work together for years without deviating from the use of surnames when speaking to each other. If an American were to use his or her natural inclination toward a first-name basis with a newly acquired Swiss colleague, it would cause the Swiss embarrassment and discomfort.

When the two parties speak completely different languages, often acquirers take special care when heeding the cultural differences. Cross-language training, cross-cultural sensitivity training and intra-company meetings can be used to help increase cultural awareness. Sometimes it is more dangerous when those within the companies think they are speaking the same language. An obvious example is a British–American transaction. The differences in language can be very subtle which means they are often missed. Consider the use of the phrase 'quite good'. To an American, quite good means very good; to a Briton it means almost good but not quite there. It is easy to see where a situation could be misinterpreted – an American says to his new British colleague that his presentation was 'quite good', meaning it as a compliment, while the Briton takes it as an insult. At a time of low trust following an acquisition, this misunderstanding may never be discussed and, therefore, never resolved.

Cross-cultural differences also provide opportunities for acquirers to understand ways of conducting business which differ from their own normal modus operandi. An example is works councils which are not used in many

Anglo-American firms but are prevalent in many Continental European companies. While an English company may not use a works council, they have some advantages including an existing communication structure which can be used for disseminating information quickly and efficiently. If an Anglo-American company is acquiring in Europe, it could be advantageous to tap into the existing structure to ensure expedient and easy communication.

INTER-COMPANY CULTURAL DIFFERENCES

There also exists the potential for huge differences in culture between the acquirer and target companies as seen in Chapter 9 (Global). In these cases, the degree of integration chosen can have implications on the new organization's culture and its effect on acquired employees. In organizations where a lesser degree of integration is chosen, the cultural upheaval may not be as pronounced due to the cultural changes being experienced by fewer employees. Conversely, in cases of merger or functional integration all employees will be affected as they must operate within the new culture. Many underestimate the role of culture. In the KPMG study, executives reported that they had not considered it enough and had done so too late in the acquisition process; in future cases they felt it should be assessed in the planning phase and not left for implementation (KPMG, 1997). Another recent study found that failure to address cultural differences was the number one reported cause of acquisition failure (Mitchell and Holmes, 1996).

The amount of inter-company cultural change an employee needs to undergo is related to the cultural differences between the two companies and the degree of integration chosen by the acquirer (see Figure 3.7). In those cases where the cultural diversity is great but the degree of integration is minimal, 'management interfacing' occurs whereby the senior target management act as a 'bridge' between the target and the acquirer. Only they must learn the cultural differences while the bulk of the changes don't effect the rest of the workforce.

The most difficult area in which to operate is 'cultural resocialization' as it requires all employees to undergo a high degree of cultural change and adaptation as they are merged into another very different culture; an example of this could be when an 'organic' company is acquired (discussed later in this chapter). It is in this environment where one can expect a good deal of upheaval and unproductive behaviour as a large number of employees try to learn how to do things differently in the new organization. In cases of high cultural differences, the acquirer always runs the risk that affected employees will not accept the new culture and decide to leave the organization.

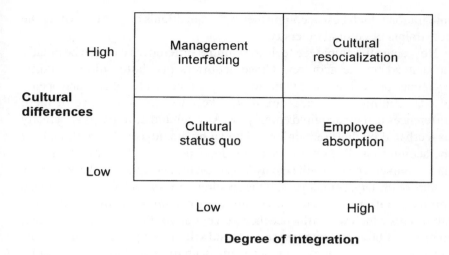

Fig. 3.7   *Cultural implications of acquisition*

One problem of culturally diverse companies is the inability to describe their culture to an 'outsider'. The sheer scope of this was seen at Global. One affected manager described the radical difference in cultural approach and his acquiring colleagues' inability to understand, let alone tackle, the issues:

> What I noticed after six months is that you were trying to join a tribe and you didn't have the right markings. I wouldn't say they are insular, like most tribal systems they are quite happy to welcome most people who they don't know but have the right tribal markings. What happens if you don't have the right tribal markings, they don't understand you and they are not prepared to make that effort because it is not part of the corporate culture to do so ... One of the problems that the tribal culture has, it just doesn't expect to have to indoctrinate you – you are either part of the tribe and you belong or else you are not part of the tribe in which case, you are not here.

The least difficult area in which to operate is 'cultural status quo' as there is a low degree of interaction between the target and acquirer and their cultures are already relatively similar. In cases of full integration but similar cultures, some adjustment of task and procedure is to be expected, but not the wholesale differences as experienced during 'cultural resocialization'. To some extent, the choice left open to the acquirer is to choose the degree of integration which best accomplishes the acquisition's objectives within the constraints of cultural diversity.

How acute the employee feels the cultural differences can also be greatly influenced by the acquirer. Those acquirers that hold cultural audits, encourage procedural and culture awareness training and explicitly and openly discuss cultural differences are more likely to find acceptance of these differences in their acquired employees. Any cultural differences are greatly exacerbated by their remaining unknown by employees. In addition, how the acquirer handles issues such as redundancy and other emotive issues during implementation will heavily impact on the perception of the acquirer's culture of the target employees. If the acquirer fairly executes its well-planned implementation, it creates a certain positive image with the affected employees which will influence their perceptions of that company's culture. In effect, it buys the acquirer some 'goodwill' as the process enhances its perceived trustworthiness and management credibility. If there is no implementation plan and poor decisions are taken in a haphazard fashion, this also creates a cultural impression and highlights any cultural differences which may exist.

One significant manifestation of company culture is the organization's name. Changing or eliminating either company's name should not be done lightly as many target employees who do not appear unduly affected by the process may react to name changes. If there is a logical business rationale for a name change, ensure that this reasoning is known to affected employees prior to the change occurring and expect a degree of sadness on the part of at least some of the workforce.

Decision Three: level of employee participation in decision making

The degree of employee participation in decision making during the post-acquisition implementation period is a critical decision for the acquirer to make. Not only may it serve a valuable purpose, but also it presents a certain tone and culture for the combined organization as it provides a positive first impression of the acquirer and how it values its employees.

There are benefits and disadvantages to having target employees participate in decisions during implementation. Target employees know more about their own company than the acquirer and as a consequence have the opportunity to make more informed, if not better, decisions. The process, if handled properly, can also be highly motivating and the most successful alternative available. The disadvantages include the fact that employee participation makes the process slower thereby prolonging the uncertainty for affected employees. The process also relies on a degree of trust between target and acquirer which may not exist during the earlier stages of the implementation process; a result may be that politics plays a major role in the decision making process. Having target employees participate and then having the process handled poorly is a worst-case scenario, as seen in Chapter 11 in the case of Infosys.

Acquirer-imposed decisions also have a good deal of merit. Uncertainty is lessened as decisions can be announced quickly – even on the day of acquisition in some cases. There is also less room for politics as the decision makers are known. The downside includes the fact that to make these far-reaching decisions without target employee participation requires thorough pre-acquisition planning and information which either may not be available or may not be within the acquirer's existing skills base to implement. Because of this, the acquirer may make the wrong decisions with regard to the target. Second, in many circumstances, current European legislation requires employee consultation prior to major changes including the transferral of businesses, as well as the ramifications such as changing working practices, including redundancies, relocations and role changes. In these cases, the acquirer cannot unilaterally impose decisions upon employees without risking legal comeback. Finally, imposed decisions may demotivate the target employees and set the wrong corporate tone and style with those employees. As this may be the target company's first exposure to the acquirer, this element cannot be ignored.

Another element which is important to employee participation in decision making is whether or not employees feel that their participation in that decision making is appropriate. Research has found that in low-trust environments or ones where they feel their involvement is inappropriate, employees will feel uncomfortable making decisions and, therefore, distrust the process. Examples of this could include deciding which head office or branches to close after merger. In these cases, the criteria for closure need to be very straightforward and methodical so that politics or subjectivity play a minimal role in the overall decision. An example of this is seen in Chapter 11 where Infosys employees commented:

I would have rather they said, 'Here is the plan, you are going to do it. You may not like it but that is your part in it.' I would have been fine. But to actually make it appear as if you are contributing to something that there was no real opportunity to influence ... I think they thought they were making it as fair as they could but I don't think they ever gave the process a chance because they had such a short timescale to deliver, it wasn't possible to consider all the options they should have done.

A suitable compromise which has worked successfully is that the overall decision to implement a certain part of the plan is imposed by the acquirer, yet how it is implemented is decided by both the target and the acquirer in a participative manner. An example of this would be the closure of an acquired company's head office. While the decisions may have been made to close the target's head office, how the relocation occurs may be left open for employees to help in the process. Similarly, an implementation group analysing cross-sell opportunities between the target and acquirer may have certain product guidelines but is able to work within those constraints to develop a jointly acceptable solution. The key to success in this environment is clearly defined boundaries or guidelines in which the employees can operate.

There are different forums available for employee participation such as joint integration groups (JIGs), weekly management briefings, and discussion groups and employee surveys. These are discussed in Chapter 5, ' The Implementation Process'.

Decision Four: speed of change in the post-acquisition plan

A related decision for the post-acquisition implementation plan is the speed at which changes are introduced to affected employees. This is related to the degree of change being implemented – the greater the changes, the greater the potential upheaval experienced by affected employees. There is a school of thought which suggests that the acquirer should spend a considerable amount of time getting to know and understand the target before introducing radical changes. Others pursue the policy that making quick decisions with some minor mistakes is better than the uncertainty that acquisition brings, as 'the most dangerous condition created by acquisition is uncertainty' (Jones, 1986, p. 33).

The immediate approach, like imposed decisions discussed above, provides a quicker process with less uncertainty and a greater clarity and certainty of action. It also plays into employees' existing expectations as they expect change after acquisition and are ready for it – to forgo the chance to introduce change at such a time is truly a missed opportunity. It does, however, require an enormous amount of highly detailed pre-acquisition planning without allowing for target employee participation. And the decisions taken could be wrong. Management at Anglo-American, described in Chapter 7, used the immediate approach suggesting an 80 : 20 ratio – by moving quickly they got 80 per cent of the changes right while 20 per cent were wrong. The speed at which they achieved their 80 per cent right more than made up for the 20 per cent of decisions they got wrong – but, as will be seen, Anglo-

American is a master at pre-acquisition planning; if one is not, the 80 per cent 'right' figure can drop quite dramatically.

The delayed approach does allow for greater knowledge of the target prior to introducing changes and provides an opportunity to involve target employees more in the process. It also allows for potentially explosive issues such as culture differences to adjust over time rather than be forced, and potentially leading to a clash. Another problem associated with delaying action is that this prolongs the uncertainty by creating a process which takes longer for results to show. It is debatable which is more demotivating for target employees – the uncertainty of the delayed approach or the lack of involvement of the immediate approach. It is likely that it depends on the decisions being taken, the length of the delay and the outcome.

In many cases, it is simply not possible to begin changes immediately due to legislative barriers such as the Transfer of Undertakings (Protection of Employment) legislation, better known as TUPE, in the UK. Under these circumstances, changes affecting employees must first be discussed with employees in a consultative manner prior to those changes taking place, thereby automatically building in a delay into the process of at least eight weeks 'post-Day One'. In Europe, the immediate approach is also not always legally available. In these cases, a delayed approach is the only option available; the length of the delay, however, need not be years, but rather only months.

The tone of consultation in this process is also worth considering. To begin a consultation process after acquisition with regard to any changes envisaged does require a degree of trust which may not exist at the early stages of the acquisition. Management can help the situation by presenting themselves as professional, prepared and willing to listen – by having a solid acquisition plan and understanding the 'human' ramifications. Entering into the first consultation process in a confrontational manner will only set the scene for future combat. It also invariably represents the acquirer as aggressive and unappreciative of its employees in the eyes of its newly acquired staff.

The likelihood of target employees remaining during times of uncertainty relies on what the employee feels is the outcome; if they trust the acquirer to treat them fairly during the process, especially if the ultimate outcome is unfavourable, they are more likely to remain and take their chances. If they do not trust the acquirer or their own chances of remaining, they are more likely to leave. An example of a high-trust relationship in which employees remained with the company is seen at Scottish Yeast in Chapter 10; their willingness to stay with the company through the changes was due to trust in the management and in the organization as a whole to treat the employees fairly. This was based partially on previous experience of acquisition and partially on the way in which the newly appointed managing director announced the changes. The use of voluntary redundancy where possible also enhanced the organization's reputation and trust with the remaining employees.

A general model comes from the research outlining the relationship between the speed of implementation and the degree of employee participation utilized (see Figure 3.8). In those cases where decisions are to be implemented quickly, employee participation may be best kept to a minimum in certain circumstances and instead, have the acquirer impose decisions (Benevolent Dictatorship). These could include where job losses are inevitable such as the closure of a head office or in cases where there are clear winners and losers (for example, one employee chosen over another for redundancy). The other variable is the degree of employee participation between the parties involved. Trust is usually low in the beginning of an acquisition where the parties are defensive and the stakes are high. If employees are asked to co-operate for the shared benefit of the new organization, it is unlikely that they will be able to do so without taking into account personal feelings or concerns. The result is likely to be highly political and destructive behaviour (Distrust of Decision and Process). This is all right if there are mechanisms

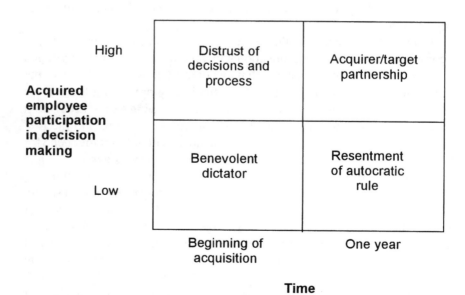

Fig. 3.8 *Relationship between acquired employee participation and time during the implementation process*

for dealing with this kind of behaviour and in fact can set a positive tone for the company if adverse political behaviour is dealt with in an emphatic manner. If not, the outcome can lead to long-term repercussions, as was the case with Infosys (Chapter 11).

The other extreme is to wait for a considerable period of time before making changes to the company. If this is done with the full co-operation and participation of the acquired employees, a 'Partnership Approach' is achieved where all involved are supposedly working together for the betterment of the combined company. If at this juncture the acquirer then imposes decisions, it will be faced with 'Resentment of Autocratic Rule' and an emotional rebellion is likely to take place.

Decision Five: integrating information and back office systems

The integration of information and back office systems is probably more related to the benefit that the acquirer perceives it can bring and less dependent on the degree of integration the acquirer chooses. For instance, an acquisition with a high degree of diversification between the target and acquirer may find there are not enough benefits to integrate the systems where a related acquisition would.

A major advantage of systems integration is the opportunity to add real value from either the acquirer or the target to the other party, either via economies of scale cost savings or the sharing of expertise. If the acquirer or the target has a real systems expertise which serves as a source of competitive advantage (by having a lower cost base or more efficient customer interface), this can often be transferred to the other company. In doing so, this transferral may have advantages such as simplifying customer transactions or interactions. It may also offer significant long-term cost benefits after the initial expenditure is made.

The disadvantages of systems integration are related to cost and planning. The initial integration expense is usually greater than originally budgeted. It also requires an enormous amount of time and energy from those affected and can take a long time to implement. It can also cause wide-scale disruption not only to employees but also potentially to customers during the transition time. This can be mitigated somewhat by thorough planning and project management as well as sufficient due diligence prior to the acquisition in order to assess precisely the cost-benefit relationship.

Another issue which arises out of acquisition is the rapid growth in size once one has acquired. When a small or medium-sized firm acquires, its current systems often cannot cope with the exponential increase in workload. This can include information systems, control systems, communication policies, personnel procedures, administration or even how one makes decisions. Thus, smaller companies can find themselves stretched systems-wise on top of having to deal with the acquisition. Whereas previously one would walk around the corner to speak to a colleague about an issue, the company's instant doubling in size could make that impossible. Similarly, signing off on capital expenditure may have been an informal procedure that needs to be formalized with the increased size of the company. Typically in small or medium-sized companies, employees know how to get things done in an efficient way. When one acquires, that same way may not be efficient any more, but instead may be chaotic. Thus some formalization of procedures such as personnel policies may be needed with the new employees, not only for the smooth running of the company but also for imparting knowledge of how things are done in the combined company.

What is recommended then is a review of processes and systems to ensure that they can cope with the increase in size. Some conduct this review prior to acquiring but others incorporate it into the integration team projects. In either case, it must be proactively tackled and not left to chance or the acquirer may find that it is incapable of dealing with the increased workload without some degree of increased systems support. A lot can go wrong during that time before those systems are fully in place.

INTEGRATING MANAGEMENT SYSTEMS: THE SECOND COMPANY LEVEL INDUSTRIAL RELATIONS SURVEY FINDINGS (CLIRS-2)

An area of potential conflict often overlooked during acquisition is that of diverse management systems. These include reporting and management structures; the role of head office, including the degree of centralization and consistency of organizational policies; and the importance of the various organizational functions. If one acquires and begins changing these business areas without fully understanding the importance to the target and the ramifications, the effect can be to destroy, or at least dilute, competitiveness in the target.

A major study conducted in 1992 analysed the differences between 198 large UK companies with over 1000 employees that acquired (called acquirers) and those that did not (called organics). While the findings are discussed in far greater detail elsewhere,[1] the results are important for understanding differences between acquiring and organic companies.

1. Results are discussed in far greater detail in Hubbard and Purcell (1993). The results discussed above were based on 85 single business acquirers and organic companies, thereby reducing the influence of diversification on business structure.

Acquirers are more likely to have decentralized decision making to business units who have their financial performance monitored by sophisticated control and budgetary systems. Budgets, financial ratios and the finance function play a more significant role in terms of overall authority in acquirers than they do in organics with other functions being perceived as less important. Return on investment is used more often than market share as the company's overall goal. This degree of financial orchestration and decentralization creates many companies with a lack of any degree of co-ordination between the operating units. Acquirers are less likely to have employee movement between different business units or even meetings between staff of different units. Personnel policies including training and development are also less likely to be consistent across the company. Even computer systems are less likely to be compatible within those companies which acquire.

Organics are more likely to have head office exert greater influence on decision making and encourage the business units to act in a co-ordinated way which supports the organization as a whole. Functions such as marketing, operations and personnel were seen to have more input and power; for example, organics are almost four times more likely to have an HR director sit on their board than an acquirer (41 per cent to 12 per cent). Organics are more likely to have market share as a main company objective than acquirers. Policies are more co-ordinated across the business, with administrative relationships, compatible computer systems, company-wide personnel and training policies, cross-company employee transfers and meetings more likely to occur.

If one is acquiring for people synergies or other synergies which require the cross-fertilization of ideas from one individual to another, this could be impaired by decentralization and the lack of consistent policies including uniform training and development policies, and co-ordinated information sharing sessions. If one is acquiring for management talent, an effective human resource department and board-level director with some input directly into the decision making processes are important for achieving a strategically valuable function. If there is a mismatch between the personnel philosophies between an acquirer and its organic target, it is possible that the acquirer and target companies will not share the same type of reporting systems, organizational policies or strategies. These fundamental differences could potentially lead to a loss of key talent and skills.

The ramifications of these findings for acquirers are important. If one is acquiring for synergy, it is important to understand the basis of those synergies before systems and structures are automatically changed in accordance with the acquirer's existing systems. This is especially true if an acquirer purchases an organic company. In many cases the acquirer begins wholesale change in terms of budgeting, financial reporting and even management structures and, in doing so, changes elements of the business which have led to its success without even realizing it.

Decision Six: the role of the target's management post-acquisition

An issue related to resource considerations is whether or not to keep the target's senior management team intact after the transaction. In those cases of well-managed entrepreneurial companies, or low integration, it often makes sense to keep the existing team intact. When there is a question mark over the ability of the target's management team, or in cases of fuller integration (within the confines of employment law), it may become a casualty of the acquisition. Other acquirers choose a hybrid approach by regularly putting at least one new member onto the senior management team (usually a finance director) in order to ensure some degree of corporate compliance and control.

In choosing which path to tread, the acquirer must consider its own resource position in terms of staffing levels. In those cases where its own staff resourcing is constrained, putting in place new management may further exacerbate the situation. As discussed above, one must also bear in mind that research has found that the greater the degree of autonomy, the greater the likelihood that the target's senior management will voluntarily remain in their posts. Likewise, fuller integrations create a 'Noah's Ark' situation where the acquirer has virtually two of everyone. This gives the acquirer a much greater choice of employees from which to pick the team to go forward. Thus, if one is 'management constrained', either a lower degree of integration or a full merger may be the answer, obviously depending on the situation (see Figure 3.9).

There are cases when target management leaves voluntarily. A more common example of this is management buyouts or when founders sell their businesses. In these cases, the acquirer must deal with its staffing shortage quickly. One option worth considering to help alleviate the problem of staffing is interim management. While not ideal, interim management makes it possible to address short-term management constraints while not becoming embroiled in longer-term staffing issues.

In those cases where target management's services are no longer needed in the business, how they leave the business becomes an important issue due to the situation's high visibility. If the exiting of senior target management occurs under negative circumstances, it serves as an example for the rest of the company to observe. Its importance is magnified as it is often so public

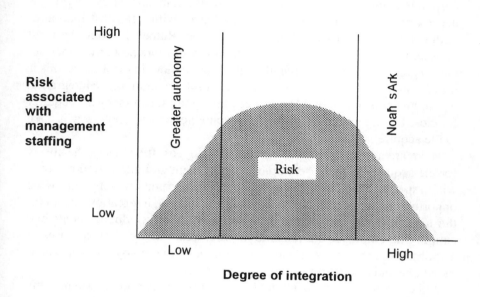

Fig. 3.9 *Relationship between the degree of integration and management staffing post-acquisition*

a decision and one early on during the life of the new company – it often is seen to indicate how the acquirer values its employees. If senior employees are unceremoniously 'dumped', it sets a very negative tone. Conversely, if it is handled sensitively and professionally, the acquirer is likely to win some quick kudos from its new employees as well as have senior management leave without causing undue damage.

Decision Seven: integrating employees

A major decision which affects every acquisition is the degree of integration chosen by the acquirer. The further the companies are integrated, the greater the necessity to integrate employees. The end results are far-reaching – this means not only the meshing of organizational cultures but also harmonizing employee terms and conditions and increasing the likelihood of intra-company differences and, therefore, potential confrontation. With culture clash thought to be a major cause of acquisition failure, it is an area that warrants a great deal of consideration.

Integrating employees can be defined as merging employees, their systems, policies, terms and conditions, management structures and, hence, their corporate cultures after acquisition. This does not mean that the merging is necessarily done in a equitable fashion, that is, with a fair distribution of both companies in the combined organization. Rather, it would be most unusual if one company, usually the dominant or more powerful, does not have a greater influence on the ultimate organization; in most cases, this is the acquirer. In cases of functional, partial or full integration, the integration of employees is inevitable. The degree of integration chosen by the acquirer for those buying for reasons other than economies of scale, however, is open to the acquirer.

There are advantages for integrating employees. It enhances the ability for the acquirer to increase employee movement and interaction not only within specific functions but also between business units, thereby improving opportunities for certain types of synergies. Second, integration allows for the unification of personnel systems consequently reducing costs and simplifying employee administration processes. Finally, in those cases of acquiring for economies of scale, the integration of employees over time is inevitable and critical for achieving that objective.

While integrating employees may be the best or only option open in many acquisitions, there are disadvantages which need to be considered. There are often additional cost implications as harmonizing terms and conditions of two groups of employees generally involves raising packages. A major objective of acquisitions based on economies of scale is the cost savings associated with partial or full integration. The upwards harmonizing of terms and conditions can quickly erode some of the acquisition's cost savings benefits. As seen at Global (Chapter 9), those companies which attempt to employ individuals working on the same site without harmonized terms and conditions can face resentment from those on lower packages.

Integrating employees' terms and conditions is also not a straightforward exercise; employee remuneration is one of the most emotive subjects facing employers. Company cars, telephones, offices and dining arrangements often take on an importance far greater than they should after acquisition because they serve as symbols to reinforce employees' status within the organization. Changing any of these elements can be seen as altering or affecting one's status or position within the firm at a time of heightened sensitivity. What can occur is dissatisfaction and, with that, resignations. Hunt et al. (1987) found that in successful acquisitions, employees' terms and conditions were significantly enhanced following the deal, while in those acquisitions considered unsuccessful, issues surrounding terms and conditions were not adequately addressed.

Perhaps the greatest disadvantage of integrating employees is the necessity to harmonize the two companies' cultures and employees' status within those cultures. This consequently highlights any potential disparities which may exist between the two companies. Employee terms and conditions are an expression of the organization's culture. High wage rates associated with extensive employee training in return for high employee commitment typifies a culture which differs from organizations with low skill/low pay practices. If one merges these employees and systems together, it is unlikely to be without considerable hardship. It is unlikely that employees used to a co-operative culture will remain in one which is confrontational. If their skills are critical to the organization's overall success, this loss will be to the detriment of the acquirer.

Related to this is the importance of status seen most notably amongst management. In those cases of high integration, the issue of relative status, especially between acquiring and target employees, needs to be managed. If the target employees are consistently placed below the acquirer's for no apparent reason and with no visible 'wins', wide-scale resentment of the acquirer is likely to occur. If mismanaged, one runs the risk that key individuals may choose to leave the organization, which again can be to the detriment of the acquisition; this is seen in Chapter 9 with Global.

Finally, when contemplating integration in some form, the organization should consider the competence of its human resource or personnel department. They should be well versed in employment law as related to acquisition, such as transfer of undertakings legislations. They also need the skills not only to determine the harmonized packages and systems but also to communicate and implement these changes effectively. If these skills are not held in-house, the acquirer should consider employing outside advisors in order to ensure these elements of the implementation process are handled professionally. If one is acquiring for economies of scale, the acquisition's success may depend on it.

Acquisition blueprint

Definition

When the operational decisions surrounding the acquisition have been made, an acquisition blueprint can be drawn up (see Figure 3.10).

An acquisition blueprint takes the acquisition overview and divides it into task specific actions which can be managed on a project-by-project basis. This in turn serves as the basis of the post-acquisition implementation plan by determining:

1. **What** action or actions are to be taken. This does not necessarily mean that the plan must be completed in terms of all changes decided and announced. Rather, if decisions are pending, the procedure for achieving those decisions must be outlined as well as the employees' role, if any, in their fulfilment. This could include, for example, outlining which projects will form the basis for joint integration groups (JIGs), the remits of the various projects and which employees are to work on the JIGs. If it is undecided which employees will be involved in the JIG process, then the procedure for selecting those employees should be outlined.

2. **When** these actions are to occur, thereby providing a timescale for change. Like the actions discussed above, it is not necessary to have precise timescales for all the decisions taken at the time of the acquisition's announcement. While it is preferable to have precise timings for changes announced, it is possible to provide an indication of timing or when those times will be announced. The key is to adhere to that schedule. If, for example, the target's head office is to close and this is announced at the time of acquisition, it may not be possible to give an exact date of closure; instead an indication of, say, within six months is usually sufficient. Similarly, if joint integration groups are to deliver results by a specific time, it is crucial that the timeframe announced is adhered to; this is in

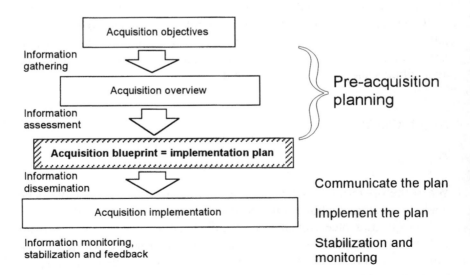

Fig. 3.10 *Acquisition blueprint as part of the acquisition process*

order to manage employee expectations vis-à-vis the process thereby reducing levels of anxiety wherever possible.

3. **Who** is to be affected in terms of employees and other stakeholders and **who** is to be responsible for implementing these changes. Both of these issues need to be addressed in the acquisition site blueprint. If employees are not affected by changes relating to the acquisition, they need to be informed as people always assume the worst in situations of high uncertainty; employees will assume they are to be adversely affected until told otherwise. An example of this occurred in the Infosys acquisition (Chapter 11) in which the employees of one division were highly concerned even though they were not directly affected by the changes. Their concerns were only allayed when they were told of the situation in an honest and open manner by their divisional head.

   Who is responsible for implementing the changes must also be decided and announced. If there is one individual or a committee responsible for the changes, it is important for employees to know who is ultimately responsible. First, employee concerns will be lowered if they can see that the process is being driven by individuals who are held accountable for the implementation's success and delivery. Second, the selection of those people also sets the tone of the deal. If it is a merger and the steering committee comprises both acquiring and target employees, this sets a certain tone. Similarly, in the case of Global's subsequent acquisitions (Chapter 9), having a previously acquired employee heading up the implementation taskforce was shrewd. Not only was he able to empathize with the target employees, he could also 'translate' Global's culture and procedural anomalies, as well as being seen as a living example of a previous Global acquisition survivor.

4. **How** the changes are to take place or the actual blueprint. The blueprint needs to be a detailed document which provides enough information for those responsible for the plan's implementation to be able to project manage the process.

5. **Why** the changes are occurring and the logic behind the changes. As will be seen in the case studies (especially Quality Guarding and Infosys), employees are very interested not only in knowing what the changes are but also in understanding the logic behind the decisions. If the acquirer does not provide this information, employees will find their own answers which they feel are logical, consequently spurring on the rumour mill. This was seen at Infosys when the rationale behind the decisions concerning the data collection site relocation and marketing department were not made public; as a result employees reached their own conclusions as to why the results were such. As expected, the

employees' reasoning was inaccurate and very negative towards the acquirer.

In many cases, the 'why' element is omitted to the detriment of the plan's implementation. In the case of redundancies, this omission can have serious ramifications in the form of 'survivor guilt'. Like other areas where the action's logic is omitted, in those cases of redundancies where employees do not understand the criteria for selection, they feel a sense of guilt relating to their own survival (see Chapter 5). This was seen very clearly in the Quality Guarding case and is discussed further in Chapter 8.

The use of the blueprint has several advantages. First, as a planning tool, it highlights those areas where information is not sufficient at present and where further input is needed in order to complete the plan. Second, it lays the foundation for the post-implementation plan and what actions are needed. Finally, the blueprint provides the basis for the information needed to communicate the plan effectively to the employees.

Blueprint tools

ADVENT AND ZENITH BUILDING SOCIETIES : AN EXAMPLE OF AN ACQUISITION BLUEPRINT

Continuing with the example of the two building societies, Advent and Zenith, it is possible to construct an acquisition blueprint using the acquisition objectives discussed above, market entry and economies of scale. If one takes the acquisition objective of economies of scale, the acquisition overview elements are:

- branch rationalization
- head office closure of Zenith Building Society
- combining some functions such as finance, administration, personnel, customer services, information technology (IT), and marketing.

Using the process discussed above, each element of the overview becomes a manageable acquisition implementation project, an example of which is seen in the branch rationalization project shown in Table 3.2. By employing this technique in all the overview projects suggested, it is possible to construct a comprehensive post-implementation plan.

Table 3.2 Acquisition blueprint for branch rationalization project (Advent and Zenith building societies)

Blueprint action plan: branch rationalization	What action is to be taken
What	The closure of those branches where there is geographic overlap and those few branches where they are not financially viable. The total number of closures is estimated at approximately 10 per cent of the combined branches.
When	The analysis over which branches would be closed would occur during the first six months of the acquisition implementation.
Who	Twelve individuals are being nominated for the joint integration group. These include: • Director of Operations (Chair and also on Executive Steering Committee) • Deputy Director of Operations • two branch managers from large branches assured to stay open (one from Advent and one from Zenith) • two branch managers from branches thought to be closing (one from Advent and one from Zenith) but whose jobs are deemed secure • two non-managerial branch staff (one from each) who are from secure branches • marketing representative to be announced • IT representative to be announced • finance/back office representative to be announced • personnel representative to be announced
How	The pool from which branches will be closed includes branches from both Advent and Zenith with the criteria for selection being based on the best branch for the combined company and not on a personal or political basis. The joint integration group will meet weekly to manage the project. Other individuals will be co-opted onto the sub-committee to help gather the appropriate information (JIGLET). The criteria for site selection will be decided within one month; a partial list of closures consulted upon will be made at three months and the full list of closures announced within six months. The first meeting is scheduled for two days after the announcement at 10.00 a.m., at the Director of Operations' office.
Why	In order to ensure the long-term success of the business (by cutting costs) and to maintain an efficient business (by reducing duplication of effort), it is necessary to close those branches which are truly redundant due to their proximity to more profitable branches or those which better serve our customer needs.

CRITICAL PATH ANALYSIS

A further tool which can be useful in organizing thoughts and actions during this point of the acquisition is a critical path analysis. This allows the user to plot backwards from a specific day such as the date of the deal's announcement giving the last possible time tasks can be performed and still completed by the chosen day. It is not uncommon for acquirers to want to achieve certain objectives by the acquisition's announcement day only to find that they don't have enough time; examples of this include getting new stationery printed, press releases out and communication packs printed. An example is given of the critical path analysis which could be used by Advent Building Society's Chief Executive (see Figure 3.11).

A Gantt chart works with the same principles as a critical path analysis. Key milestones are highlighted and relationship between events can be charted. With current project management software, interrelationships between different ongoing projects can also be linked which is ideal for the larger or more complicated acquisition.

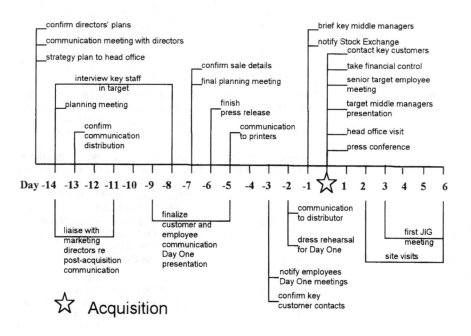

Fig. 3.11   *Example critical path analysis: Advent Building Society*

Day One, one day, one week, one month, one quarter and one year plans and measures

Built into any pre-acquisition plan must be milestones such as what should occur at various stages of the acquisition. While it is acknowledged that all acquisition plans must be fluid, one must start off with a strong idea of what one is hoping to achieve and at what juncture. Thus, milestone dates such as 'Day One', one day, one week, one month, one quarter and one year all can be used to identify which tasks one wants completed by those times. Against those times should be listed defined outcomes and tasks, with those individuals responsible for their achievement, and hopefully measures for ensuring their achievement. These can be in the form of cost savings, employee headcount, sales forecasts, or 'softer' outcomes such as the acceptance of the company's new mission statement or core values. In any case, the more concrete the outcome, the greater the ability to measure and monitor its progress. Built into the milestones should also be several 'quick wins' (these are discussed in more detail in Chapter 5). 'Quick wins' should be apparent not only to those on the acquisition teams but also to other employees. They are used to show, as soon as possible, that the acquirer says what it is going to do and then does it. The sooner this occurs during the acquisition, the better; after all, it is a cornerstone of managing employee expectations. It is also a fundamental and critical part of pre-acquisition planning.

Risk and issue logs

A good way of keeping track of cross-functional or company-wide issues is to list them in a risk or issue log. The log works by flagging up any issues which are unresolved. Issues or risks can then be discussed in the appropriate forum and the intended action and owner of that action can be added to the list as the issue is resolved. This process also works very well in dealing with implementation issues (discussed in Chapter 5), especially in ensuring that issues or risks do not fall between the boundaries of two related implementation teams.

CONCLUSION

The greatest benefit pre-acquisition planning brings is the opportunity to sit down and think about why one is buying the business and how this is going to be achieved. Until this is decided, it is impossible to convey this message to anyone else. It is getting the balance right of planning and communicating what you have planned which enhances acquisition success. With either part missing, the positive elements of both remain hidden and the effect is lost.

The next stage of pre-acquisition planning is the construction of the communication plan in which the format for disseminating those key decisions is decided. Although this is a fundamental part of pre-acquisition planning, it is discussed in the next chapter, which outlines the process for effective communication management during acquisition.

4 Communication: The Binding Force of Acquisitions

INTRODUCTION

Flatter organizational structures, empowered employees and advances in information technology have focused the corporate mind on the ability and necessity to communicate more effectively. There has been an increasing acknowledgement of the important role communication plays in corporate life in delivering performance and business efficiencies. Chief executives are increasingly willing to acknowledge that communication can affect the 'bottom line' by increasing the organization's efficiency, employee morale and commitment.

During times of change, communication takes on an even greater role as it is used to convey the ramifications and transformations brought on by change as well as in managing the day-to-day business. During acquisition, communication needs to convey vast amounts of information in a thoughtful and timely manner. Thus, communication during acquisition or merger is more complex and more important than it is during an organization's normal working environment. In the acquisition process, the step which links the pre-acquisition planning phase and its implementation I call the Information Dissemination phase, or communication of the plan to its stakeholders; it is fundamental to acquisition success (see Figure 4.1).

THE IMPORTANCE OF COMMUNICATION DURING ACQUISITION

Communication is a crucial element of the acquisition implementation process. Studies have found that in the months following acquisition adequate communication correlated highly with employees' feelings of personal control, organizational commitment, lower uncertainty, increased performance and job satisfaction. When the communication stopped, employees experienced increased distraction, guilt, intent to be absent and job insecurity (Davy et al., 1988; Napier et al., 1989). My research found that acquirers who failed to communicate effectively saw a drop in employee trust, in feelings of fairness during acquisition implementation and in management credibility,

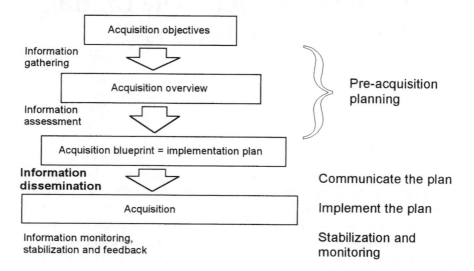

Fig. 4.1 *Information dissemination as part of the acquisition process*

and an increased intention to leave the organization. Other findings are similar with under-communicating being reported as probably the single most important cause of poor motivation, general discontent, and rumour generation during acquisition (Mitchell and Holmes, 1996).

A comprehensive communication strategy is fundamental to the acquisition process outlined in this book. It serves to manage employee expectations during acquisition implementation by announcing the planned intentions of the acquirer prior to the actions taking place. If this vital step is missing, employees have little hope of understanding or judging the acquisition plan of the acquirer. A vital element of pre-acquisition planning is the employees knowing that the acquisition has been planned; it makes the acquirer look professional. As mentioned before, the acquirer may have the best plan in the world but if employees do not know of it, much of its value is lost as employees do not know the acquirer has planned so carefully.

COMMUNICATION IN THE PRE-ACQUISITION PLANNING PHASE

The communication plan as part of the overall business plan

An effective communication plan begins as an integral part of the overall acquisition business plan. In order to ensure their most effective use, the method and media used to disseminate the communication plan must be included in the plan. As seen in the previous chapter, research has found that only half of companies do *any* acquisition planning whatsoever. As over two-thirds of companies did not involve the HR department until the deal was signed (Hunt et al., 1987), it is likely that only a small percentage of companies have a well-integrated communication strategy as part of their overall acquisition plan. In many cases, those companies which do have a communication plan, incorporate at the last minute; a study in the US found that almost three-quarters of acquirers who did communicate, did so at the last possible moment in order to 'avoid disruptions' (Schweiger and Weber, 1989).

Communication planning especially when dealing with complex transactions such as public bids or those which require wholesale change such as mergers takes on an even greater importance. The overall co-ordination of acquisition communication planning is important for four reasons:

1. **To maximize the likelihood of successful communication on the day of announcement**. If one is intending to communicate on 'Day One' of the acquisition (which is highly recommended), the communication plan must be a co-ordinated and planned effort. In those acquisitions where changes are to begin or be announced on the day of completion, vast amounts of strategic and communication planning is required prior to the announcement day in order for it to be implemented smoothly. This includes the proper mix of media and message.

2. **To cope with the necessity of increased information**. Especially during the planning stages, many executives find they are trying to organize pre-acquisition planning often in a secretive environment while continuing to perform their day-to-day jobs. This doubling of information requires increased communication co-ordination, especially if the acquisition is commercially sensitive or a public bid which attracts a high degree of media attention.

3. **To co-ordinate internal and external messages**. A potential problem of acquirers is the inability to co-ordinate internal and external communication messages. The only way an acquirer can guarantee its co-ordination is to sufficiently plan for the two to complement each other in a timely manner. An example of this occurs when the acquirer raises funding to purchase the target; it is human nature to paint an aggressive picture to ensure the funds are forthcoming. Similarly, public offer documents designed to pursuade the target company shareholders to sell their shares gives an overly optimistic impression in terms of returns

and value added by the acquirer, often in the form of a lower cost base and synergies. In doing so, the internal and external messages are often out of sync and need somehow to be reconciled. It is only through integrated pre-acquisition and communication planning that a realistic balance between external media and internal communication can be achieved.

4. **To allow for contingency planning if leaks of negotiations or the deal occur**. A major concern for public deal acquirers or those who wish for negotiations to remain secret is the possibility of a leak occurring prior to the deal's announcement. There are many ways to stem information leaks or to deal with them once they have occurred but all approaches require a consistent and planned approach. One such solution is to have all enquiries (for those employees who know of the deal) passed to a centralized location, designated manager or outsourced communication advisor who has a prepared written script detailing the information which the acquirer deems publicly appropriate. That information should be factually accurate within legal and commercial confines. It is not appropriate to say that no discussions are taking place if the deal has been agreed; if this approach is taken employees and other stakeholders are less likely to believe future corporate communication. What is more appropriate is either a 'no comment' statement, a statement confirming that the company is in discussion with a number of parties or that any of the businesses are for sale at the right price. With the current acquisition boom, it is unlikely that a general but honest statement would cause undue upset with employees, customers or shareholders. What is imperative, however, is a uniform approach by both the acquirer and target, which can only be achieved via careful communication planning.

A definition of communication

Communication encapsulates not only formal verbal and written communication but also informal communication, actions, gestures and feedback; even no communication is in itself communication. It can be used for many purposes within organizations:

- to disseminate information
- to facilitate working and groups
- to sway employee opinion
- to manage employee expectations

- to fulfil legislative or legal requirements
- to make the receiver of the communication feel important
- to build a foundation of trust and believability amongst employees, management and the company,
- to set a tone within an organization.

Yet there are many problems inherently associated with communication. All people receiving information have a perceptual bias which colours how they perceive it. Second, not all those responsible for disseminating information share good communication skills. Third, some use information as a source of power by retaining sensitive information rather than passing it on. Research has found this to be prevalent in ambitious people who perceive that withholding information strengthens their position. Finally, in those cases where there exists a large differential in status between employees, there is less effective communication between the parties. Because of these problems, the message sent is quite often not the message received, suggesting that 'what is obvious to the sender is obscure to the recipient' (Dubin, 1976, p. 32).

A model of communication

The best framework for effective communication during acquisition comes from a study conducted analysing communication during large-scale organizational change (Smeltzer, 1991). Smeltzer analysed 43 companies and found the following results:

1. Only four of the 43 companies studied, or less than 10 per cent, had a written communication strategy for announcing the changes. Management generally felt that communication of the changes was not an important issue; therefore, a written plan was unnecessary. A symptom of this was the overwhelming propensity of management to deliver just one message to all employees without an audience breakdown to those employees affected and those not affected by the changes.
2. There were major symptoms of communication failure in over 80 per cent of announced changes; in those cases where there was communication planning, the symptoms of failure were far fewer. In the 80 per cent of cases where failure was evident, there were big differences between the intended changes and what actually occurred.
3. The biggest cause and indicator of communication failure was seen by employees as the presence of negative rumours. Indeed, their presence

was what most differentiated effective and non-effective announcements. This result came as a surprise to management as they did not feel rumours were an important issue prior to the research. Likewise, they were surprised that employees knew of the changes prior to their announcement through extensive rumour circulation.

4. It is likely that the rumours were caused by poor communication timing. Timing, or poor timing, was seen as the topic most discussed by employees after the change announcement. In those cases where the change announcement was poorly timed, employees spoke of hidden agendas and not being given the complete story by management. This was exacerbated by many of the companies' management not giving honest and forthright announcements, but instead, speaking in euphemisms.

5. The second biggest cause of communication failure was employees learning of the changes from informal sources such as the press or via 'the grapevine'. In those cases, feelings of resentment were commonplace, which in turn led to damaged management credibility. Interestingly, this was seen most noticeably in employees who were not directly affected by the changes but were watching from 'the periphery'.

6. The context of the communication was deemed more important than the content. In other words, the timing, method and channels of communication were seen to be more important in determining how employees viewed the communication's success rather than the actual message being conveyed.

There are some important lessons from Smeltzer's research which can be applied to acquisitions. During acquisitions, communication is important in setting a tone as well as conveying a message to the affected parties. As it is often the first contact that acquired employees have with their new owner, its impact is even more pronounced. Messages for affected employees during acquisition will differ: in some cases employees will experience dramatic change; in others the changes will be less pronounced, even within the same business unit. What is key is to differentiate between these messages to the affected employees in an honest and timely manner. Smeltzer's findings also highlight the need for timely and accurate communication during times of change. When this is present, negative rumour spreading is kept to a minimum. Finally, as we will come back to again and again, it is the delivery, not the message, which is the key to communication success.

Based on these findings, Smeltzer developed a model for communication, the three elements of which are communication content, channel and timing. They are integral parts in the dissemination of information surrounding change (including acquisition) (see Figure 4.2). They are affected by the nature of the changes taking place as well as the way in which the organization operates. For example, in a highly decentralized and geographically dispersed operation such as a bank, timely and accurate face-to-face communication directly after acquisition, while desirable, is highly problematic. Instead, alternative communication sources such as written documentation should be considered at least to augment any face-to-face encounters. Similarly, if during acquisition, wide-scale redundancies are to occur, the sensitive perceived nature of the change should dictate more detailed and multichannel communication in order to ensure the greatest number of employees receive and understand the changes and the reasons behind them.

Getting the three elements of the model right are important to ensuring effective communication during acquisition. For example, take the issue of timing. Research has consistently found that successful acquirers 'took control' of the target during the first two days of ownership. This includes those acquirers who implemented changes immediately or communicated a procedure and timescale for doing so. During acquisition, the earlier one is able to reduce uncertainty by giving an honest and clear communication, the more successful the communication will be perceived to be, in spite of the message.

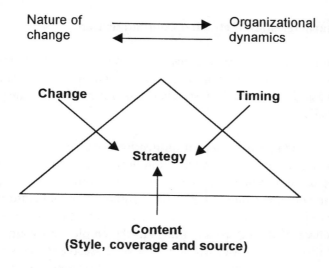

Fig. 4.2 *Model of communication during change (Smeltzer, 1991)*

The channel element of the model is also a vital component during acquisition. It is a mistake to believe that the best form of communication is always spoken. When large amounts of detailed information must be conveyed to a large number of employees, written communication is most effective. For example, changes in terms and conditions or pensions should, at least in part, be written down in order to guarantee accuracy in dealing with lots of detail, but also to allow employees to refer to the changes at a later date if desired. Redundancies should be discussed face-to-face with those affected and never handled solely via written communication.

Similarly, content comprising coverage, style and source must be also considered. A legal document outlining changes to pension arrangements following acquisition is not an appropriate method of informing most employees – it needs to be translated into laymen's terms in order to be understood by the majority of recipients. Announcing redundancies in a flippant or covert manner is also inappropriate and should instead come from a suitable source, such as senior management, followed by written confirmation, thereby reflecting the gravity of the situation. Finally, with the potential of *over-communicating* following acquisition, it is prudent to consider coverage issues for certain information. For example, one should consider if it is suitable for shopfloor employees to know the share option arrangements of the senior management team in minute detail.

Other characteristics of effective communication

In addition to those characteristics of communication discussed above, there are others which can increase an acquirer's communication effectiveness. These were discussed in Chapter 2 and include the following characteristics.

1. **Honesty and precision of communication** is perhaps the most important element of effective communication during acquisition. Studies have repeatedly shown that employees value honesty in communication more than any other attribute. Employees scrutinize available information in order to judge its honesty. In those cases where it is proven to be true, the source of the information rises in the employee's estimation and credibility; in those cases where it is proven false, the source's credibility falls. Research, including my own, has found that employees would much rather know all information including bad news rather than know nothing, be told incorrect platitudes from management or hear of future

events in euphemistic terms. This includes learning of redundancies, relocations and changes in status and job performance.

2. **Consistency of information** is a key factor in the process of managing employee expectations and in successful acquiring. This includes consistency of internal messages as well as consistency between internal and external communication. In those cases when communication is inconsistent, the acquirer may be accused by employees of hidden agendas, secrets, and political manoeuverings within the context of a low trust environment. When employees don't get a consistent answer, they make up their own – which is usually wrong and highly negative. This is discussed further in Chapter 5 and can be seen most explicitly in Chapters 8 (Quality Guarding) and 11 (Infosys).

3. **Believability of communication** is another factor which emerged from the five case studies as being critical to the acquisition process. An example of communication being unbelievable occurs when management state that it is 'business as usual' after acquisition while knowing that changes are imminent. In this context, believability is closely related to honesty of communication. An example of this is seen in Chapter 8 (Quality Guarding). One employee recounted:

> At the moment, clients don't believe it is 'business as usual'. If in the paper a statement is made that we are going from 4 to 10 per cent and you tell clients that nothing is going to change, they aren't going to believe you. That 10 per cent will be achieved, it will come.

Determining communication audiences

The model and characteristics of communication discussed above recognize that different audiences need to receive distinct messages often by differing channels of communication while the acquirer balances the need for consistent information. This can be achieved by developing an overall communication plan which can be used to segment the various audiences. A first step in effective communication planning is to understand three factors: the message, the audience and the most appropriate medium or media to be used.

The message

While the message should become clear from your acquisition plan, there are several factors to consider:

- is the message consistent to all stakeholders?
- will it be logical to most hearing it?
- are there legal ramifications for communicating the messages immediately (TUPE)?
- how many messages do you have (is it a complicated story or straight-forward)?
- what percentage of employees (target and acquiring) will be affected by any changes?
- which stakeholders will be affected or benefit from the changes anticipated due to the acquisition?
- can you make the message public knowledge or is it commercially sensitive?
- is the message all good news, all bad news, or good to some stakeholders and bad to others?
- does the communication need to be phased over time or can it be disseminated all at once at the time of the transaction's announcement?
- will major decisions affecting stakeholders be made soon after the acquisition's announcement or will they occur during the implementation phase?
- what is the timeframe for changes to be made and announced?

These factors will shape the complexity of the communication plan. If the plan is complicated, with mixed messages affecting a large proportion of employees and decisions and communication to be phased over a period of time, and it includes commercially sensitive information, it is clearly a more complex plan than that of a low degree of integration acquisition.

The audience

If one takes employees alone, deciding your communication audiences can be complicated, but when one also factors in the other communication audiences which could be affected by acquisition, the number of recipients and messages increases dramatically. Others which could be affected by the acquisition include a wide host of organizational stakeholders who could need communication:

1. **Target employees including senior management, middle management and non-managerial employees**. These employees are all different groups with potentially different message needs. Additionally, there may be geographic or functional distinctions, again

causing a differentiation in the messages. For example, the combining of back office functions or closing of head office would warrant different messages to sub-groups of employees on the same level of an organizational chart depending on their geographic location or function. Another element of communicating to target employees prevalent in European acquisitions is the consultation with local or national works councils. Works councils can be seen as a negative or positive force: negative if they impede management's ability to push through changes relating to acquisition but positive if they can aid in the downward (and upward) communication process. This latter potential of works councils is often forgotten by Anglo-American acquirers who are generally not used to a co-operative employee representative process.

2. **Acquiring employees including senior management, middle management and non-managerial employees**. In cases of full, departmental or functional mergers, it is common to have acquiring employees affected by acquisition; it is less common to have these employees prepared for the subsequent changes. In the Infosys case discussed in Chapter 11 the acquiring employees complained of a 'reverse takeover' as they never expected to be affected by any changes due to the acquisition. After all, they were the acquirers! A good communication strategy informs all affected employees by outlining realistic expectations of impending or potential changes. In cases of acquiring employees being affected, the message needs to be repeated several times in order for it to be understood, especially as it is not what is expected by those employees.

3. **Customers**. Few plans incorporate effective communication to customers. While an acquisition which consolidates an organization's market position may be positive for the financial institutions and shareholders, it may not be positive to customers if it means higher prices and fewer choices. Whatever benefits the acquisition brings, be it more efficient service, expanded product range, or lower costs, these benefits can serve as the basis of a communication message. At the very least customers should be kept informed in a timely manner of the transaction and any changes which may effect them. To ensure a uniform response to customers, all customer facing employees in both companies should be briefed on the message they should convey if queries are raised; this can be done via a customer briefing script or release (see below).

4. **Suppliers**. What is true for customers is also true for suppliers. There are cases where suppliers and customers in long-term service agreements legally stipulate that they are to be informed of any potential acquisition or merger prior to its agreement. In these cases, effective consultation

and, thereafter, communication needs to take a high priority so as to not lose that vital element of the supply chain or customer.

5. **Shareholders**. Shareholders play an integral role in acquisition and merger activity whether by voting directly for the deal to proceed in public deals or by voicing disapproval if it fails to bring about satisfactory returns. While many investors remain passive during the majority of deals, those cases which require shareholder approval (such as contested deals) necessitate a carefully planned external communication strategy. There are numerous cases where the communication strategy was seen as instrumental in swaying public opinion to accept or reject a hostile or contested bid (Granada/Forte, Lasmo/Enterprise). One difficulty associated with external communication to shareholders is that it can be highly optimistic in order to pursuade shareholders to approve the acquisition; it can be misleading as subsequent actions may not meet these expectations. When employees are also shareholders, it can be a confusing time where the acquirer talks of cost cutting and increased profits but at the expense of employees' job security. This communication should be honest and not inflammatory or overly optimistic. In the cases where it is the latter, the acquirer is in danger of winning the bid but failing to deliver during its implementation.

6. **Competitors**. While it would be extremely rare for an acquirer to communicate directly to its competitors about an acquisition, it is common for competitors to use acquisition to target key customers and recently acquired employees as the acquirer takes its 'eye off the ball'. Thus it is important not to lose 'the business thread' when acquiring. If forced to make redundancies post-acquisition, a few sophisticated acquirers contact competitors via the media or trade press to try and find their redundant employees alternative jobs. This is unusual but sends a message to the remaining employees that the organization is trying to behave in a highly fair and responsible manner.

7. **Media**. It is not uncommon to find inconsistencies between internal employee-focused communication and external communication during acquisition. As discussed above, in many cases external communication focuses on the financial benefits of the deal and, in doing so, creates great uncertainty within the target employees on how these benefits are to be realized. In addition, what is positive for some of the audiences mentioned above may not be positive for employees or customers. For example, reducing employee overheads presented in an unsympathetic manner can send a negative message to affected employees and customers, yet send an acceptable message to investors. An example of this is seen in the Quality Guarding acquisition discussed in Chapter

8. When the Chairman's claims of doubled margins were discussed in the press it created a reasonable degree of unease in employees. When these proved to be correct in direct contradiction to internal communication, the credibility of the divisional management who had made the inaccurate claims suffered. One senior Quality Guarding manager said:

> They made 4.5 per cent and Cummings wanted to take it to 10 per cent to justify the money. Now clients are more suspicious, they are less comfortable with Quality Guarding. At the end of the day, we will be a more profitable organization if we don't lose all our employees or customers.

8. **Financial institutions**. As with shareholders, communication directed at financial institutions can be overly optimistic, especially when securing the deal relies on the raising of funds to pay for it. In these cases, it is not unusual for the acquirer to make inflated or best-case scenario claims in order to secure financing. It is also common for these claims to mirror those in the media which can create further problems for affected employees. Bid documents are a prime example. An overly optimistic bid document can potentially create expectation conflict at a later time by creating a picture for analysts and investors which is negative for employees. In these cases it is likely that figures won't be met, as it is likely that management attitude post-acquisition would be unco-operative and investor expectations high.

9. **Government bodies**. The communication needed for governments and industry regulators has increased significantly within the European arena in recent years. Not only do country-specific government and industry bodies require communication, but European regulators do as well. The increased use of lobbying within Europe demonstrates an increasingly sophisticated attitude towards ensuring an overall business case is put forward – this may prove vital in cases of certain acquisitions which could warrant anti-monopolistic approval.

10. **Local communities**. Often overlooked during acquisition is the possibility that the related outcomes can dramatically affect local communities. The closure of sites and downsizing of the workforce can have a negative impact, while site expansion can be regenerative for a region. In some cases, the loss of a significant proportion of the workforce can traumatize the local community and bring an adverse media reaction. Careful 'courting' of the local press and workforce can help alleviate this situation; a genuine management effort to retrain,

relocate or assist affected employees can present the organization in the most sympathetic light in what is a most difficult time. This occurred at Scottish Yeast (Chapter 10) where a carefully planned communication campaign aimed at the local community was used when reducing the workforce by 40 per cent. The result was that what could have been a 'negative media frenzy' was averted and the downsizing occurred without major incident or long-term repercussions.

In each acquisition, the extent to which one communicates depends on the number of audiences, the number and complexity of messages, and the amount of time and resources the organization has available to achieve its objectives. Audiences may be prioritized in order to ensure the most important receive adequate communication. For instance, if time and resources are constrained, key customers may be targeted for certain more labour intensive communication while smaller customers may receive less. Similarly, key customers may receive communication from several media sources, such as face-to-face meetings in conjunction with written correspondence, while less important customers receive only the latter.

The media

When planning an effective communication strategy, a variety of media should be employed for four main reasons. First, as discussed above, some media are more appropriate for certain messages than others. Second, time and cost considerations will necessitate using a variety of methods to cover the majority of affected stakeholders. For example, in large organizations, face-to-face meetings cannot be held with all employees and other stakeholders on 'Day One' and, when discussing subsequent changes, therefore, other methods must be employed weighing up the cost, effectiveness and coverage of these media. Third, different employees retain information through different means. Habbe found that 60 per cent of employees retain information from reading things while 40 per cent gather information from hearing it (1976). If management communicates repeatedly while using only one source of media, it is effectively missing half of its employees. For those messages which are very important, the use of more than one medium with consistent messages should be used in order to reinforce the central messages. Finally, not all employees are good communicators. If one relies solely on people to cascade communication down through the organization, it is guaranteed that the message will be inconsistent and patchy. The use of more than one channel of communication for important messages, therefore, increases the likelihood that the messages get through. A combination of verbal and written communication, such as team briefings and bulletin board releases, for example, is generally effective.

An example of internal communication audiences and media

The example of two building societies discussed in Chapter 3 will be used to highlight an effective communication plan.[1] Advent Building Society is buying Zenith Building Society for a variety of reasons including economies of scale and market share enhancement. Achieving economies of scale will require the closure of Zenith Building Society's head office and those smaller branches of both Advent and Zenith with geographic overlap. It is not known precisely which branches will close; joint integration groups working during the six months preceding the acquisition will determine exactly which branches would be affected based on a variety of criteria including: sales per square foot, profitability, lease details and gross sales. It is estimated that this would affect around 10 per cent of branches. A few non-profitable branches would also close; it is estimated that this will include around eight branches. Branch staff were generally not long-serving, so consequently any redundancy payments they were to receive were not considered enough to guarantee the retention of staff until the site closed. Because of this, staff who remained until their site closures would be given loyalty bonuses. Talented managers from the redundant branches would not necessarily be made redundant but endeavours would be made to find them another suitable branch assignment. They would be accommodated where possible by the early retirement of some managers and the voluntary redundancy of others. No managers from branches not closing would be made redundant mandatorily. Non-managerial branch staff from branches earmarked for closure would be made redundant without the opportunity to relocate unless vacancies were available. The bulk of Zenith's head office is comprised of back office and administrative staff, none of whom will be needed once the systems are moved to Advent's location and integrated six to twelve months after the acquisition. It would be hoped that staff would remain working for Zenith's head office until the site closed; for the same reasons as the branch staff loyalty bonuses will be awarded to those employees who remain. The only exceptions are ten IT/back office/

1. This communication plan is based on the information available but does not necessarily comply with current TUPE legislation regarding the transferral of work and consultation with employees prior to job changes. It is used only to illustrate the point.

finance managers who are considered key to ensuring the transition to the new systems is successful and to the long-term future of the company.

Senior management from both companies would be affected as there would be one senior director and a deputy taken from the two societies; the chairman (formerly Zenith's CEO) and managing director (from Advent) were to pick the team equitably based on who was best for the job. Senior directors were assessed as to their ability, interviewed, and chosen accordingly. Who held what positions was known to the affected managers but was to be made public only on the announcement day.

In six to twelve months' time Advent's head office staff would also be affected as they would be working with an increasing back office workload and potentially new systems. In addition, they would in all likelihood have at least a few new colleagues in the ten managers, some of whom it was anticipated would move to Advent's head office. The remaining branches of the combined Advent/Zenith Building Society would also be affected by an influx of new customers as the redundant branches are closed and customer accounts moved to the remaining branches.

Concentrating first on the internal communication aspect, affected employees include not only Zenith Building Society's head office and branch staff but also some branch staff from Advent's branches which are to be closed. Therefore, the internal audiences would include:

- newly appointed directors and immediate team
- newly appointed deputies and immediate team
- Zenith branch managers
  - those not affected by closures
  - those who will be affected by closures
    - made redundant
    - targeted to remain
- Zenith branch employees
  - those not affected by closures
  - those who will be affected by closures and will be made redundant
- Advent branch managers
  - those not affected by closures
  - those who will be affected by closures
    - made redundant
    - targeted to remain
- Advent branch employees
  - those not affected by closures
  - those who will be affected by closures and will be made redundant

- Zenith head office staff
- the ten key managers needed from Zenith's head office to remain with the company and relocate
- Advent head office staff.

Due to the complex nature of the various audiences, it would be impossible to send a blanket statement via one communication channel to all employees and have it be effective. As the ten key managers from head office are deemed critical for the merger's success, it would be advisable to see them individually for a personal talk as soon as legally possible. The senior management from both sides will have already had some hand in determining their positions as functional head and deputy. Their immediate teams, however, would need communication about the changes in reporting lines and any related changes. If any branch managers are known to be 'high flyers' within the firm, an informal verbal communication from a senior manager could be made to those employees reassuring them of their job security within legal constraints.

In this case, external stakeholders would include shareholders, the City, media, suppliers, local communities and, of course, customers. Suppliers could be seen as those who supply one or both of the existing building societies and probably would not be seen as a high communication priority. Local communities of those branches with overlap would differ from those without because there is the likelihood that one of the two branches would be closing in time. Similarly, the community serving the head office is another affected stakeholder and would rate as a high communication target. Finally, a large number of customers from both societies would see changes – especially if the name, the product offered or the business procedures change, or if they bank with those branches which are closing and will be asked to move to another branch. In addition, there may be large customers or those whom management feel warrant further specialized communication. As customers are deemed critical shareholders, they would be the focal point of the external communication effort.

Methods of communication and a communication audience chart

The methods of communication used in this case would vary as it would not be efficient or most effective to offer face-to-face communication with all employees. The next step becomes determining the affected stakeholders' media mix.

Those employees who are deemed most critical for the acquisition's success are those who warrant the most care and attention when it comes to communication strategy. In this case, they are the newly appointed directors and deputies and the ten target managers who it is hoped will stay with the company. The behaviour and attitudes of the former are critical for setting the right tone and in demonstrating what are acceptable actions for their teams. They will be under close scrutiny by all affected employees to see how they react to the changes and their new appointments. Sufficient effort must go into explaining this to the directors to ensure their full co-operation and support of the changes, and this should come from a most senior executive in a face-to-face meeting. Meetings with the ten target managers if conducted by the new Chairman or MD would also impress upon those managers the importance of their role in the new entity.

An example of an audience communication chart makes explicit the appropriate messages and communication media for each audience (see Table 4.1).

Table 4.1 Audience communication chart

Audience	Message	Media
Directors (both Advent and Zenith)	Will be changes in work roles Must work fully with deputies Employees looking to you for guidance and to set an example	Face-to-face meetings with MD and/or chairman
Deputy directors (both Advent and Zenith)	Opportunities in company for advancement Big player in a bigger company Will be changes in work roles Employees looking to you for guidance and to set an example	Face-to-face meetings with MD and/or chairman
Branch managers (Zenith)	Some branches to close (10 per cent in total) Most branches not affected Keeping good managers even if branch closes Will look after redundant staff Need (and will reward) loyal staff	Written communication Meetings with director/manager
Branch managers (Advent)	Some acquirer's branches to close (roughly 10 per cent in total) Most branches not affected Keeping good managers even if branch closes There will be redundancies but will look after redundant staff Need (and will reward) loyal staff	Written communication Meetings with director/manager

Table 4.1 continued

Audience	Message	Media
Branch staff (Zenith)	Some branches closing (roughly 10 per cent in total) Most branches not affected Closing branches' employees made redundant but will be well looked after Loyal staff needed (and rewarded)	Written communication Branch managers' talk
Branch staff (Advent)	Some branches closing (roughly 10 per cent in total) Most branches not affected Closing branches' employees made redundant but will be well looked after Loyal staff needed (and rewarded)	Written communication Branch managers' talk
Head office staff (Zenith)	Head office to close in six to eight months Employees made redundant will be looked after Loyalty needed (and rewarded)	Written communication Visit by MD and chairman on Day One or Day Two
Ten key head office managers (Zenith)	Head office is closing but we want you to remain with the company and relocate You are key to a smooth transition and future with the new integrated systems You will have career opportunities with the new company Loyalty needed (and rewarded) even if you do not relocate	Written communication Face-to-face communication with director or chairman/MD if possible on Day One
Head office staff (Advent)	No job losses There will be new colleagues and some new procedures and systems Tolerance and understanding of new colleagues important	Written communication Talk from functional director if time
Other staff (Advent and Zenith)	No job losses May be changes in working practices, new colleagues and culture	Written communication

The next logical step in communication strategy planning is to add the action steps for the various audiences. In other words, what outcomes are needed in order to ensure that the intended messages and outcomes are received by the appropriate audiences? In some cases, it can be the further development of the communication plan and package, in others it may be to structure the redundancy and loyalty bonus packages. As a tool, this provides the acquirer with a written reminder of what steps are still needed by the day of announcement and, therefore, aids in developing the implementation blueprint.

In the example given, the following action steps could be used by the acquirer to further develop the communication plan and implementation blueprint discussed in Chapter 3 (see Table 4.2).

Table 4.2 Communication action chart

Audience	Message	Media	Action
Directors (both Advent and Zenith)	Changes in roles Must work with deputies Under scrutiny	Face-to-face meetings	Pre-acquisition meetings to gain consensus Get involved with acquisition and communication planning ASAP
Deputy directors (both Advent and Zenith)	Career opportunities Bigger company Changes in roles Under scrutiny	Face-to-face meetings	Pre-acquisition meetings to gain consensus Get involved with acquisition and communication planning ASAP
Branch managers (Zenith)	Some branches to close but keep good managers Will look after staff Need (and will reward) loyal staff	Written communication Meetings	Joint integration groups Finalize communication packs Prepare fair redundancy packages Determine loyalty payments Define voluntary redundancy terms Brief on role during acquisition communication to branch
Branch managers (Advent)	Some branches to close but keep good managers Will look after staff Need (and will reward) loyal staff	Written communication Meetings	Joint integration groups Finalize communication packs Prepare fair redundancy packages Determine loyalty payments Define voluntary redundancy terms Brief on role during acquisition communication to branch

Table 4.2 continued

Audience	Message	Media	Action
Branch staff (Zenith)	Some branches closing Will look after staff Loyal staff needed	Written communication Managers' talk	Prepare fair redundancy packages Finalize communication packs Define loyalty payments Keep staff informed of changes
Branch staff (Advent)	Some branches closing Will look after staff Loyal staff needed	Written communication Managers' talk	Prepare fair redundancy packages Finalize communication packs Define loyalty payments Keep staff informed of changes
Head office staff (Zenith)	Head office to close in half year Staff will be looked after Loyalty needed	Written communication Visit by MD and chairman	Prepare fair redundancy packages Finalize communication packs Define loyalty payments Keep staff informed of changes
Ten key head office managers (Zenith)	Head office closing but we want you Key to a smooth transition and future Career opportunities	Written communication Face-to-face communication	Finalize communication packs Prepare relocation packages Finalize new job descriptions Prepare loyalty packages if they do not relocate but remain Joint integration groups
Head office staff (Advent)	No job losses New colleagues and systems Tolerance and understanding	Written communication Meetings	Finalize communication packs Keep staff informed of changes Prepare staff for new colleagues and systems via additional communication or training
Other staff (Advent and Zenith)	No job losses Changes in practices, colleagues and culture	Written communication	Finalize communication packs Keep staff informed of general changes

The same exercise can be conducted for external stakeholders. The City and the media would receive the message of a good geographic fit and increasing coverage. The combining of back office functions and the roughly 10 per cent rationalization of overlapping branches would be used to illustrate how economies of scale savings would be made. The local community surrounding the head office would need some sensitive communication, perhaps outlining what would be happening, the timeframe and any positive steps Advent Building Society would be taking to help with future employment for those potentially redundant employees.

Some communication to customers would be highly advisable. This could include personal visits for big clients and letters to clients of both Advent and Zenith. The information given could outline the positive elements of the acquisition by citing more branches and wider coverage, perhaps new products but the maintenance of the same personal service. If more efficient billing or back office is anticipated, this could be mentioned. A hotline telephone number also could be provided for customers with related queries. The vast majority of customers would not use it but it presents a professional and well-managed image to the outside world.

Designing the 'Day One' communication package

A communication action chart can facilitate the design of an acquirer's 'Day One' communication pack as the actions highlighted in the plan indicate what issues should be decided upon prior to its announcement. A communication pack is written information provided for target and acquiring employees at the time of acquisition. The objective of the communication pack is to provide the employees with as much accurate information as is available at that time. The more information provided, the lower employee concerns about the uncertainty brought on by the acquisition. A communication pack is only effective if it reaches employees in a timely manner, which is generally within 48 hours of the acquisition's announcement.

Research has shown that the amount and type of communication received by acquired employees at the time of acquisition varies greatly. A UK study found that just over half of employees received a talk from the acquiring chairman (51 per cent), 22 per cent received written communication from the acquiring chairman and 8 per cent from a senior executive, while 33 per cent received an acquisition newsletter. A further 11 per cent received no communication whatsoever concerning the intentions of the acquirer and the deal (Hunt et al., 1987).

How much information an employee received was also heavily related to their position in the organizational hierarchy. A US study found that, not surprisingly, senior employees received far more communication on changes than middle managers or the hourly paid (Schweiger and Weber, 1989). As seen in Table 4.3, while senior management received wide-ranging communication in many areas, other employees, especially the hourly paid, did not. An example is the announcement of redundancies; while 95 per cent of senior managers were made aware of a reduction in the workforce, only 77 per cent of middle managers and 60 per cent of hourly paid were informed. This suggests that employers were not communicating to employees in an open and honest manner.

Table 4.3 Information communicated to which level of employee at the time of announcement

Message communicated to employees	Senior Managers (%)	Middle Managers (%)	Hourly Paid (%)
Reasons for acquisition	100	83	77
Nature of agreement	98	52	35
Change in strategies	90	72	51
Change in benefits	90	88	79
Reduction of the workforce	95	77	60
New work environment	71	67	49
Change in salary	73	60	40

Source: © Schweiger and Weber (1989)

This study also highlights the dilemma faced by many middle managers during acquisition. Middle managers generally do not get the whole story from their senior managers, yet because they are receiving more information than non-managerial staff, the latter often cannot accept that middle managers do not know more than they really do. Accusations of hidden agendas and political behaviour can occur, especially in cases of low trust or threatening situations. Open and honest communication is the most effective means for dispelling this behaviour.

For maximum impact, communication packs should be consistent both across the acquirer's and target's employees as well as between the various documents. Inserts for organizational charts and personalities may be included on a function-specific basis or further briefing documents included for managers who are required to cascade information down the organization. If only certain divisions of the acquirer are to be directly affected by the acquisition, it is a more efficient use of resources to target only those employees affected with the information pack. Other divisions may not require the entire pack but instead are usually adequately served by a press release outlining the events. If employees are to have some contact with the target company and its employees, then a longer version can be provided including a history of the target company, what actions will be occurring, their timeframes and what the acquiring employees can expect in terms of contact.

A communication pack could include any or all of the following:

1. **Welcoming letter(s) from the acquiring chairman or CEO and also from the target management (especially in cases of agreed bids)** are important as they are usually the first point of contact the new employees will have with the newly acquiring management. Letters should be individually addressed to each employee. In one recent acquisition, the acquiring managing director personally signed each of the 3000 letters that went out to the target and his own employees. When the target employees received the communication packs and letters, they were very impressed not only that someone so senior had written to them personally but also that he had bothered to sign the letters himself. This was helped by the fact that the employees had never remembered receiving any individually addressed correspondence from their own management. Their perceptions of the new managing director's professionalism were enhanced and their goodwill towards the acquirer rose enormously. It is also imperative that any letter sets the tone that the acquirer intends to carry throughout the acquisition process. It is difficult to strike a balance of positive attitude yet tactful diplomacy when dealing with an acquisition which includes employee redundancies. If the balance is wrong, the acquirer can look callous or arrogant.

   It is also useful to have a letter from the target's senior management, although this is most likely only to happen in cases of agreed acquisitions. It is only effective, however, if the writer of the letter is going to stay with the combined firm. This type of letter can alleviate some of the fears of target employees because it is from a familiar person and can serve as an introduction to the acquirer's employees.

2. **An outline of the company vision** gives the reasoning and logic behind the acquisition and provides a framework of how the companies will develop in the future. This could include, for example, if the target is part of an ongoing acquisition strategy and where the target 'fits' in the organization. A timeframe and schedule for future changes can be outlined in this section. As seen in the Schweiger and Weber (1989) study, this information is often not passed down through the organization

– but even the hourly paid are interested in the logic behind the deal, if only to appease their unease about the future.

3. **A history of both companies** can be provided to both the acquirer and target employees. If either company has a long or interesting history which has influenced its culture, it is useful to include this information as it may 'explain' certain attitudes and perceptions to the other party as well as providing a source of interest.

4. **A question and answer (Q&A) sheet**, with the most commonly asked questions relating to acquisition answered, is one of the most important elements of the communication package. The bulk of employee questions generally come under the domain of the human resource department: terms and conditions, redundancies, relocations and changes in working practices. Even questions such as what will happen to the office Christmas party are questions which employees will ask and need to be answered in time, although the 'Day One' Q&A need not go into that level of detail.

5. **Press releases** can be included for customer- or media-facing employees. In some acquisitions where many employees come into contact with customers, it is worthwhile to give the press release to everyone in order to maintain continuity of information. These can be used in answering any externally generated questions; often the press release serves as the foundation for other external messages such as the customer briefing documents.

6. **Customer briefing Q&A** is usually based on the press release and offers those employees who have customer contact some answers to questions the customer may pose. Questions regarding levels of servicing, changes in contracts, pricing and employee point of contact should be covered. A central telephone number and contact name can be given if customers have further questions – this helps to maintain continuity in response and makes the acquirer look like it is firmly in control of the process.

7. **A manager's guide to employment law** is recommended in cases of functional or full merger in order to explain to managers why decisions have to be taken in a certain way. This includes referring to the transaction in certain ways (such as a proposed acquisition prior to regulatory approval) and in selecting employees (picking the best person for the job and not necessarily your existing team). This is discussed in more detail in Chapters 3 and 5.

8. **A code of behaviour for the implementation process** is a useful addition to the communication pack outlining what behaviour and practices are condoned in the new organization, especially during the

implementation process. In one acquisition, the target was perceived as being a highly political organization whereas the acquirer was not. In the code of behaviour, it was specified that only non-political behaviour would be tolerated – that decisions took place in the meeting room and not in the hallways. By stating this, the document set the tone for the implementation process. In order to be effective, however, future action must consistently back up the written code. In addition, the acquirer must have a good idea of its own culture and values (and not just at board level) in order to communicate them to another party.

9. **A timeframe for changes or when those changes will be announced** is essential information in creating a foundation for employee expectation management, reducing uncertainty, and creating some 'quick wins'. Publicly announcing certain milestones (and then adhering to them) is the cornerstone of a successful implementation process. If there has been adequate pre-acquisition planning the first public announcement of milestones can be in the communication pack. Key to its overall success, once again, is the ability of the acquirer to adhere to its written message in terms of timing and delivery of outcomes.

10. **How decisions are going to be made** (such as joint integration groups) and who will be involved with those changes (or in the integration groups) can be included in the outline of future events or as a stand alone document. In either case, like the timeframe, this document serves not only as an information dissemination document, but also in tone setting (professional and thorough management) and in employee expectation management.

11. **An organizational chart** is useful to include on an organization-wide or functional basis if the organization has a complex structure or if the structure has changed radically due to the acquisition. In the example of Advent and Zenith, this would be beneficial to highlight the new director and deputy director positions.

12. **A brief biography of some of the people you may come across** at the two companies or within functions is also useful in some cases, especially in those where functional or company-wide merger is to take place very soon after the acquisition announcement date. This would be most appropriate as an insert done on a function-by-function basis.

Co-ordination of external and internal communication and internal media

Once the deal has been approved by the shareholders and relevant regulatory bodies and the acquirer takes control of the target, it is time that communication to acquired employees begins in earnest. Most of the work, however, will have occurred prior to the day of announcement. On 'Day One', employees receive their information pack and, in many cases, hear a talk by a senior acquiring manager. They also receive information from a variety of other sources including the external media. Consistency of information is a theme common to successful acquisitions and includes both internal and external communication. The Quality Guarding example discussed in Chapter 8 is a prime example of differences in internal and external communication; the chairman stated in the press that margins would be doubled while the internal communication stated it was 'business as usual' with employees being informed of changes as they occurred. When the former turned out to be the more accurate, the internal communication's source was damaged in terms of credibility.

In the case of smaller acquisitions, there may be little external media interest; however, in larger or public deals it is to be expected. The press comments regarding the acquisition will be based on several sources of information: company-issued press releases, individual sources and press speculation. The acquirer, therefore, has some influence over what will appear in the external media. The acquirer can not only release its own press statement but it is suggested that it co-ordinate releases with the target company's management as well. This is more important if it is a subsidiary sale as it is common for both companies to put a positive spin on the sale; the acquirer says it got 'a bargain' and the seller says it sold at full price. What should be released is a mutually agreed basis for press communication.

In many cases, if the deal is a public bid or reliant on funding, the external message will be optimistic. If this optimism is based on cost savings achieved via redundancies, how this message is handled must be carefully planned. While this is good news for shareholders, it isn't necessarily so for employees. Especially in these cases, communication must remain honest and consistent, both internally and externally. If job losses are to be expected, then they must be declared. If the acquirer discusses them in an empathetic or sensitive manner, it sends a different message than if the acquirer's reaction is less sympathetic.

Consistency of information is also important in internal communication – research has consistently found that those sources which prove the most accurate gain credibility, while those which are inaccurate decrease in credence. Not only does this inconsistency damage the source of the communication in the longer term, it also weakens the immediate communication message and increases the likelihood of rumours. An example of this was seen in a service company which bought a major competitor. While the written communication pack was excellent, it referred euphemistically rather than directly to the redundancies which were to affect less than 5 per cent of the workforce. At the deal's announcement, the charismatic and straightforward managing director toured several of the operating locations and answered employee questions. When asked about redundancies, he replied honestly that they would occur and would affect a small but significant percentage of the employees. While this did not directly contradict the communication pack, it was a far more direct response. While this enhanced the managing director's credibility and perceived honesty, it unnecessarily blurred the overall communication message at the time while also creating rumours. Instead, the written pack should have discussed more openly the impending redundancies.

The legal mechanics of acquisition communication in the UK

As outlined in Rule 19 of the Blue Book (the legal code for public deal acquisitions in the UK), it is illegal to provide any stakeholders (including various shareholders, employees or customers) with preferential information which could affect the price of shares; this includes information on any potential acquisition or merger. Thus, the same information must be made available to all stakeholders simultaneously and the stock exchange must be notified prior to the release of any public information. The ramifications of this are that it is impossible to discuss any acquisition with employees until it becomes public information. Those deals which require a shareholder vote (public deals) necessitate the potential acquirer going via the existing management to the shareholders in agreed bids or to the shareholders directly in contested or hostile bids.

In any public deal, the bid will be public knowledge prior to its approval for at least 60 days (the statutory minimum allowed for a share purchase) and in cases of referral to a government agency or contested bid, much longer. These two months can be a time of intense media speculation and, consequently, high uncertainty for affected employees. While the acquirer usually cannot contact employees directly, the information available publicly via the media is part of the overall communication strategy and can present a balanced view of what the acquisition will bring for the various stakeholders, including employees.

In some cases when market speculation concerning a merger or acquisition is affecting share prices, the stock exchange may ask the company in question for a public statement. The company may state that it is in discussions with another organization over the possibility of an acquisition or merger, but without naming the other party. The media usually then begins speculating with whom the talks are occurring. Obviously this can also be a time of increased anxiety for employees as they read press speculation about the potential partners. Under current legislation, however, the company in question or acquirer is in no position to directly make denial or allay employee concerns at this juncture.

Similarly, many acquisitions require industry regulatory approval which can also take up to 60 days to be granted. During this time it is often possible to communicate directly with target employees and customers with the approval of the target's shareholders. If this is the case, it is important to communicate to employees as soon as possible and explain the delay as most employees will not understand the nuances of regulatory approval.

The legal constraints surrounding private deal communication are less onerous. The parties can announce the deal at any time, be it during discussions, at reaching agreement subject to due diligence or when the acquirer is about to take control. As long as the parties have a communication strategy in place to deal with the time of announcement, the appropriate timing depends on the circumstances and preferences of the parties involved.

THE RUN-UP TO ANNOUNCEMENT: PLANNING TOOLS

Perhaps the biggest difficulty prior to the 'Day One' announcement is ensuring that everything is adequately planned. Acquisition communication is always difficult as it relies on so many other elements of the process – pre-acquisition planning, decisions from different functions, and management and legal approval. Because of this, the process benefits from a project management discipline. This can include using critical path analysis, project management software, and Gantt charts estimating the amount of time needed to finish each step along the way. (See Chapter 3 (Figure 3.11) for a critical path analysis of Advent and Zenith.) As can be seen, there are many steps which are often forgotten in the hectic few days going into the deal's announcement.

A key employee chart is another tool which can be used to ensure that no key employees 'slip through the net' of either the acquirer or target during the implementation (see Table 4.4). The chart also ensures that employees are not being overstretched in terms of their joint integration group commitments. The acquirer can ask its managers to fill in the chart with those employees they feel warrant special communication (be it a managers' briefing, individual interview or participation in joint integration groups). If the acquisition is friendly, the acquirer can ask the target management to do the same. In either case, it is likely that the acquirer will want to choose participants on the basis of their current positions. The acquirer must bear in mind the risk that there may be political bias over who is chosen in both companies. Validating who the 'key employees' are by a variety of means reduces the problem to a greater extent.

Table 4.4 Key employee chart: Advent and Zenith building societies

Company (A or Z)	Position and function	Employee name	Joint integration groups?	Which ones?	One-on-one interview?	If yes, with whom and when?

As the time approaches for the 'Day One' announcement, those managers who will be speaking on behalf of the acquirer should go through a dress rehearsal. This is especially helpful if those managers are intending to take questions from the newly acquired employees and those questions will be on difficult topics such as redundancies. Various questions could be asked to which the speaker responds; while this does sound 'stage managed', the fewer surprises one has to face on 'Day One', the better.

During this time, those in charge of communication should also be developing contingency plans for if the acquisition announcement is made prematurely or is held up by regulators. While this may not apply to many acquisitions, those involved in the deal's communication must consider all the possibilities and have solutions in hand if things do not go accordingly to plan. An example could be if the deal looks like it will be concluded on a Friday afternoon. From a communication sense it is far preferable to have the news embargoed until the following Monday to ensure that employees hear of the deal from management and not from the weekend newspapers.

As discussed in Chapter 3, the critical path analysis and project management technique of 'Day One', one day, one week, one month, and so on, can also be readily applied to communication planning. During the run-up to the deal's completion, it is very difficult to manage all the communication threads without using some kind of project management tools and techniques. As communication is so critical to the employees' initial impressions, they are highly recommended tools.

ONGOING COMMUNICATION DURING IMPLEMENTATION

Although this section could be covered in Chapter 5 ('The Implementation Process'), it is really a continuation of the communication process. Because of this, it is included in this chapter. Other communication issues relating to implementation will be discussed in Chapter 5 as well.

Typical communication problems encountered during implementation

We have seen in Chapter 2, the ability to communicate effectively during acquisition is reliant on several factors such as consistency of action and communication and believability of communication. Yet time pressures and work constraints after acquisition often make it impossible to communicate in such a manner. The problems which can arise as a result of this during acquisition implementation include:

1. stop-start communication
2. rumours and gossip
3. inaccurate communication
4. distorted messages
5. difficult communication between the acquiring and target employees.

These will be discussed in turn.

Stop-start communication

A major problem for many acquirers is the ability to keep the momentum going with communication during the implementation process. As will be seen in the Quality Guarding case study, management can begin with the best intentions of communicating to staff but the dual pressures of day-to-day workload and acquisition implementation intervene. The information needed to run the company becomes more complex as it is needed for both running the business and facilitating the acquisition implementation. This can be further complicated by new procedures, policies, culture, organizational and communication styles which come with the new target company. Consequently, it is not uncommon for management to begin communicating and then over time find that other issues become a priority. When formal communication stops, the 'rumour mill' begins in earnest with employees spending increasing amounts of time discussing the acquisition and its ramifications with their colleagues. During this time, the ratio of formal to informal communication can be at its lowest point and in the void created by the lack of formal communication, informal communication and rumour can run rampant, especially via employees' informal groups.

Another factor which often impedes effective communication is actually waiting for information to be communicated. While there is a flurry of activity on announcement day of the acquisition, there can be an information lull while implementation groups and the steering committee work to produce findings which are the basis for future action. What happens is an 'information void' where employees are expecting communication yet none is forthcoming. This was seen at Quality Guarding; one manager commented:

> We got a memo saying 'business as usual' and this is what Service Conglomerate had agreed, we will keep you informed and then that was it, then complete silence. Personally, I think if you send a letter out of that sort, you have to follow through with more information. You are building hopes of more information and then none is forthcoming. The next bit of information we received was the date of the reorganization eight weeks later.

A common response from the acquirer is: 'I didn't communicate because there was nothing to communicate.' While this may be true, the affected employees do not know this and assume decisions are being made without their knowledge; accusations of 'hidden agendas' can develop. The answer is to communicate when employees expect it, even if you have nothing concrete to say. If an answer is expected on a certain day and the decision is delayed, communicate anyway stating that the decision is delayed, the reason why and when the decision will be announced.

Rumours and gossip

Employees always want more information than they are given during an acquisition; as Buono and Bowditch suggest, the 'rumor mill and grapevine work overtime, leading to more anxiety and, in many cases, counterproductive behaviors' (1989, p. 257). When employees do not receive adequate formal communication they rely on rumours and informal communication. In many cases, over two hours of every working day is lost through gossiping or unproductive behaviour during acquisition. Yet employees would rather have information from management instead of having to rely on rumour and gossip. One Scottish Yeast shopfloor employee commented:

> We would rather be told by management rather than listen to the grapevine because when you listen to the grapevine, you don't know whether or not it is true. At least if they [management] tell us, you hope it is true.

Rumours are defined as 'information usually of local or current interest intended for belief' (DiFonzo et al., 1994, p. 50). They are unconfirmed and spring from collective employee concerns and interests. US-based research found that rumours during the early stages of acquisition are more nebulous and based on general anxiety in target employees and, in some cases, the acquirers surrounding the situation (Ivancevich et al., 1987). Once the implementation phase begins, the rumours change, becoming more clear and detailed in speculation as word leaks out into the organization. The level of employee stress is related to employees' appraisals of the situation, rather than the actual intent of the acquiring company at this point; thus, rumours fuelling employee speculation can be especially damaging at this point during acquisition.

The truth contained within rumours is often made more difficult to detect as it is buried amongst a great deal of factual information. Rumours are accurate 80–90 per cent of the time; however, the 10–20 per cent of inaccurate information is very damaging (Davis, 1977). Rumours are almost always negative, thereby increasing employee concerns and anxiety rather than reducing them; they are usually based on a worst-case scenario and portray the worst possible motives of those in charge.

Related to this is the issue of confidentiality during acquisition. There is simply no such thing as confidential information during the implementation process. As soon as a meeting takes place, a telephone conversation overheard, a document photocopied and the original left on the machine or a memo dictated, the word is out in the open as employees are desperate for any information they can find. Thus, in order to control rumours and the flow of information, it is easier and more effective to make information available to all staff as soon as it is possible. This was seen in Quality Guarding: all the employees knew the meetings amongst senior directors were taking place. It would have been better to confirm and manage employee suspicions rather than let them run wild and unchecked.

Inaccurate communication

Organizational communication can be poor even at the best of times, but accurate information during acquisition can be very scarce. Two types of inaccurate communication can arise during acquisition, that which is inaccurate due to changes in the plan and that which is simply not true from the outset.

In those cases where formal employee communication is wrong from the outset and it is later discovered by employees, the effect can be seriously damaging. In fact, this has been found to be more damaging than receiving no information at all. Further ramifications can include decreased trust in management and perceived fairness of the acquisition process. In some cases an increased questioning of the new organization's culture as well as intention to leave are outcomes. This was seen at Quality Guarding.

In those cases where the implementation plan changes, the original intention may have been communicated whereas the abridged version is not. If the changes are not communicated, the dichotomy between communication and action can confuse employees and lead to expectational dissonance. One Infosys employee summed up this feeling:

> People would have accepted the changes more readily if they had explained the changes; they may not have agreed with them but they would have accepted them more readily because they would have understood the rationale behind them.

The issue then becomes an adequate explanation for changes to the perceived or expected plan which remains a cornerstone of managing expectations. When adequate explanations are provided for employees even retrospectively, employees are more likely to accept the changes. If it is not given, not only can management credibility be damaged but the outcome can be seen as flawed; the result is rebellion in light of the decision. This concept, procedural justice, is discussed further in Chapter 5.

Distorted messages

Noise is defined as any factor that causes the message sent by a source to distort and be misinterpreted by the receiver (Mitchell and Holmes, 1996).

It is a common phenomenon of acquisition that communication messages can become distorted due to a variety of means. These can include:

- misinterpretation of motives
- wrong first impressions
- hearing influenced by wishing
- words having more than one meaning
- missed communication
- stereotypical thinking
- high emotions
- distrust of the sender
- defensiveness and/or
- an unshared set of assumptions (ibid.).

The end result is that the message that was intended is not the message received. An example of how noise can distort a message was seen in a recent service company acquisition. A few weeks after the acquisition, the acquiring operations director drove to a target site to give a presentation to the employees and answer any questions they might have. Upon arriving late at the site, he found no available parking spaces so he doubled parked. When he met the site manager, he explained his parking problem and asked if the site manager would mind moving the car for him if someone wanted to get out. He said he didn't want to leave the meeting and interrupt any employees during the presentation or question time; the site manager gladly agreed. Within two weeks, the rumour going around the company was that the acquiring operations director walked into the site, flicked his keys at the site manager and said: 'Park my car, that is your job now.' The surprising aspect of this acquisition was that it was going very well with a great deal of effort being expended from the senior acquiring team to ensure its success. In spite of their work, these kinds of rumours flourished.

Difficult communication between the acquiring and target employees

Some acquisitions create situations where communication between employees becomes difficult. Examples of this include when individuals are vying for the same job or others by virtue of previous history, mergers of fierce competitors, or hostile acquisitions. In these circumstances, communication between elements of the firms is likely to be strained or inaccurate. Research has found that in cases where the informer did not trust the recipient, the result was evasive communication where the distrust distorted the relevant information. Power also served as a communication block with ambitious people withholding information that they perceived as strengthening their position. This differential in information can, in turn, become a source of conflict in some cases as it creates feelings of power and defensiveness.

The Infosys case discussed in Chapter 11 is a good example of this. The two most senior executives were put in an organizational structure which demanded a great deal of liaising, honest communication and trust, yet their own personal positions were ambiguous. They also had not had time to develop a solid working relationship. It is very unlikely that these two ambitious professionals would ever have been able to work effectively in such an illogical post-acquisition management structure. Both could see there was only one job and two suitors; as such it was doomed to failure. A directly reporting manager commented:

> I went through it earlier today and the organizational chart makes no sense whatsoever at the moment. Whose job is it? Isabelle Saunders who runs the business or Glenn Johnson who has got some vague strategic role?

Techniques for implementation communication

Communication problems are more the norm than the exception during acquisition. There are several methods and techniques, however, which can be used to help alleviate the problems associated with ongoing implementation communication. These include:

1. realistic merger previews
2. communication vehicles
3. communication awareness and training for managers
4. team building between target and acquiring parties.

These will be discussed in turn.

Realistic merger previews

Realistic merger previews are based upon the concept of realistic job previews which are used to socialize new employees into a company upon joining. They are effective in combating rumours and inaccurate or distorted information by expressing both the positive and negative aspects of a specific organizational role, either verbally or in written form, to new employees prior to their commencement of employment, and by managing new employees' expectations of the impending work experience.

Realistic job previews are seen to work for four reasons. First, they foster a belief that the organization is trustworthy, honest and it cares about its employees. Second, in engendering these feelings the employee's commitment to the organization can be strengthened. Third, realistic job previews reduce role ambiguity. Finally, they allow for employees to adjust to the realistic levels of expectations prior to joining the firm.

The research shows that new employees who receive realistic job previews are 'more satisfied with their jobs and more committed to the organizations, experience less stress, and are less likely to leave than employees socialized through more traditional methods' (Schweiger and DeNisi, 1991, p. 112). In addition, realistic job previews have been found to have a positive effect on turnover, job satisfaction, role clarity, job performance and organizational commitment.

The concept of realistic job previews has been translated into merger previews in order to achieve many of the same objectives. A merger preview provides information as well, portraying the acquiring organization in a positive light in terms of honesty and trustworthiness. It can be achieved via a comprehensive communication package containing the elements discussed above. It may, however, cause some employees to leave the new organization rather than undergo the socialization process, especially during times of low employment, for example. This could either be a positive or negative factor for the acquirer – positive if the acquirer would have had to make people redundant at a later time after incurring training and redundancy costs, or negative if those individuals leaving are key to the company's success.

To date, there has been only one major study on realistic merger previews involving two plants whose owners had recently undergone an acquisition (ibid.). One plant received a realistic merger preview containing information on why the merger had occurred and the expected positive and negative outcomes, including redundancies, while the control plant received no information. The results were that the acquisition raised employee concerns over uncertainty and levels of stress. The plant that did not receive the realistic merger preview experienced a decrease in job satisfaction, commitment and intention to remain, as well as perceptions of the company's trustworthiness and honesty. Importantly, these feelings increased rather than decreased over the course of the acquisition's implementation. A merger preview comprising realistic communication helped employees to cope with the uncertainty and to better understand the process. Furthermore, when a realistic programme of communication was introduced at the control plant, the levels of perceived company trustworthiness and honesty, as well as performance, improved over time (ibid.).

Communication vehicles

The acquirer has a choice of channels through which to communicate to employees during the implementation process. All the channels discussed below, when used effectively and consistently, can help the acquirer in addressing the potential problems associated with implementation communication discussed above.

1. **Newsletters** are often used to keep employees informed as information becomes available. Two characteristics an effective newsletter will have are that it is timely with regular distribution and that it covers the relevant issues in a sympathetic manner. If an acquirer states that a monthly newsletter is to be produced, then it should happen monthly even if it is thought there is nothing to communicate. Whether or not decisions have been taken, timeframes for decisions and other information can be discussed. If the acquirer does not have sufficient internal manpower or expertise to regularly produce the document, the process can be outsourced to a professional communication specialist.

2. **Hotlines, both telephone and e-mail**, offer employees – and more importantly, customers – a means of asking questions and gaining information about the acquisition. They also provide a forum for continuous and consistent communication on the part of the acquirer, thereby reducing rumour. In return, they provide feedback to the acquirer on the types and levels of employee concerns. Their success relies on being staffed by people with expertise in the dynamics of acquisition as well as their having access to the most up-to-date information on the implementation process as it becomes available.

3. **Acquisition co-ordinators**, like hotlines, offer a single source of formal communication from which to give and receive information. An acquisition co-ordinator must have sufficient understanding in the dynamics of acquisition; as many of the queries will be human resource related (terms and conditions, redundancies, role changes), an HR staff member can often perform this job. They must also have the time to perform the job adequately which usually means it being a full-time position, at least at the beginning of the acquisition. If they sit on the acquisition steering committee or have good access to decision makers, their ability to gain information in a timely manner is enhanced.

4. **Bulletin board releases** are a useful and inexpensive means for keeping the workforce informed. While this method does not allow for any form of feedback nor personal interaction, it is effective in those businesses with highly geographically dispersed sites and for those

companies whose managers are not universally good communicators. It is best used as a form of back-up communication in conjunction with verbal communication.

5. **Acquisition surgeries** promote two-way communication and give management a strong indication of what employee concerns are within the organization. A senior manager can hold private sessions on site and answer personal questions being asked by individuals who make appointments. As the questions being asked often pertain to HR issues, it may be advisable to have a human resource staff member visit the sites.

6. **Regular acquisition meetings** do not have to be anything elaborate but can serve as the conduit between the decision makers and the rest of the workforce. Forums can include office meeting rooms, canteens, and even the company car park. If weekly management briefings are already part of the organization's existing communication programme, this can be used to cascade down related acquisition news. Meetings offer the opportunity for employee feedback and questions, both of which are useful for management to gauge employee feelings and concerns. It is important that the meetings occur at regular intervals and that the people speaking are well versed in communication skills, especially if difficult issues are being discussed. Road shows are a more formal type of acquisition meeting and can offer employees the opportunity to meet and hear the senior people outline the company vision and future as well as field questions.

Communication awareness and training for managers

Communication training just after acquisition is not the most opportune time, as in many cases managers will be grappling with an already increased workload. But research has consistently found that the average manager is generally not an effective communicator. During acquisition, this may be exacerbated by an unwillingness of some managers to communicate as they are too worried about their own security to communicate to their subordinates. What would help is communication training prior to the acquisition as part of a general management training programme. Management communication training can help alleviate rumours, distorted and inaccurate communication, as well as help managers deal with difficult communication between acquired parties. In addition, more than one type of communication channel should be used to reinforce any messages and ensure that employees working for poor managerial communicators receive at least some communication.

Team building between target and acquiring parties

As discussed earlier, communication between acquired parties can be strained for a variety of reasons including low trust, role tensions and 'them and us' perceptions. In order to promote effective communication between the parties, it is important to understand why communication is poor. Often it is an underlying symptom of another issue, for instance, outstanding role issues or organizational hierarchy decisions to be decided. If this is the case, it is impossible to ensure effective communication until the underlying problem is rectified.

If communication is poor because there is low trust between the target and acquiring employees, team building exercises which promote communication may be advisable. Examples of this can include having managers work together on projects not directly related to the acquisition, via business games, or by promoting extracurricular activities such as sporting tournaments which require the two companies' employees to mix. Another example is to have a competition whereby teams are asked questions about the other company and the only way to find out the answers is to talk to the other employees. All the exercises are designed to promote intra-company communication in a non-threatening environment.

CONCLUSION

'We should have communicated more' is a management response heard so often after acquisitions. While it is easy to say this, it is much harder to deliver. It requires a consistent and dedicated effort to ensure that employees feel they are receiving adequate communication. As it is a 'softer issue' it is often disregarded or given a low priority, yet it is a fundamental part of successful acquiring. It is possible to be a poor acquirer and communicate if the planning and implementation do not come up to standard, but it is impossible to be a successful acquirer and not communicate effectively to your workforce.

5 The Implementation Process: Where the Work Begins

INTRODUCTION

By the time the contracts are signed, employees look anxiously to the acquirer for direction and the way forward. The three months following taking control have the greatest impact on whether or not the deal is a success and the ability to influence this phase's success rests almost entirely with the acquirer (see Figure 5.1). Those who understand its importance and approach it professionally will stand a greater chance of being successful. Those who take it lightly do so at their peril. But by the time the acquirer gets to this stage, its fate may already have been decided – has management meticulously planned the process and communicated it to those affected or entered into the arrangement without sufficient thought? If it is the latter, they are already doomed. If it is the former – they have all to play for during the implementation phase.

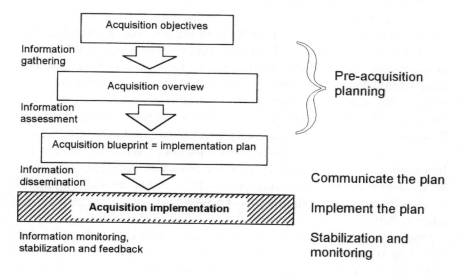

Fig. 5.1 *Implementation as part of the acquisition process*

'DAY ONE' OF THE ACQUISITION

As discussed in the previous chapter, regulatory or shareholder approval may delay taking control of the business immediately and the implementation process. If possible the acquirer may be able to communicate directly to employees and customers during this time with the permission of the target shareholders. This is an option worth pursuing when possible as most employees and customers will not understand the nuances of approval and will expect some form of communication at this stage, if only to acknowledge the time delay. If the deal is public and the transaction is completed at an awkward time (such as a Friday afternoon), it is also worth considering embargoing the news of the deal's completion. This allows the acquirer the opportunity to dictate the timing of the news breaking so that it can be co-ordinated with internal communication such as site visits.

Announcing the deal

How employees first hear of the acquisition's announcement is important. Wherever possible, it is important that employees learn of the deal internally before they hear of it via external sources for several reasons. First, hearing it internally presents a far more professional image of the acquirer and indicates that the process is under control and being run competently. Second, it allows the acquiring management to put their point of view across first or to 'paint the first picture' in the eyes of affected employees. Third, it allows employees to understand the deal and its ramifications before talking to customers. Employees find it very uncomfortable to hear of acquisitions from clients rather than first-hand – not only does it look unprofessional to both the employee and client, but it means that a uniform response to clients is impossible. Finally, employees will be bombarded by questions from clients, suppliers, competitors and perhaps even the press. If they are to provide a consistent story which highlights the positive aspects of the deal for the respective parties, they must have that information at hand. It is important to remember that acquiring as well as target employees will be asked questions by clients and suppliers. Thus, customer-facing employees from both companies should also be provided with relevant support documentation.

Employees heard about the acquisition from outside sources at Quality Guarding (Chapter 8). Through no fault of the acquired management, employees heard of the acquisition from the radio, clients and other affected employees. The end result was a confused and disjointed message both to employees and clients, one which the acquirer had to overcome before being able to communicate effectively with the acquired employees. One Quality Guarding guard commented:

> At the start it could have been a lot better if they had timed it properly and the press would not have had it first. It took two to three days for us to find out and it could have been done in a day. Clients were coming up to us and asking questions and we didn't know; we were only speculating. It makes them uneasy because they don't know who they are dealing with.

A manager added:

> You are getting questions from staff and other managers and clients and you think you are stupid because they know more than you do because they heard things on the radio.

The role of senior staff during the first few days

By the time the transaction is completed, the senior management team is usually exhausted from the negotiations. Yet unfortunately for them, the work has just begun. After the deal is announced, target employees naturally look to both the acquirer and their own leadership for direction. Hopefully, employees will have been given a written communication pack which answered most of their questions. But there is a huge amount of follow-up action that is needed during the first days of the acquisition, especially by the most senior management.

The first necessary action is to take financial control of the target: the cheque books, specified spending limits and the treasury function. This can be done relatively quickly but clear guidelines on what is expected and allowed in terms of spending and limitations by the target need to be outlined. Some acquirers impose immediate spending freezes until they have had a chance to assess the target's current position, after which time different guidelines are put into place. Not only is it financially prudent, it sends a message that the acquirer is professional and in control.

It is also wise to remember the 48 hour rule – you have 48 hours to take psychological control of your target, especially if you want to effect change. That doesn't mean one needs to tell affected employees the exact outcomes of the implementation process, but at the least you need to tell them a timeframe of when you plan to have answers about what areas are being examined. This can be done personally via face-to-face communication individually for key employees or in groups of varying sizes. It can also be done using the acquisition communication pack described in Chapter 4. As this is probably the majority of target employees' first exposure to the acquirer (other than perhaps via the press), it is critical to make a professional first impression. After that first impression is made, all subsequent encounters will only be modifications of that first perception. Thus, senior management have a vital role to play in the first few days after the deal.

As the principal communicators during this time, senior management disseminate information, set the tone, make the receivers feel important, serve to build trust and believability, and manage employee expectations. They do this not only in what they say but in how they say it: their choice of words, their body language, gestures and tone. In those companies where the senior management are effective communicators, it is critical to have them meet as many employees as possible. If the acquiring management can talk honestly and professionally it will enhance the acquirer's credibility. A short 'visionary' speech followed by a question and answer session allows for an open dialogue between the acquiring management and target employees – if the former listen to employees and answer questions honestly, the process can be mutually beneficial. Management gets an understanding of employee concerns while employees get an opportunity to have their questions answered and 'test the water' with their new owners. Forums which are likely to be used include: large group meetings, smaller meetings for more senior or key managers or one-to-one meetings for the most important employees.

Face-to-face communication has consistently been found to be important to acquisition success. A UK study found that in two-thirds of successful acquisitions, a senior member of the acquirer communicated the essentials of the acquisition to the newly acquired company employees; in two-thirds of unsuccessful acquisitions, they did not (Hunt et al., 1987). A most important element of this process was for senior management to provide a clear vision of the company and its future direction. A large-scale US study found that employees saw honesty and providing a clear vision as the two traits they most liked in their managers (Shaskin and Williams, 1993). It is not surprising to find that during acquisition these characteristics were highly prized in senior management.

The results from the five case studies were the same, with employees impressed by the visionary talks given by the heads of Anglo-American, Scottish Yeast and TeleCable Group. While their styles differed, the positive impact did not. A director hearing Alistair Anderson of Anglo-American commented:

We went to the meeting and listened to Alistair Anderson. They had clearly done their homework and were laying down where Home Products had gone wrong over the years, where they could improve it, the next course of action and the course it would take over the next few months. It was a very impressive meeting.

PROJECT MANAGING THE IMPLEMENTATION PROCESS

The role of senior management during the implementation process

As with communication, the role of senior management during the implementation process is vital to the acquisition's success. During the few weeks of an acquisition, employees focus upon senior management as they look for guidance and direction. Senior management will find themselves under intense scrutiny as employees assess whether or not they are worthy owners. These first impressions are critical.

There are certain ways that acquiring management can increase the likelihood that acquired employees feel that they are credible. First, as discussed above, acquired employees will look to senior management to provide vision and the way forward not only for the acquisition but also for the business in general. If management are able to provide a clear and logical vision then their credibility is enhanced. Second, senior management can gain credibility if they have a technical expertise which the employees value. Related to this, employees respect senior managers who are seen to be knowledgeable and well prepared – this is seen in the Anglo-American case. Third, if senior management are seen to be honest and open communicators, this also adds a great deal to their credibility; this was the case at Discovery. Finally, impartiality also is seen as a great credibility boost.

It is always best to have a very senior manager in charge of the implementation process, perhaps as head of the steering committee (see below). His or her involvement signals the importance of the acquisition to the affected employees and ensures that the process is going according to his or her plan by the philosophy espoused. The difficulty comes with the already overstretched workload of the average chief executive. If the chief executive is too busy to devote the time necessary to see the process through, it is better to have an appointed deputy who can devote the time necessary and yet keep the executive informed of the implementation's process. Paramount must be delivering the outcomes in a timely manner.

Implementation behaviour: organizational justice theory

As discussed in Chapter 2 and seen in the case studies, it is often not what is implemented nor the amount of change but how it is implemented which shapes success during acquisition. Comments such as 'It just wasn't fair!', were heard in two of the cases, Quality Guarding and Infosys. The issue of fairness becomes critical during acquisition if how changes are implemented becomes more important than the changes themselves. To understand what employees mean by 'fair', it is useful to understand the concept of organizational justice.

Organizational justice is divided into two related elements: distributive and procedural justice. Distributive justice is the perceived allocation of organizational judgements (that is, are they made in an equitable fashion within the organization?). Procedural justice is the perception of how fair are the procedures used to allocate those outcomes; it comprises three elements: the decision making procedure, the explanation of that procedure, and finally the treatment of individuals during the implementation of those outcomes (Greenberg, 1990). Procedural justice means that the process of getting to the result is often more a determinant of employee reaction than the result itself. When comparing the Scottish Yeast and Quality Guarding acquisitions, more people were made redundant in the former, yet, as the procedure was generally considered fair, there was less of an uproar over the redundancies. Thus, even if the outcome is negative, the impact can be mitigated if the procedures for arriving at that result are considered fair. Although individuals may be unhappy with the actual outcome of a process, if they understand the process through open and honest communication and perceive it has been fairly determined and implemented, they will accept it more readily than if it was handled badly. This is especially the case if the outcome is negative (as in redundancies).

There are several factors which can influence the perceived fairness of the process and its subsequent result. First, the amount of input into the decision making process can affect the outcome – clearly, if employees have some hand in determining the outcome they are less likely to perceive it as unfair. This, however, is reliant on the employees' ability to communicate their views and opinions openly during the decision making process – the more open and participatory the forum, the greater the likelihood of the procedure being perceived as fair. On the other hand, if employees have given their input only to have it ignored in the decision making process, it has a detrimental effect, a feeling called the 'frustration effect' (Greenberg and Folger, 1983). In these cases, acquirers are better off not having employees involved at all rather than involve them then ignore their input. Second, individuals are more likely to perceive an outcome as being fair if the procedure is seen as being without bias and applied consistently. Finally, the fair, courteous treatment of those affected by the decision is also seen as a key determinant of the outcome's perception.

When employees judge the procedure to be fair, a 'fair process effect' can be seen in which employees respond positively about organizational fairness, employee loyalty, job satisfaction, commitment, management trust, performance, and trust in leadership (ibid.). Reductions in turnover and intention to quit also have been related to perceptions of fair process.

The ramifications of organizational justice are very important for managing employees in acquisition. Acquisition often leads to radical organizational change, including restructuring and redundancy. If these potentially damaging events are dealt with in a fashion that is deemed 'fair' by those affected, it is likely that the remaining employees' views of the organization will not be adversely affected and, in fact, may be enhanced. The impact on the remaining employees cannot be underestimated; those who remain will carefully assess how those being made redundant were treated. If they were treated fairly and generously, then the remaining employees feel no threat with remaining – if they are subsequently made redundant they think that they, too, will be treated fairly. If they see their colleagues treated badly, they will leave before undergoing the same ignominious outcome themselves. The result can be a haemorrhaging of employees – and they are usually the competent ones with ample opportunities.

Employees also accept that the integration will not always go according to plan and that it must be able to change in respect to environmental fluctuations and unforeseen circumstances. The reasoning behind these changes as well as its communication to those affected, however, is an integral element in ensuring a fair perception. If the communicated plans are changed (especially to the detriment of the workforce) and no rational explanation is given, feelings of injustice and exploitation will result. Yet if explanations for change are given, employees are more willing to accept the changes, even if they are negative, without long-term detriment to the organization.

Good and bad implementation practices

Every acquisition implementation process is different depending on many of the choices made during the pre-acquisition phase:

- What is the degree of integration chosen?
- What is the level of employee participation in the implementation phase?

- How quickly will the implementation process move?
- Are there any cultural implications for the acquirer?
- What is to be the role of the target's management in the post-acquisition company?
- Will employees be merged?
- Will systems be merged?
- How receptive are the target employees to the acquirer?

Bearing in mind the uniqueness of the implementation process in light of these factors, each acquisition differs. But there are a dozen 'golden rules' which enhance the acquirer's chances for success during implementation.

Project manage the process and measure progress

Pre-acquisition planning should have included the design and detail of the various integration teams. A crucial part of this process is how they are then project managed. There are various techniques for ensuring that it proceeds on a smooth and professional track. These can include using outside facilitators, using tools which expedite the process such as project management software, managing conflict (discussed below) and allowing employees enough time to devote to teamwork. A project management approach to implementation is paramount to ensuring it delivers on time and within budget; fundamental to its success is building in measures and milestones along the way. These can be in the form of cost savings, sales targets, head counts or other objective criteria; attaining certain milestones can be as meaningful. These could include conducting an employee opinion survey and feeding back the results; agreeing a combined company culture and mission statement or a new branch structure in the case of Advent and Zenith Building Societies. What outcomes and milestones the acquirer chooses to measure in terms of success is not really the issue; they should measure *something*. Without using forms of measurement, it is impossible to assess the transaction in terms of its success and ultimate outcome; it also hinders the ability to learn for future acquisitions.

The use of integration teams works well within a project management context with each team working on a separate acquisition issue. Each team should have an overall objective and operate within the bounds of the accepted code of behaviour. It is possible to measure the team's success on how well they achieve that overall objective or any sub-objectives which may be deemed appropriate. Within the teams, work can be sub-divided with individuals being made responsible for completing specific tasks; overall co-ordination can be driven by a team leader or sponsor.

Build in some 'quick wins'

As discussed in Chapter 2, after acquisition target employees are usually somewhat cynical and wary of their new owner. This will depend in part on their relationship with their existing owner and how that company treats employees – are there existing claims of hidden agendas, political manoeuvrings or words spoken and not meant? Or are the target's management perceived as honest and good communicators? Either perception is problematic for an acquirer for different reasons. In the latter and more unusual case, the incumbent owners are a hard act to follow; in the former and more common scenario, acquiring management will want to demonstrate that they are different (and better) than the previous owners or managers. The quickest way to differentiate themselves from previous owners is to show that if management say they are going to do something, they deliver. A good way of demonstrating this is to build into any plans a series of 'quick wins'.

'Quick wins' can come in several forms. They can be further information given out to employees on a specific date, repainting offices, pre-arranged site visits – anything which is visible and tangible. The important element of this process, however, is to have those affected know of the event prior to it happening, that is, have it well communicated and an expectation set that it is going to occur. After acquiring management communicates and then delivers when they say they will, even cynical employees will grudgingly admit that acquiring management is believable. They may not like them or trust them but at least they believe them. This is the first step towards building a working relationship between the acquirer and its new employees. Thus, it is important not to communicate everything on 'Day One' but build in some future steps and then communicate these when you have said that you will. This was done at Gas Appliances. A manager remembers:

> When they stood up and talked to us, a lot of things before with Home Products were, 'Yes, we are going to do it', and then it didn't happen. But with this it was, 'There will be skips arriving on Monday and there will be bags all over the place and by the end of the week, this place will be cleaned up.' And then there were skips coming in left, right and centre.

In the Advent and Zenith Building Society acquisition an example could be communicating that the integration teams are being put together and that a full list of their responsibilities and team members will be announced three weeks after the acquisition. The crucial element of this process is ensuring that you then deliver; if you don't you are just like all the rest in the eyes of the employees.

Be seen to add value to the target either through investment or other means (orphan syndrome)

Research has found that the ability to 'add value' as an acquirer is a positive step in the implementation process (Hunt et al., 1987). This can be achieved through inward capital investment (as seen in Scottish Yeast and Gas Appliances), through management expertise (Anglo-American), through a transfer of technology or infrastructure, or even through the acquirer providing 'an understanding parent'. This latter situation, 'orphan syndrome', is seen in many diversified conglomerates where the subsidiary often feels that the parent company doesn't really 'understand' their business and as a result cannot add significant value. As conglomerate buyers in the 1960s divested, many 'orphans' found new understanding in related business acquirers who fully understood their business and its potential. They in turn felt like they 'fitted' in the new company. The result was a happier and more productive co-existence. The case of Infosys (Chapter 11) was an interesting one. The acquisition was well received at first by many of the employees; part of the reason for that was the belief that they were finally going to be owned by a parent company whose management understood their business. This positive predilection was to change, however, as the implementation proceeded and did not meet employees' positive expectations.

Both Anglo-American and Scottish Yeast were seen to add a great deal of value to the businesses they acquired for which employees felt grateful. In the case of Scottish Yeast, the value added in terms of capital investment by Discovery generally outweighed the negative aspects of wholesale redundancies being necessary. One Scottish Yeast shopfloor employee commented:

> Discovery has put a lot of investment into the site. Between £12 and £20 million already has been spent and it has been great, not for everybody because we have lost a lot of people but for those who made it.

Another manager added:

> The business is going well and it has been positive, it is turning around. Discovery has invested heavily. It is wonderful. There is a long-term future for the site so not just for us here but for the whole community which

will benefit from this investment. Here at least we believe there is a plan behind it, we do know where we are going.

Being realistic on what you can achieve

A major problem associated with acquiring is the inherent doubling of workload as those managing the process become engulfed in not only the day-to-day operations of their own business but also the implementation process. This can stretch even the most well-organized managers to the limit in terms of time, energy and work volumes. The only way to approach this process is to delegate wherever possible to other able-bodied managers. If, as senior management, you feel you don't have such managers, I would question whether or not you are in a position to be buying another company – your priority should be getting your own house in order.

An inherent part of delegating authority during acquisition is to ensure that the entire team is aligned in their philosophy and support of the acquisition. There is nothing more divisive during acquisition than different members of the top team sending different signals to the target employees. The result is that target employees become confused over what is the generally agreed way forward. If the top team cannot agree wholeheartedly about the acquisition and how it should be handled, don't enter into the transaction, at least until it can be agreed, as it simply will not work.

There is a great tendency during the implementation process to over-promise in terms of deliverables and timescales. This should be avoided at all costs – it is impossible to effectively manage employee expectations without adherence to realistic timeframes and outcomes. Employees will tolerate some slippage due to the process (especially if reasons why it has occurred are communicated) but if it is the norm rather than the exception, they become rather more jaundiced and cynical towards the acquirer and its ability to deliver. Acquirers must be realistic in what they can achieve in terms of outcomes and the time it takes to deliver them. If anything, it is wise to overstate the timescales and then deliver before they are expected as employee concerns always crescendo immediately prior to anticipated change announcements.

If you use the example of the two building societies, Advent and Zenith, you tell employees that you are planning to announce those branches earmarked for closure within three months. You then plan to have the information available in ten weeks – if you overrun for any reason then you are still within the communicated timeframe. If not, you make the announcement early – prior to employee concerns beginning to escalate.

At worst you have met employee expectations, and at best you have exceeded them at a time when they did not expect it.

Another major problem during the implementation process is the tendency for momentum to wane. While many acquirers begin the process with the best intentions of seeing things through, the burdens of everyday work begin to take their toll. Projects begin to drag on, deadlines are not met and a domino effect of failed outcomes piles up. The perception this gives to acquired employees is one of 'firefighting' management style, incompetence and management who is 'all talk'. With this impression it is difficult for employees to trust management or find them credible. One Quality Guarding recipient commented:

> The communication that we did have was like a marionette thrashing about – that is how it came through – we will issue one of these and one of those, very disjointed. It didn't come from one source, it wasn't planned, and if I am perceiving this, God knows what the other people on a higher level are seeing, God knows what the clients think.

One way to ensure this does not happen is to give individuals or a team the task of implementing the acquisition. In order to be fully successful, however, those people need to have adequate resources in terms of time, money and training to ensure they do it properly. This means making some of those people involved in the project work full time towards its completion. They can then be assessed against predetermined success criteria to measure their success. If the organization is too small or 'lean' to adapt this approach, outside help in terms of outsourcing or project facilitation may be the best answer.

Use line managers

One of the most underutilized assets during acquisition is the affected employees' line management. Not only do line managers have a deep understanding of their own organization and its foibles, they also are likely to have their subordinates' trust already. Acquirers are more likely to have their communication believed if there exists trust of the source (the line managers) rather than communication just coming from a new source, the acquirer. Line managers are also often opinion leaders who can sway their subordinates' opinions with their comments. If the acquirer can gain line managers' emotional commitment, their enthusiasm often can be cascaded down the organizational hierarchy. Additionally, communication forums such as daily or weekly staff briefing meetings already may be established which allow for line management to speak effectively with the staff and may be used to disseminate acquisition news. As poor communication remains a fundamental flaw to most acquisitions, using line management is an opportunity to delegate responsibility to those managers, thereby reducing senior management workload in what is already a hectic time. By doing so, the result is likely to be a motivating influence for those line managers as they prove themselves to be important to the implementation process. Anglo-American made good use of line management in its Gas Appliances acquisition. Not only did this spread the workload, it served as a motivational force. One Gas Appliances manager commented:

> It was good and an exciting time because you could see change all the time and everyone was working towards a goal. It was nice that you were part of the team that was changing the face of Gas Appliances. People were asking questions and they knew they could ask me and I would tell them.

In order to get line management committed, it is useful to include some line managers in joint integration groups. By being involved, they have first-hand knowledge of the events as they unfold and can pass this information on accordingly. Second, it is also important to use some kind of a formalized briefing session guideline or procedures in order to ensure line management is well informed in a timely manner of changes as they occur. Finally, not all line managers are good communicators. If one is anticipating needing their support during an acquisition, communication skills training prior to the deal is beneficial. If there remains any doubt over any line managers' communication skills (which invariably there will be), parallel channels of communication (such as using briefings and memos) should be used in order to ensure the message gets delivered to all employees. This also serves to reinforce the messages if they do get through via the line management which, in turn, increases both management's and line management's credibility with employees as being honest and informative.

Keep your plan fluid but do not lose sight of the 'big picture'

One must always remember the importance of the acquisition plan in its role as the foundation for the implementation process, but it is also worth remembering that all plans change and evolve over time. If it makes sense to change the plan because of unforeseen circumstances, then change it. There is an important caveat to this, however. If the plan changes, the changes must then be communicated to those affected. It is not worth thinking that they should remain 'high level' and employees do not need to know. If the communicated plan changes and employees are not told of the rationale behind the changes, they will make up the rationale themselves. As discussed in Chapter 2, the perceived rationale behind the changes is likely to be based upon a worst-case scenario and will include a belief in 'hidden agendas'.

While changes to the plan are inevitable, it is important not to lose sight of the overall objectives of the transaction. It is tempting to let individual personalities dictate structure and decisions; generally it is not advisable. In these cases, the 'big picture' often becomes distorted as politics creeps in. When this happens, comments of 'hidden agendas' take on a more realistic meaning. This was seen at Infosys on several occasions. First, the organizational structure was changed at the top to accommodate Isabelle Saunders; ultimately these changes signalled an untenable and illogical working relationship between Saunders and Johnson. Second, the decisions surrounding data collection and marketing also contradicted the previously believed logic of the deal. The changes were never explained and the process greatly damaged the credibility of TeleCable Group and made the process seem poorly managed and the outcome illogical. As one Infosys employee commented:

> People still do not understand why their jobs are going and why data collection is moving to the South Coast. It would have made people feel much better if they had understood it.

Another commented:

> If there were really some overall plan, if it were really cheaper in the South Coast (for data collection), that would make more sense. For people in their jobs for twenty years to be going whereas they need people on the South Coast being trained up again, it just doesn't make any sense.

The bottom line is that although the plan must remain fluid, do not lose track of what you are ultimately trying to achieve.

Manage conflict between acquiring and target employees

Once the dust has settled after the acquisition, employees will eventually get to the stage where it is once again 'business as usual' and a 'normal' working environment is restored. This state of normality is much more difficult to achieve if the inevitable conflicts which arise during the implementation process are not properly managed. Conflict during implementation is inevitable especially as decisions are taken in which there are clear 'winners' and 'losers'. These types of decision are prevalent in cases of full merger or functional integration where either one person, unit or location is chosen over the other. If the conflict which arises out of these situations is handled badly, the acquirer can experience a mass exodus of disenchanted employees – usually the vanquished, but also in many cases those watching disillusioned from the sidelines.

An example of poorly managed conflict is seen very clearly in Chapter 11 (Infosys) where key decisions were mismanaged concerning the locations of the marketing function and data processing unit. In the latter example, there were clear 'winners' and 'losers', yet the process for handling the related conflict went unmanaged. Some of this was due to the yet unresolved (and some would argue, conflictual) relationship of those at the top. The conflict remained unchecked and future working relationships were seriously put at risk due to the comments made during the heat of the moment. One manager involved commented:

> There was a lot of bad feeling (in the meetings) which no one managed and these people are going to have to work together. This is what has caused the conflict – nobody was there to manage constructively what was very negative, soul destroying and destructive.

There are ways for dealing with conflict positively. Facilitators can be used for meetings where conflict may arise, for example, in acquisition teams. An accepted code of behaviour (discussed in Chapter 4) can outline what is the company's policy towards aggressive behaviour or rebuttal. It is effective only if the code is then enforced consistently and publicly. Open and honest discussion concerning any discord which may arise will also serve to diffuse it more convincingly than if it is denied or ignored. Finally, it is how one reacts to conflictual behaviour that really causes the damage. In those cases where an employee gets away with behaving badly, the damage can be significant (see Infosys). On the other hand, if it is punished swiftly and decisively, the effect can be a positive indication of what is and what is not acceptable behaviour in the new company. Word gets around the businesses very quickly that the acquirer is serious about what behaviour is acceptable and what is not. The usual outcome is a drop in unacceptable behaviour.

Manage employee expectations

If acquirers follow the process outlined in this book, they are already managing employees' expectations. This is achieved by carefully and comprehensively planning and communicating the process and procedures that the implementation process will follow including time scales and expected outcomes. The key is acting upon them in a fair manner. Once the acquisition implementation process is underway the need for expectation management is even greater. Employees will concentrate on the most minute detail as they try to gather information – if this is provided by the acquirer, anxieties and uncertainty will diminish. Not only should this result in relative increased employee productivity and commitment, it should also increase the likelihood that the implementation upheaval is shorter and less traumatic. The end result is a quick return to 'business as usual' in the new organization.

The process of managing expectations can also be applied to the implementation process. Instead of pre-acquisition planning, the integration groups construct an operational plan related to their element of the acquisition blueprint. Once this has been approved by the steering committee, the plan is communicated to the workforce via the acquisition newsletter and monthly acquisition meeting conducted by line managers (or whatever communication forum the acquirer chooses). The plan is then implemented in a fair and professional manner and the results monitored.

Because of the low trust and general uncertainty which usually pervades the average acquisition, it is important for acquiring management to realize that its messages will be distorted and misunderstood. Bearing this in mind, it is critical for senior management to constantly repeat those key messages that it really wants employees to understand. These include the rationale for the deal and the important outcomes and their respective timescales. For really important messages, it is important to use more than one medium in order to ensure employees have received the message. While the involvement of line management in the communication process is crucial, it is also important to supplement the communication with another medium as not all managers are equally competent communicators. This increases the chances that employees are getting the message which is an important element of expectation management.

Make no assumptions

It is incredible just how many assumptions are made during the implementation process. First, acquirers tend to assume that target employees are inferior to them purely because they are the target and not the acquirer. As a result, target employees are often automatically downgraded in respect to their equivalent positions in the acquirer (see Global). Second, many acquiring employees assume that nothing negative will happen to them – after all, they are the acquirers. When it does (as it did in TeleCable Group), there are cries of injustice because they were simply not prepared to be affected. Third, acquirers seem to think that target employees will understand the procedures, culture and foibles of the acquirer with nobody needing to explain them. As seen at Global, this is never the case. Someone must take the time to explain the new company and its procedures, however simple, or expect the target employees to continue operating as they did in the past. Finally, acquirers assume that things will stay the same in the acquirer: the top team, systems, culture, management style and company atmosphere. After acquisition you can assume nothing and take nothing for granted. There will be changes and employees need to be told this repeatedly from the start.

Expect strange behaviour and be ready for it

Acquisition never ceases to surprise people due to the strange behaviour it engenders. An important lesson for acquirers to remember is to expect the unexpected and be ready for it. As seen in Chapter 4, even in acquisitions which are agreed and going well, intended communication and actions can be wildly distorted via the rumour mill and 'noise'. Employees can be hostile and defensive for no apparent reason. Non-political colleagues can become political animals overnight when they feel threatened by the possibility of change and all the uncertainty this brings. Everything becomes exaggerated and, in many cases, unrecognizably so. While it is impossible to predict the extent to which this behaviour will affect the implementation process, it is worthwhile remembering that it will occur even if the process is going very well. The moral of the story is to be prepared for it and, if possible, recognize the behaviour and the reasons for it without holding it against the offending employees. An example of this can be seen in a recent acquisition where a target employee became aggressively defensive with an acquiring employee. The latter replied that she understood that the acquisition was difficult for the acquired employees and that when things settled, she hoped they would be able to work well together. Rather than rise to the bait, the acquiring employee diffused a potentially confrontational situation by responding in an understanding manner and thereby laid the foundation for a positive working relationship in the future.

Remaining visible and 'out of the bunker'

During the hectic post-acquisition implementation period, it is quite common for senior executives to reduce their number of site visits. Some retreat into themselves, especially if they are worried about their own positions. Often, however, it is due to management trying to keep both the business and the implementation running on schedule. Unfortunately most employees affected by acquisition are so consumed by their own concerns and the situation that they don't realize that is what is occurring. Instead, they only see (or don't, as the case may be) that management is staying away, or, as many refer to it, 'keeping their heads down and hiding in the bunker', with the bunker usually being the boardroom. Senior management should use the opportunity of the acquisition to visit the newly acquired locations and if possible meet employees and answer their questions.

In one recent acquisition, the managing and operational director visited every newly acquired site – 48 in all – within the first three weeks of the acquisition. At many of the sites, employees had never seen the previous management as they had never been on-site. In addition, the directors answered all employee queries and questions in an open and honest manner and listened to employees' comments. Thus, the visits made a considerably positive impression on the target employees and reinforced the message of a professional and proactive management team in the acquirers. Some employees commented afterwards that they had misjudged the acquirers and that they weren't as bad as they expected – if that visit had never occurred, that ill-judged preconception would have remained. The visit by the Service Conglomerate Chairman highlights this. Upon visiting the Quality Guarding site, he spoke to all the employees and listened to them with interest; he made a lot of allies of employees who previously were wary of him and the company.

Keep an eye on the ball and don't forget the customer

A common problem associated with acquisition is the introverted perspective that naturally comes with internal change. Everyone becomes so engrossed with the daily gossip and goings on of the acquisition that they forget that they are employed to do a job. The stakeholder who suffers most as a result is usually the customer. Most employees forget that although there may be turmoil and change going on internally, the image the world must see is one of a smoothly operating professional company which is firmly in control. The usual image is one where the cogs and wheels have ground to a resounding halt.

This cannot be the case. It is important for the acquirer to keep their eyes on the ball and everything in perspective. The target may be one-quarter the size of the acquirer but that means that the acquirer has four times that amount of business outstanding that needs to be serviced professionally. It is important not to lose track of that perspective.

Competitor's acquisitions also present an opportunity for those in the industry. If the process is not being handled well, one can use this chance to try and poach prized employees. Service levels to clients may have deteriorated and, consequently, present scope to win key accounts. Competitors will try to do it to you when you acquire. Be prepared and don't let them succeed.

MOTIVATING KEY STAFF DURING CHANGES

Ask most acquirers what is the most difficult time during the implementation process and they will say that it is trying to keep staff motivated when colleagues are being made redundant. While redundancies are always difficult, there are some steps acquirers can take to mitigate their negative aspects. Some acquirers can even use this time as a source of motivation to those employees remaining in the firm, although this is never achieved without a great deal of planning and effort on the acquirer's part.

Who are your key staff?

One of the most difficult aspects of any acquisition is trying to determine which acquired employees are considered key and which are not. Related to this, is trying to understand the relative importance and performance of acquired employees vis-à-vis any target employees where there is overlap and potential rationalization. If the deal is agreed, you may have access to employees prior to its completion; however, this is not always possible. Instead, it is likely that acquirers have two choices for choosing the top team. The first is to make a judgement prior to the purchase as to who are your key employees – those people one wants motivated to remain with the company during the implementation process and afterwards. The second is to delay any decisions until after the acquisition and one has the chance to assess employees. If one is not planning to implement the bulk of the acquisition changes until much later, this does not pose a huge problem other than creating undue and prolonged uncertainty for affected employees. But for those acquirers keen for a speedy implementation period yet who want to involve key employees via participatory mechanisms, certain decisions need to be taken as to which employees are to be involved and in which capacity.

Acquirers may be able to gain access to information prior to the deal's completion. Others may choose to rely on the personal recommendations from senior people of fellow employees in the target with whom they have contact. This assumes that the acquirer values the opinions and judgements of the senior management team. It also increases the risk of politics playing a bigger role during the process. Second, employees may be considered key due to their positions and not necessarily their competence. This is a common means of selecting key people for acquisition participation post-transaction. It does run the risk that some of those people may become redundant during the implementation process if they are not as good as their position may warrant vis-à-vis employees in the other company. Third, performance reviews on target employees are likely only to be available after the deal's completion if they exist at all. Fourth, any experience of the target employees garnered during the negotiation process can give an indication of key employees. At the very least, it may give an indication of which target employees' opinions you trust to tell you who are the key players. Finally, industry knowledge is also a useful means of assessing some of the more high-profile employees being acquired.

Another means of choosing which people are to be considered key is personal experience via initial employee meetings. An example would be to hold an initial acquisition workshop meeting within two weeks of the deal's announcement with managers invited to attend based on their positions. During the workshop, senior management can assess the performance of those participating and their importance in the new organization. Communication released on 'Day One' can say that integration teams will be formed during the first two weeks of the deal and announced on a certain date. If other employees are needed during the implementation process, they can be co-opted onto the teams where they best add value at a later date.

Ideally, one should use as many sources of information as possible to assess which employees are important to the new organization and which are good to involve in the implementation process. If one is going to get employees involved in the implementation, it is important to find out which employees can influence colleagues, have a skill base which is useful during the implementation process or who the acquirer feels are important and wants to retain after the deal's completion and get them involved.

Project management and participation techniques

Most acquirers are not able to implement all their wide-scale changes immediately after the acquisition due to the sheer scope of such an undertaking and legislative requirements to consult employees prior to major changes. Because of this, most acquirers use some form of project management technique during the implementation period; often it involves teams of acquiring and acquired employees working together on a project-by-project basis. As discussed in Chapter 3, employee input during the implementation process can not only serve as a valuable source of knowledge but can also motivate and emotionally involve employees. It also increases the likelihood that employees will accept the decisions being taken if they play some part in creating it.

There may be certain employees who the acquirer may find beneficial to include in the implementation process. These can include employees who are seen to be influential amongst their colleagues – perhaps opinion leaders, trade union or employee representatives. While some may be inclined to exclude these employees, it is advantageous to involve them. Employees will turn to these colleagues for information whether or not they are involved; if they are, they are more likely to have accurate information to pass on. Additionally, they are less likely to be in a position to criticize any decisions taken if they themselves have some hand in making them and feel some ownership of the process.

There are a variety of project management techniques which run from sophisticated multi-tiered integration teams to a simpler acquisition manager approach which are discussed below. What is important, however, is that the techniques chosen fulfil the purpose for which they are created – they motivate and allow employees to participate in genuine decision making. Having teams analyse issues and submit proposals for decisions which have already been taken is not a good use of employee skills or time. The end result is a backlash of resentment which is far worse than if the participation techniques had never been employed.

Acquisition manager

An acquisition manager is the employee ultimately responsible for its project management and encourages its successful completion. As time management during acquisition is at a premium, freeing up one individual to run the implementation process on a full-time basis is often the most efficient means. A senior retiring employee can often make a good acquisition manager if he or she leaves their position and works as acquisition co-ordinator for his or her remaining time in the company; those employees also often have the opportunity to rise above any political manoeuvrings as they have less of a political agenda themselves.

An acquisition manager fulfils several key roles. First, he or she can project manage the process by dovetailing projects and personalities and thereby ensuring the most efficient output with the least amount of conflict and overlap. To do this effectively the acquisition manager can serve as the head of the steering committee (see below) or as a member. Second, the acquisition manager often acts as a first point of contact for affected employees if they have any queries. Finally, the acquisition manager can fulfil almost a diplomatic role for the acquirer if he or she remains impartial and above politics as the process is driven forward – this can serve to promote the professional nature of the acquirer especially if the acquisition manager is the main point of contact with affected employees.

Thus, acquisition managers need to have certain skills. Having project management training is a bonus (ex-management consultants often make good acquisition managers). Sympathetic employees who are good communicators and with good 'people skills' also tend to make good acquisition managers. In the case of Global (Chapter 9), the acquisition manager joined Global via a previous acquisition; this natural empathy combined with his good interpersonal skills made him a very effective choice to run the project. According to one acquired employee:

> The head of the task force was wonderful, he is honourable. When he tells you, 'Don't worry it will be sorted out', people came out believing that no matter what happened, he would sort things out for them. So he was ideal.

Another commented:

> One Global manager was universally respected even by those who were made redundant. They said, 'I know I have been made redundant but he has really been fair about it.' He had a job to do but he was fair and respected.

The acquisition manager must also have authority and the respect of key decision makers to get things done and gain access to the relevant information in a timely manner. Finally, an acquisition manager needs the time to perform the job well – on a full-time basis rather than trying to do two important jobs at once.

In a recent acquisition, the target's entire board left, with two exceptions. One of the exceptions was a senior employee who made it clear that he did not plan to stay with the combined organization in the long term. As he possessed excellent project management skills from a previous stint as a management consultant, he was asked to serve as the acquisition manager. He was persuaded to remain and serve as acquisition manager throughout the implementation process, after which time he was given a sizeable bonus based on its success. This approach worked very well as he knew the business well including its positive and negative elements, had the trust of the target employees, had the right skills base, was incentivized to perform and had a window of opportunity.

Acquisition co-ordinators

An acquisition co-ordinator operates in less of a project management capacity but rather serves as a communication point for the integration project and employees. The role is more administrative and less leadership driven than that of an acquisition manager. Employees with questions can contact an acquisition co-ordinator who can answer in accordance with the company's position. This greatly reduces the potential for rumours and lends a general feeling of professionalism to the process. In order to be effective, however, the acquisition co-ordinator needs to be at the front line of decision making in order to ensure his or her receipt of the information is timely.

Acquisition teams

An acquisition team is usually a central unit which works full time on implementation issues with selected skills being co-opted onto the team for specific acquisition projects. Team members will have a variety of functional disciplines and other skills can be brought onto the team when needed. It is hoped that by working full time on acquisitions team members build up an expertise in implementation techniques honed over time. Similarly, an acquisition team can 'use a formula' chosen by the acquirer in order to instil uniformity across subsequent targets. Having a full-time acquisition team, as seen in the Gas Appliances acquisition (Chapter 7), has many advantages; however, the cost of having such a team is prohibitive to the average company unless one is acquiring large targets or making several acquisitions per year.

Integration teams

Integration teams are a common means of employee participation during acquisition during the implementation process. There are two approaches. Employees can stay in their current jobs while taking on the extra workload associated with the implementation process, or they can be seconded to work full time. It is far preferable to have employees working in a full-time capacity so that the 'day job' does not distract the participants. The feasibility of this happening, however, depends heavily on the current staffing levels of both the target and acquirer. The level of sophistication in integration teams varies enormously depending on the size and complexity of the companies and the implementation plan. It is ideal to base acquisition teams around those issues which arise out of the acquisition overview and blueprint (see Chapter 3).

In order to be effective, integration teams should have clearly defined parameters. These include the topic being assessed, timeframes, outcome deliverables, and expected behaviour in achieving the objectives. Second, in order to serve as a motivational influence, the teams need to work genuinely towards a solution – they cannot just 'go through the motions' if a solution has already been decided. In cases where this happens, the process just adds weight to any rumours of hidden agendas and political manoeuvrings. Third, which employees are members of the integration teams also sends a clear message to the workforce – if it is dominated by one side (usually the acquirer), the effect can be to demotivate the target employees. Having an equal or sizeable representation of target company employees sends a positive signal to the remaining workforce. Fourth, as discussed above, conflict which naturally arises out of the process needs to be managed carefully but firmly as this, too, sends a message to observers. Finally, it is important to know which employees are key to the acquisition's success and get their involvement in the teams.

Sub-integration teams and information gathering teams can also be used and report to integration teams which then take on a more steering committee role in the process. As the process gets more complex or the deal larger, integration groups can take on a more co-ordinative role as they, in turn, co-ordinate the teams working below them.

Steering committees

A steering committee serves to co-ordinate the various integration teams throughout the course of a larger or more complex acquisition. Not only does this reduce any duplication of effort, it also sets the tone of the implementation process by having an open discussion forum and discouraging political behaviour. Ideally the chief executive heads the steering committee but if time constraints make this impossible, a close deputy can chair the committee. Some acquirers who use an acquisition manager have that person chair the committee – this is effective as long as they have the relative authority to do the job properly.

Like integration teams, the steering committee's composition requires a great deal of thought as it says a lot about the organization: is it functionally biased, top-heavy with no junior representation, or does it exclude target employees? Those steering committees which are most effective comprise less than ten people. It is ideal to have one representative from the steering committee working on each integration project in order to ensure the overall co-ordination of activities. This is usually done by the project's sponsor whose involvement with the project is usually in a part-time capacity.

As discussed above, how the steering committee operates will often serve as a role model for behaviour in the integration groups – this includes political behaviour. Similarly, conflictual behaviour is inevitable but it needs to be channelled into a positive business experience and not a negative manifestation with long-term ramifications (see Infosys, Chapter 11). This can be achieved by communicating and adhering to the agreed code of behaviour as discussed in Chapter 4. By doing so, management's reputation for impartiality and professionalism will be enhanced in the long term.

External consultants/facilitators

When an acquirer does not have the time or in-house expertise to lead the implementation process, outside facilitators can be used. In some cases this can be the most efficient means for ensuring the implementation process proceeds smoothly: consultants are likely to be able to work full-time on the project and have the commensurate skill base. They should also be up to date on the latest best practices for acquisition integration. In addition, it is often cheaper to employ consultants rather than keep full-time acquisition specialists on hand if one is not acquiring with regularity.

There are some disadvantages, however, to using outside consultants. While at first glance consultants may be considered impartial, if the process does not go well, target employees will invariably argue that they were either a 'hatchet men' or reliant on the acquirer to pay their fees. Second, and especially in times of uncertainty, consultants are often used as political pawns by senior management who are involved in internal power struggles. Third, consultants are not cheap, but to be fair their fees in terms of a percentage of the overall deal cost are minimal, especially when considering the cost of getting the acquisition wrong. Finally, even if outside consultants are used, management cannot abdicate responsibility for the acquisition and decision making – consultants are there to facilitate and advise, not to dictate. A good consultant should work closely with senior management advising them on the process while ensuring the process reflects well on the acquirer and not the consultant. In any case, a process handled well and led either internally or externally will reflect well on the acquirer – it is far better to have acquisition implementation handled well, aided by consultants, than done badly by internal sources alone.

Surviving redundancies

Historically, employees are made redundant in roughly three-quarters of acquisitions. In the current age of 'economies of scale' acquisitions, this figure is probably even higher. Bearing this in mind, how the acquirer deals with redundancies and other related bad news can play a vital role in the acquisition's overall success. In many cases how the acquirer handles redundancies is the target employee's first real exposure to the acquirer. In essence, target employees are seeing how the acquirer fares under stress and how it treats its employees. If the acquirer treats them well, employees watching their colleagues being made redundant are more likely to remain with the company even if times get tough again in the future, knowing that they too will be treated fairly if their time comes. Consequently, if the acquirer handles the redundancy process well, employees are more likely to remain with the company as long as their skills are needed.

Communicating the bad news

A major problem associated with restructuring during acquisitions is how to deliver the negative messages of closures, redundancies and relocations. While many of the employees who remain with the firm will benefit from the changes including greater job security and increased profitability, for those being made redundant the message is not positive. How the acquirer communicates the redundancy message can have a great impact not only on the perceptions of those employees who go but also on those who remain. Consequently it is imperative to communicate the message in a way which is palatable to all employees. One Quality Guarding manager recounted 'Black Monday':

> We are not naive ... we know this is a fact of life and that if we are treated correctly within the procedure we will accept that. All we want is to be treated right and fairly and that didn't happen on that particular day.

A major issue is the time between announcing and implementing acquisition-related redundancy. If announcements are made early with plenty of notice, the majority of employees do not leave early. Legislation requiring employee consultation notwithstanding, the timely announcement of redundancies and changes in employee circumstances has been found to be a positive rather than negative occurrence in the acquisition process as long as the announcements are made with plenty of notice prior to the changes and they are then implemented fairly.

A major concern on the part of acquirers is that those employees targeted for redundancy will leave prior to the time anticipated by the acquirer. As seen in the Discovery chapter (Chapter 10), this is not usually the case. If employees are provided with an adequate explanation, given plenty of notice, and then treated fairly and generously, the majority of employees do not leave early. Loyalty and incentive bonuses, generous redundancy packages, outplacement, CV workshops and counselling are all additional costs to the employer when closing a site. The positive goodwill left with the remaining employees, however, almost certainly far outweighs the costs associated with a poorly orchestrated closure.

Some companies give as much as 18 months' notice for the closure of a site. Long timescales are effective for two reasons. First, the extended timeframe ensures that rumours and information leakages are kept to a minimum. The channel of such announcements must be appropriate; a senior director personally speaking would be suitable, during which time affected employees could ask questions and receive honest answers. Second, announcing changes all at once is more settling for employees and reduces uncertainty far more than a 'drip feed' of redundancies every few months. In the case of the former, employees can get over the news and get on with their jobs rather than continuously feeling nervous over the next round of redundancies. Again, the content and style should also fit the situation, with the executive sympathetically explaining the reasons why and what steps will be taken to help those affected.

An example in the positive communication of negative news is seen in Greenberg's study (1990). Greenberg studied three plants in which two of the three were given a temporary 15 per cent wage reduction and the third plant served as a control. One plant was given a full, honest and rational explanation for the wage cuts – that the cuts precluded any need for layoffs and that they would be shared by the entire site. The presentation to the staff was done by a very senior executive and was conducted in a respectful and sensitive manner. The second plant received only a cursory unapologetic talk by a middle manager. The plant that received the pay reduction without adequate explanation saw an almost threefold increase in pilferage when compared to the control group. The plant receiving adequate information also experienced an increase in pilferage, although it was significantly less than the former. However, it was in the area of job resignations where the difference was most noticeable – the plant in which employees received the poorly handled explanation experienced a turnover rate of 23 per cent whereas at the plant which received the sufficient explanation the rate was only 5 per cent. The conclusion drawn was 'the use of adequately reasoned explanations offered with interpersonal sensitivity tends to mitigate the negative effects associated with the information itself' (Greenberg, 1990, p. 566). This reinforces the procedural justice findings – what you say is less important than how you say it.

The Discovery acquisition discussed in Chapter 10 is an example of where positive delivery largely mitigated the negative message being communicated. While the plant was to get new investment, its automation meant that almost half of the workforce was to be redundant. The combination of honest and thoughtful communication and a fairly implemented policy generally outweighed the highly negative message. One shopfloor worker commented:

> [The MD] said that the change is going to keep going and going and with new technology we will be out of more jobs. That is what has happened so far; I have never made any bones as long as I know the truth. With our previous owners we didn't have that certainty, now we have it more at least – they seem to be honest. Now people aren't exactly happy with what they have done but at least they know exactly where they stand and they don't make any bones about it.

Picking the employees who remain

In almost all acquisitions, it is not the spectre of redundancies which haunts the acquirer for months afterwards but the way in which they are handled. Part of that problem is the determination of who remains and who is made redundant. Some acquirers only use voluntary redundancy; others operate a straightforward LIFO policy (last in, first out). Scottish Yeast in Chapter 10 used early retirement and voluntary redundancy where possible and then tried to pick the best employees by using a system which retrospectively measured their performance in terms of timekeeping and other indices. Their approach was not successful as it was seen as being 'unfair' to judge employees retrospectively without their knowledge. Quality Guarding in Chapter 8 tried to pick employees who would cause 'least client disruption'; this was a logical reason for employees to be kept although it wasn't communicated properly (and, consequently, wasn't understood by affected employees) nor implemented in a way considered 'fair' by affected employees.

In essence, it almost doesn't matter how the acquirer chooses the employees it makes redundant other than the reasoning has to be very logical and clear so as to be seen as fair. The process, including the reason for selection, needs to be well communicated not only to those affected but also to those employees who remain with the firm and then the process should be implemented in a professional manner. In the case of Scottish Yeast, they would have been better off sticking with voluntary redundancies and using natural wastage and the anticipated increase in production to attain the appropriate staff numbers. Quality Guarding would have been better off communicating that redundancies would need to occur including the criteria for selection, and then implementing the redundancies in a professional manner.

The process of fully merging two units together is one which, due to its sheer magnitude, can create a great deal of upheaval and trauma for those affected. TUPE legislation requires that the acquirer must take the most appropriate person for each job and, in doing so, must not favour either its own or target employees; the process of selection must be fair and impartial. One selection technique which is time consuming but can be very fair is to have all employees reapply for the new jobs. For this to work it is important that the process is seen as fair. Some acquirers use outside recruitment firms to assess the candidates to ensure it is done objectively. It is an expensive option but takes away any doubt of bias. To be considered fair, the selection process and criteria must be known and impartial; for instance, all employees should use the same new application form when reapplying.

Alternatively, it is possible to take an entire unit based on them either reapplying for their jobs or being chosen as to their ability if there is some kind of external ranking system available which assesses their performance. This could be used in banking, for example, where departments are ranked on their performance against the industry norm. This has the advantage of ensuring that employees are used to working together. There is a quicker assimilation period and, therefore, a shorter time of lower productivity associated with employees getting used to working with new colleagues in a new work environment. There are two disadvantages of using this type of system: you may end up with distinct cultures throughout the organization as different work groups do not have to amalgamate into a new culture, and also you may lose good individual performers who happen to be in a poorer performing work unit. The bottom line is to pick the team logically and fairly and communicate your criteria openly and administer the redundancies sympathetically.

Some acquirers fail to understand the importance of treating redundant employees fairly even if it costs more to do so in terms of redundancy pay, outplacement and counselling. In almost all cases those employees being made redundant are friends with those employees who stay. In many cases, they are friends with your clients, and in some cases they may be consumers of your products. Why poison the patch unnecessarily when it costs so little in time and money to do it right? This was not taken into account at Quality Guarding. One manager recounted:

> I was extremely upset because a friend had been made redundant and treated badly. Also the letter that went out to clients offered insufficient information,

very cold. I had a lot of feedback from clients saying this letter isn't very nice. They all knew my boss personally and the letter didn't explain why my boss was made redundant, it was just one line saying that he will no longer be with us. If the reason had been there and a bit more caring approach clients would have felt better.

Dealing with survivor guilt and offering survivor support

Any criteria used in selecting those earmarked for redundancy should be made known to all employees, including those who remain. There exists in acquisitions a phenomenon known as 'survivor guilt', where those employees who remain after redundancies feel guilty for being selected to keep their jobs. This is a little considered but highly potent emotion which features in many acquisitions, including the Quality Guarding acquisition discussed in Chapter 8. One Quality Guarding employee summed up the feeling as akin to being in the trenches during the First World War:

You go through the cycle in the trenches and you go through this survival thing because all of your friends have just been shot beside you. You go through this terrible, 'Christ, it wasn't me.' Then you get all happy because you made it and then you feel all guilty because you felt happy. None of this was taken into consideration during the acquisition.

Unless all employees – both those going and those staying – are told the criteria for selection, the amount of guilt felt by remaining employees can be overwhelming and debilitating. If employees are told that, for instance, the acquirer kept those employees who it was felt were the best based on their job evaluations, the negativity of redundancies is diminished. Similarly, if employees reapply for their jobs and the selection criteria is known, those employees selected must understand that they are the best people for their jobs. Choosing those employees who are the longest serving to remain also can be easily understood by those affected as a legitimate means of employee selection, although this doesn't necessarily create the best team for the new entity nor aid in manpower planning. What is essential is to have a logical means of assessing employees for redundancy. This was a problem at Scottish Yeast – using a retrospective system for mandatory redundancies was not perceived as fair by the employees affected; because of this, it was not an accepted result and Discovery's credibility, which until that point had been high, suffered. The irony was that employees participated in deciding the redundancy selection criteria through their trade union's involvement and yet they still felt aggrieved. One shopfloor employee commented:

It was the way they did the redundancies it was terrible. Most companies recognize last in, first out, but they wanted to do people's timekeeping and absenteeism so there were people who had only started in the last two years and they are still here and other guys who had been here for fifteen or twenty years that you get on with and they are gone. I think that is wrong because some of these people were absent through genuine illness or through injury and we thought surely they can't take that as a measure, but they did.

Getting the employee numbers right

Another typical mistake during acquisition occurs in manpower planning, especially in the light of redundancies. Many acquirers fail to take into account natural wastage in employee turnover figures when determining manpower requirements for employee redundancies. Those acquirers who take into account employee turnover tend to do so at the average employee turnover rate for the organization. Whatever the employee turnover rate is during 'normal' times, the rate following acquisition is sure to be significantly higher. The result is that many acquirers make employees redundant only to have to rehire them – typically as consultants or back into their old jobs – after having paid out redundancy packages. Not only does this negate some of the benefits of downsizing, it makes management look ill-prepared and potentially jeopardizes the organization by depleting it of critical skills.

Lamalie Associates found that almost half of top employees left after the first year and 75 per cent in the three years following acquisition (1985); Walsh found that over 60 per cent of managers leave their company within five years of acquisition compared to a market norm of 33 per cent (1988). If this level of turnover is not taken into account, it is likely that acquirers will downsize too radically. This was seen in the Quality Guarding acquisition (Chapter 8) in which employees left voluntarily during the implementation phase, thereby requiring Quality Guarding to try and rehire some of the employees it had only just made redundant. Not all those made redundant were willing to return to working for the company again; it also coloured the perceptions of the remaining employees.

The Quality Guarding acquisition also highlights another problem in manpower planning often experienced by acquirers – more employees leave voluntarily during a badly handled implementation than they do during one implemented in a professional manner. This was seen when comparing the five case studies. As discussed in Chapter 2, employees were asked, if they were offered another job with the same career opportunities, the same salary and at same distance from their house but without the complications of the acquisition, would they take it? When the process was handled well, such as at Anglo-American, employees tended to want to stay. When it was handled poorly, such as at Infosys or Quality Guarding, there was a greater percentage of employees looking elsewhere. And those employees who leave are the ones being offered jobs – they are the better performers.

Incentivization of leaving employees

Some acquirers incentivize employees to remain while a business location or function is being 'run down' towards closure. The reason for doing so is a worry that employees will leave before the time anticipated by the acquirer. The most likely form of incentivization is a bonus payment. Using bonuses as an incentive has advantages and disadvantages. A bonus can be a good motivator and generally works in keeping employees up to the time they are no longer needed. This is especially the case when affected employees are not long serving and, therefore, would not receive substantial redundancy payments upon the site's closure. But the down-sides must be considered. In order to motivate, the payment must be a sum of money which makes it worth the employee's while to stay. Second, there must be strict guidelines for who is eligible and what is required to earn the payment. Third, there may be some resentment of those undergoing change but not eligible for the payment. Fourth, bonus payments do not necessarily reflect productivity during this time period, so the acquirer may end up with ineffectual employees. Finally, it can be costly and unnecessary in some cases, especially if redundancy packages are generous.

ADVENT AND ZENITH BUILDING SOCIETIES

Following the example of Advent and Zenith building societies, which was discussed in Chapters 3 and 4, an outline of a potential structure for the implementation phase is shown below (Figure 5.2). They could have several integration teams looking at issues such as:

- back office delivery
  - billing
  - account administration
  - customer services
  - back office closure (this may be a separate workstream or contained under the overall project of back office delivery)

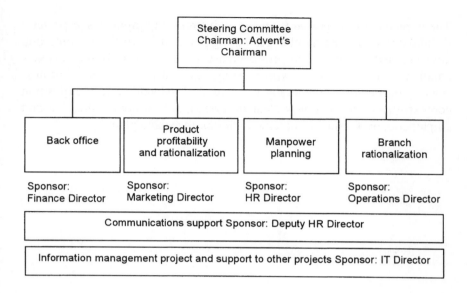

Fig. 5.2 *Diagram of the Advent and Zenith building societies implementation structure*

- product profitability and rationalization
- branch rationalization
- manpower planning
  - staffing levels and competencies
  - training for new systems
  - looking after key staff.

Both communication and information management would run as 'cross-boundary' projects as they relate to all the different integration teams. All the teams would report to a steering committee headed by the new chairman of the combined group. All teams would be 'sponsored' by a senior director, all of whom sit on the steering committee. It would be the task of that steering committee to ensure co-ordination across the various projects. It is the task of the chairman to act as the final adjudicator in disputes and to be the 'honest broker' of the implementation process. Each project or sub-project would have specific objectives outlined and measures of success highlighted.

CONCLUSION

The implementation period is one of high stress for employees, especially if there are wide-ranging changes taking place. It is worth remembering, however, that employee concerns decrease during this time if the process is handled well – employees expect change and if it is implemented professionally, the outcome is generally accepted. Professionalism in an acquisition context means transparently clear processes, honest communication and empathetic, professional implementation of the stated plan.

6   When the Dust Settles: The Stabilization Period

INTRODUCTION

There will come a time during the life of the acquisition process when those involved stop and think that the whirlwind changes and pace of the last few months is finally drawing to a close (see Figure 6.1). This time can be spent constructively appraising how well the acquirer's management performed during the acquisition and what they could do better the next time. Unfortunately, most acquirers fail to assess their actions post-acquisition and as a consequence make many of the same mistakes in subsequent acquisitions rather than learning during the process.

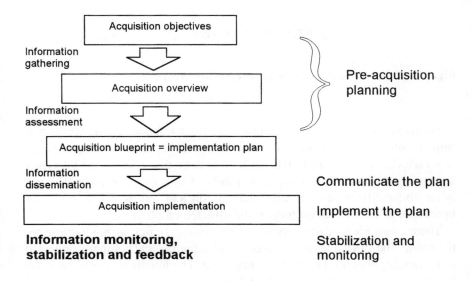

Fig. 6.1 *Monitoring, assessment and stabilization as part of the acquisition process*

MONITORING AND FEEDBACK DURING IMPLEMENTATION

It is very difficult to break acquisition into neat compartments because of the overlap. For instance, planning and implementation are inextricably linked; communication must occur throughout the process to be effective. The processes of monitoring, feedback and stabilization are also related but do not necessarily run concurrently (see Figure 6.2). They all do, however, follow the implementation period. Because of this, information monitoring, feedback and stabilization are all discussed in this chapter.

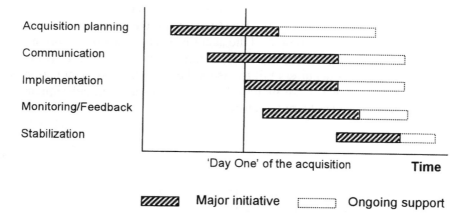

Fig. 6.2   *A general timescale for the acquisition process*

As discussed earlier, misinformation is a common failing during acquisition implementation. In order to ensure that the correct message is being received, several techniques can be used in addition to those discussed above including surveys, questionnaires and acquisition audits. Collecting employee feedback is an underutilized activity after acquisition and one which is mutually beneficial to both the acquirer and the affected employees.

There exists a legendary story which may be fact or fiction, but it illustrates the point. The story goes that a large US pharmaceutical company acquired a smaller, highly entrepreneurial competitor. The intention was to keep the innovative and creative research and development department as a stand alone entity but ensure it had all the resources it needed to continue its excellent work. The other departments were to be made redundant as the larger acquirer had them already in situ. One by one the acquirer made the marketing, finance and administration departments redundant. Abruptly the research and development (R&D) department resigned en masse to join a competitor rather than have the same fate befall them – no one had bothered to tell them that they were the entire reason for the acquisition. Clearly, if the acquirer had channels for feedback and if it had monitored employee concerns, this incident could have been avoided.

Employee audits are confidential employee feedback methods used to get a clear understanding of employee feelings and views of the acquisition and its success. Methods of feedback can include: personal interviews, focus groups, employee attitude surveys, hotlines and exit interviews (discussed below):

1. **Personal interviews** are a good way of gathering information from key employees. The benefits from using interviews rather than focus groups is that employees are more likely to be honest and open and less in need to 'perform' in front of their colleagues. Thus, for trade union representatives, directors and some managers, this is probably the best form of information gathering. It is, however, time consuming and does not offer the opportunity for 'brainstorming' with the other group participants.

2. **Focus groups** are an excellent means of getting a great deal of information in a short period of time. Groups of up to ten employees can discuss the issues, often fuelling each other with their comments. They must be carefully facilitated, however, as they run the risk of bravado rather than honesty for all participants.

3. **Employee attitude surveys** can cover a lot of ground, especially if the acquirer wants data to compare with its own existing survey data. It can also cover a whole host of topics with great anonymity. However, surveys are expensive, slow to administer and slow to show results, and do not give employees the same sense of participation that an interview or focus group does.

4. **Hotlines** or other upward feedback mechanisms can be used in larger or more geographically dispersed acquisitions where employees may have specific questions that need answering. A good point about a hotline is that the types of queries can be monitored and answers fed back to all employees on those topics. They also give a strong indication of overall concerns across all employee groups and can be relatively anonymous. They are often underused by employees, however, and cannot provide too much in terms of general feedback and perceptions from employees. They are best used in conjunction with another form of feedback mechanism.

5. **Exit interviews** are a bit like 'closing the stable door after the horse has bolted' but they do serve a purpose. Employees are asked a series of questions about the organization and why they are leaving. Issues such as career opportunities and employee grievances can often be discovered at this stage. What the acquirer does with this information is important – it could be used to address the situation rather than simply to satisfy idle curiosity.

The objective of feedback is to get an accurate picture of employee sentiment and concern about the acquisition, the implementation process, and the two companies. It is useful for gathering perceptions of the other company and of how employees see themselves, which allows for comparisons between the two to be made. This form of information collection offers a non-confrontational way of addressing sensitive issues.

Employees may find a face-to-face dialogue more satisfying than filling out a written questionnaire – however, this must be weighed against the issue of anonymity. If employees are worried about confidentiality or repercussions based on their comments, they will not speak openly. External consultants can provide a valuable service as an unbiased bridge for employees being interviewed and the acquiring management.

While the facility for feedback may exist, its effectiveness may be impaired if employees are too afraid to speak openly for fear of redundancy or the adverse implications of speaking out. In these cases, they would rather accept the status quo and not voice their concerns, objections or anxieties. Senior management unaware of employee problems can incorrectly assume that as employees are not voicing concerns these concerns do not exist. Thus, management is left believing that employees are comfortable with the situation simply because they fail to say otherwise. It is a dangerous assumption to make. The use of external or anonymous means of upward feedback can alleviate this problem to a greater extent.

The most important issue for any employee feedback is how the findings are used and presented. If they are only for senior management to use, the result is rather dissatisfying for not only those who took part but also the other employees who will undoubtedly have heard of the process. If the results (both positive and negative) are generally released for all employees, the message sent is that the senior management team values their employees' opinions, has an open communication style, is interested in positive outcomes and is not just 'going through the motions'. This was seen at Quality Guarding. While perceptions of management suffered a great deal during the acquisition implementation, they recovered well by having the acquisition audit conducted and then publishing the results internally for all to see.

Employees saw this as courageous on the part of management and as an indication that management valued their opinions as employees. It went a long way in easing some of the acquisition angst.

TIMEFRAME FOR STABILIZATION

The stabilization period is the time after which the implementation and corresponding change has occurred and a period of relatively little change begins. There is no time estimate for when the integration finishes and the stabilization period begins and ends. It varies enormously due to the amount of change experienced by employees and the degree to which employees feel traumatized by the changes. Research in the US has found that during the stabilization period employees experienced a reduction of uncertainty, ambiguity and stress in employees (Ivancevich et al., 1987).

It is not necessary for all of the changes to have been implemented in their entirety in order for employees to feel more secure in this stabilization period. Ongoing projects which would be likely to continue after an acquisition could include information systems, back office realignment, developing the combined corporate culture and the harmonization of employees' terms and conditions. Those projects that are continuing, however, must take on a more 'ongoing project feel' in order for employees to feel totally comfortable. This means that employees' questions regarding their own job security and that of their colleagues, their general role in the new company, and an understanding of the new company's culture and procedures must be answered satisfactorily. In essence, employees must agree emotionally to continue forward with the new owner – that the changes so far are acceptable and that they are willing to enter into a new psychological contract with the acquirer (see Chapter 2).

While the amount of change influences how quickly employees enter the stabilization period, it is more often how those changes are implemented which dictates the speed at which stabilization is reached. If the process was well handled, employees adjust more readily to the changes and settle down to their organizational routine more quickly, almost in spite of the levels of change. In these cases, the stabilization period can begin within six months of 'Day One' of the acquisition. This is illustrated in the case studies (discussed in Chapter 2) where employee concerns and their intention to leave the company stabilized more quickly when the process was handled well, even if it meant more change (including job losses) in the process. In cases where the implementation process was handled poorly, employees remained apprehensive and unsettled for what was a considerably longer period of time. During this time, concerns did not settle and employees either looked for alternative employment or emotionally detached themselves from their current job. Issues which engendered these negative feelings in employees were the acquirer's inability to manage employee expectations, the breaking of any promises on the part of the acquirer, perceptions of unfairness, little communication and any unpredictable behaviour on the acquirer's part. In these cases and in others, employees can remain in an unsettled state for years. Symptoms include employees using phrases like, 'I am keeping my head down and watching my back', and a refusal to speak openly about contentious subjects. This was seen at Quality Guarding where some employees interviewed were told by their managers not to say anything contentious which could draw attention to them.

LEARNING DURING THE STABILIZATION PERIOD

Assessing one's performance after the event

There are several means for assessing one's performance once the nirvana of stabilization has been reached. The first way is to assess the financial success of the acquisition by comparing the objectives of the transaction weighed against any budgetary information available. For those acquirers who have built in performance measurements for their implementation, this can be done by seeing which targets were met or missed and their costs. Unfortunately the majority of acquirers omit this crucial step; KPMG's European study found that 55 per cent of respondents did not know what their budget was for the acquisition of acquirers; another 17 per cent said that there had been no budget set aside for the acquisition (1997). Of those who did budget, half reported that costs had overrun by up to 60 per cent of that budget (ibid.). When asked what elements caused the overruns, the five most common responses for those who knew were:

- staff allocation costs were higher than expected (11 per cent)
- complexity of the organization (11 per cent)
- understanding cultural backdrop was a problem (8 per cent)
- underestimated the scale of the reorganization and rationalization (8 per cent)
- were too optimistic (8 per cent) [ibid.].

These findings suggest a wholly unsatisfactory approach to budgeting for most acquirers and a fundamental lack of understanding of the basic issues surrounding the implementation process. Three of the five findings point to a lack of awareness of the importance that 'people issues' play as part of the process; other research findings bear this finding out.

An often underutilized means of judging acquisition success is to conduct a post-acquisition audit. This can be achieved using an external facilitator to get an unbiased sense of how the acquisition went. Audits can be performed via interviews for key employees and focus groups to get an overall feel of employee sentiment and suggestions of how it could have gone better. From this process an objective profile can be developed and fed back to management and, ideally, employees. Management can then learn how what they did was perceived and lessons on how they can improve for any future acquisition. The process then becomes a key learning tool to ensure improvement. This approach was used extremely successfully at Service Conglomerate. Where the Quality Guarding acquisition had not gone as well as planned, further acquisitions both by Quality Guarding and its parent have gone extremely well, due in part to using the knowledge gained in assessing the Quality Guarding acquisition process.

At a bare minimum, acquirers should have a management team debriefing session to assess how they did and what they would do differently the next time. Through this process, acquirers can capture quite a few suggestions to ensure that they improve every time they acquire. Some companies use external coaches to ensure that learning is captured throughout the process. Unless there is a resourcing problem on the part of the acquirer, externally hired coaches rarely have to come in more than twice to help an acquirer learn how to master the acquisition process.

Some companies capture lessons they have learned during acquisition through documenting their process. This is a great advantage if one is planning on acquiring again or if a subsidiary is about to undergo an acquisition and some of the knowledge can be captured for future use. In addition, while there is a process to acquiring and tricks related to that, many of the lessons learned during acquisition are relevant for most businesses' day-to-day operations and can be useful as such.

Getting ready for the future

Whether or not future acquisitions are anticipated, the acquirer can use lessons learned from the acquisition experience in its ongoing business development. Included in this are lessons learned regarding the process itself, assessing management shortcomings or talents, and requisite training.

Lessons learned from the acquisition process should not be used solely for acquisitions. Many of the keys to acquisition success are also salient to management change in general: managing employee expectations, communication and project management skills. Rather than 'compartmentalize' those skills and disciplines learned solely for acquisition, it is worth spending some time understanding how they can be transported not only to exceptional times but also to everyday management. One area to which this readily applies is leadership management.

Leadership management comes under fire during times of stress and change; acquisition is an obvious example of this in action. If one has found management's skills lacking during acquisition, one can use the stabilization period for further training in this area. If future acquisitions are planned, one can assess how managers performed during the previous acquisition and tailor a training programme to address these needs for the future. The likely areas where middle management training can add value for future acquisitions are communication, leadership during times of change, acquisition project management skills and understanding employee behaviour during acquisition.

There are also certain cases where further acquisitions occur during the stabilization period. This can be very unsettling for affected employees, much like a second large wave engulfing them soon after the first – they feel tossed about and not terribly in control. If it is possible to avoid this, do so. If not, try to limit the down-side by ensuring key managers are secure in their jobs, their roles and responsibilities. Try to involve other employees in the new acquisition while giving those who worked hard on the previous one some time off to get back to their day-to-day responsibilities. By all means, use their knowledge and skills, but let them return to a 'normal' working environment. And use the skills learnt on the previous acquisition to ensure the next one goes better. By undertaking this process of learning after each acquisition, the expertise built up over time increases incrementally as one continues to acquire.

EMPLOYEES LEARNING HOW TO COPE

The acquisition process affects some employees more dramatically than others. Some employees just do not have the ability to deal with uncertainty to the same extent as others. Those more pragmatic employees tend to find the uncertainty associated with acquisition easier to bear than those who crave structure. The process of acquiring can, however, teach employees to cope with change and become more comfortable with the concept of working in a constantly changing organizational environment. If employees undergo a well-managed acquisition and implementation process, organizational trust is enhanced. Consequently, employees are more likely to be willing to trust the company in the future. This means they are more willing to stick with the company during future times of uncertainty knowing that management is professional in its dealings and in any event, it will treat employees well. This is a source of huge competitive advantage; it means that employees are more able to deal with periods of uncertainty, restructuring, role changes and a more fluid working environment because they trust their employer to look after them.

This sense of coping can only come through experience. If employees have had a positive change experience (such as successfully undergone a major acquisition), they are more relaxed about future ones. Conversely, if their only experience of major change is a negative one, such as through a mismanaged acquisition, they are more likely to react adversely to potentially related situations in the future. Part of the process of employee coping is that the employer must accept that these emotions exist in employees. As seen in Chapter 2, senior management's concerns and emotions differ from those of middle managers and the rest of the workforce. Because of this, workforce emotions are often ignored by senior management. Senior management must realize that employees will display a whole host of emotions throughout the entire process including the stabilization period. These have been related to the emotions seen by Dr Elizabeth Kubler-Ross in people confronted with loved ones dying. Though this sounds far-fetched, employees during acquisition go through anger, denial, frustration, sadness, and finally a period of acceptance. When this final emotion occurs, it often marks the beginning of the stabilization period. It is at this point that employees are ready to 'move on' and get on with their jobs. This doesn't mean that employees will not still react when confronted with a loss of a company name or brand but it does mean that they are not quite as emotionally involved as they were during the implementation period. Acquirers can help during this process by behaving sympathetically towards this gamut of employee emotions and understanding that they will occur.

CONCLUSION

Employee feedback and monitoring throughout acquisition is an undervalued yet important step in ensuring that 'the message sent is the message received'. Without it, acquirers run the risk that major misunderstandings with key employees or units can damage the acquisition. It takes very little effort but the rewards in using feedback and monitoring methods are well worth it.

While the stabilization period marks the end of the acquisition, it is an important time in the process. It offers the acquirer the opportunity to assess and understand what went well and what could be improved upon. Without this vital step acquiring management run the risk that they will repeatedly make the same mistakes again and again with every subsequent acquisition. In addition, the acquirer must understand employee sentiment and emotions with regard to its former company. While compassion costs nothing more than thought and perhaps some time, it can go a long way in showing employees the 'human face' of their new employer.

7   Anglo-American Industries plc and Gas Appliances

INTRODUCTION

While over half of the cases discussed in this book show acquisitions which were not as successful as they could have been, this first Anglo-American case outlines how acquisitions can be handled in an efficient manner, thereby eliminating much of the uncertainty and angst which can accompany the process. While not all acquirers have, or need, a specialized acquisition team, the principles demonstrated by the team in following a systematic process of acquisition implementation can be adapted by other acquirers.

BACKGROUND TO THE ACQUISITION

This case study analyses the 1991 acquisition of a global home and building products conglomerate known as Home Products plc by a larger UK-American conglomerate known as Anglo-American Industries plc. The price paid was £330 million and it was a publicly quoted company transaction.

Anglo-American enjoyed a meteoric rise from a small British-based company to a £1 billion turnover public company in the span of ten years, due primarily to its highly successful acquisition technique. At the heart of the company's success was its clear acquisition strategy; companies were acquired which could benefit from capital investment, changes in working practices and from a defined 'fit' with the existing Anglo-American businesses. Because of this, the degree of integration pursued by Anglo-American was that of improving the business then running it with financial controls with little to no integration with the other Anglo-American companies. Synergies were achieved at head office via purchasing and customer power and selected cross-fertilization of ideas in research, production efficiencies and marketing.

Home Products possessed brands which included some of the most famous in the world, of which Gas Appliances was one. While under Home Products ownership, insufficient capital had been invested to build upon its brands. The operation, therefore, did not fully utilize its existing assets or systems and, in fact, relied on milking the assets. Home Products plc's long-standing chairman summarized his business philosophy in a comment made to the Anglo-American CEO:

> [Peterson] said there is a difference between you and me. He said, 'The difference is when you see a window in a building that's loose and rattles, you will put immediate effort into stopping the rattling, seal it, and make it good for the long term. When I see a window in a building which rattles, I will just watch it till it falls out.' Now he thought I was wrong which tells you all about the differences in culture. They had owned the business; they had spent very little on any of the businesses and they had given very little attention to them whatsoever.

Home Products plc had been led during the previous 35 years by its colourful chairman, Hugh Peterson. Peterson had ruled the conglomerate in an autocratic fashion; he did not decentralize control and ran the business as he saw fit. As one colleague commented: 'Hugh Peterson had run Home Products in a very poor way from the small team in the centre.' In addition, Home Products had made a series of acquisitions through the years and in the process acquired some prestigious brand names, but never managed to take full advantage of them. As one Home Products director put it, 'Our acquisitions turned out to be poor judgments or the implementation never fulfilled expectations as a general rule.'

Home Products plc had been a highly attractive takeover candidate for almost a decade. In fact, an earlier merger bid with another well-known home product conglomerate had only failed well down the course of negotiations due to differences in management styles. Anglo-American had expressed an interest in Home Products as early as 1989 with the advances being rebuffed by Peterson. Allegedly Peterson was demanding that he be made chairman of Anglo-American which, due to historical reasons and his management style, was out of the question. By the mid-1990s, Peterson was reaching retirement age and perhaps because of this was more amenable to the acquisition. Home Products plc was acquired by Anglo-American in an agreed bid of £330 million which was consummated after several months of negotiations between the two companies' managements. Peterson joined the board of Home Products, a position he held for six months before his retirement.

A related conglomerate, Anglo-American had a strong home products division in which it was considered Home Products would fit nicely in terms of both product fit and customer base. A key success factor for Anglo-

American had been its management team including its chief executive, Alistair Anderson, which had taken the company from its inception to its current size. A special unit in charge of acquisition implementation was kept separate to the organization's day-to-day operations and reported directly to Peterson. This unit contained specialists in various disciplines who were responsible for implementing changes in the newly acquired companies. By the time of the Home Products acquisition, the special acquisition unit had integrated approximately 40 acquisitions and had developed an implementation routine which had proved to be highly successful in quickly and efficiently bringing those companies in line with Anglo-American's standards. As these professionals were deemed as not having the usual perks associated with other managers of their standing within the firm, such as secretaries and offices, they were given sports cars as a sign of their status. These cars came to symbolize the unit; Alistair Anderson also had a sports car as the honorary head, and spirit, of the acquisition unit. When the negotiations were underway between the Home Products and Anglo-American managements, the employees at Gas Appliances were aware of the talks through internal rumour and press speculation, especially the reports detailing the famous Anglo-American acquisition team and their sports cars.

Gas Appliances' primary manufacturing site was located in central England and employed approximately 450 employees. Gas Appliances manufactured a range of appliances for home use which was a highly seasonal business; 80 per cent of their sales occurred in the three winter months. The factory, like the rest of Home Products plc, had not been given the resources to maintain its market leading position and, therefore, was not run at optimum efficiency. This included overstocked finished goods and inventory stores, a disused derelict warehouse, out-of-date plant and equipment, and antiquated and compartmentalized offices and dining facilities. The shopfloor and communal areas reflected this: they were untidy with cardboard boxes separating work spaces and empty tins and food containers sitting on the production lines. The workforce adopted this attitude and behaved less than professionally – it was not uncommon to have employees visiting or eating while working on the line. One shopfloor worker commented: 'Everyone would do their work but if they finished at 3 o'clock, they would stroll around and read the paper and make tea – it needed a boot really.'

The shopfloor workforce comprised primarily women, many with long-standing service; some had worked at Gas Appliances for over 25 years. Historically, Gas Appliances attempted to deal with the seasonal nature of the products in two ways. First, it stockpiled large quantities of finished stock during the summer months which was stored in a warehouse. This was not ideal as it was quite common for finished stock to get damaged while in store and require refinishing on the line when ready for sale; it also strained the company's cashflow. Second, sub-contracted employees worked during the winter months when demand was at its highest. When full-time jobs fell vacant the sub-contracted employees were given priority in hiring. This was also less than satisfactory as it was considered that the seasonal employees were less motivated and diligent in their working practices than their full-time counterparts.

THE ACQUISITION

Within days of the sale, all Home Products directors throughout the world were summoned to England to meet the Anglo-American team and hear about their futures. A two-hour presentation was made which was thought to be cold and stark; it was, however, considered highly professional and inspired a great deal of respect in those directors attending. The presentation had been put together by the central acquisition team of Anglo-American and clearly showed the amount of pre-acquisition planning and detail which had gone into the acquisition. The presentation included a video of Anglo-American, their history and growth; it also included a very detailed analysis of Home Products' strengths and weaknesses and the reasons for the acquisition, including where Home Products would fit into Anglo-American's structure. The presentation was considered impressive because of its detailed information on Anglo-American and its analysis of Home Products. The presentation style was also exemplary; the Anglo-American chief executive, Alistair Anderson, conducted the proceedings with extreme professionalism. This immediately engendered respect in all the directors interviewed, respect for the company in terms of industry knowledge and respect for the management in terms of leadership ability. One director described the meeting:

> I found at the start that there would be no questions so I took a transcript down of it. I was thinking this guy is a metronome because he did it without a script, surgically, humourlessly, utterly professionally, his presentation was absolutely awesome. But taking the notes down made it so easy to pick out the themes going through it, and there were the messages so clinically and clearly expressed, you couldn't help but be utterly impressed, almost overwhelmed. His analysis of our company, the politics in the company were all honestly dead on the button. It showed that they had done their homework exceptionally well. It was done to leave people

thinking seriously. Alistair Anderson is brilliant, they are Oscar candidates, the psychology of it for the time was absolutely perfect.

At the close of the meeting, all those attending were given a copy of an Anglo-American video which outlined the company and were encouraged to show it to their subordinates. The coverage of that video being shown after the presentation was mixed, with the majority of middle managers at Gas Appliances being shown it. The rest of the workforce, however, were less likely to have seen the video.

Employee concerns at this point were relatively high and were being fuelled by press speculation as to the post-acquisition implementation style of Anglo-American. The press were keen to point out the positive aspects of the acquisition but also revelled in the macho image of Anglo-American and the sports cars. Many of the employees interviewed at Gas Appliances were not familiar with Anglo-American as a group because it was company policy to keep its subsidiaries highly independent. Once told of the companies owned by Anglo-American, however, the general reaction was one of surprise that Anglo-American owned so many prestigious brands. But it was the image of the sports cars that remained most firmly in the employees' minds. One middle manager said: 'I read about it [the sports cars] in the paper on Sunday, and thought it can't be that bad, and you turn up on Monday morning and there they are, four or five of them lined up outside.'

ACQUISITION IMPLEMENTATION

Within a week of the initial meeting, the acquisition team in their sports cars, including Alistair Anderson, arrived at the initial locations to assess the business units. The acquisition team's first job was to evaluate the company's top management, a process which was to take several weeks. While it was company policy to retain top management, Anglo-American management felt that the incumbent management evaluation process was an important initial step of the acquisition's implementation. Any management not willing to do things the 'Anglo-American way' would be asked to leave. The Gas Appliances management team consisted of long-serving finance, commercial and marketing directors, and newly appointed managing and operations directors. The initial meeting consisted of the acquisition team questioning the directors for several hours over their previously poor performance, to which they responded. At the conclusion of the meeting it was made clear that the management team would be kept intact and evaluated over the next few weeks. They would, however, be operating the 'Anglo-American way' and must be open to new management techniques and greater accountability, to which they agreed. One director said of the meeting: 'That first day you feel like you have had a working over but sitting down after they left I thought, "Yes, these people are professional" so it hurt my pride and it was an incentive.'

The following day the Anglo-American acquisition team of five people began a formal review and transformation of the operations, a process which was to last six months. Within two weeks of arriving on site a formal presentation was made to all employees by the acquisition team via the existing management team. Anglo-American was committed to using line management for communication; it did, however, offer a great deal of assistance to those managers to ensure that the message sent was consistent with Anglo-American's strategy and objectives of the next six months. This presentation included the video on Anglo-American followed by an outline of future implementation plans. The latter element was clearly outlined as being in four points. First, senior management was asked to complete a comprehensive post-acquisition analysis of their business. This included a full financial, product and profit margin analysis, and a comprehensive listing of all plant and equipment, as well as copies of all building leases. Second, the site would be cleaned up, including the demolition of the disused warehousing and removal of all rubbish and non-essential papers. Third, the offices were to be refurbished and modernized in an open plan office style with the overhauling of the central reception and meeting areas. The Anglo-American rationale for these changes was that if Gas Appliances was a market leader it should look like one. Finally, the shopfloor was to be reorganized with the introduction of certain total quality and short cycle management techniques which would radically change working practices. Thus, Anglo-American built in and communicated some highly visible 'quick wins' to show employees that they delivered on their promises.

The information session was one of information dissemination and offered no opportunity for employee questions. Those employees attending the meeting were of two opinions when hearing about the organizational changes. Approximately half were happy to be included in the change announcement and were interested in the video's content. One middle manager said, 'They actually came down and did a presentation here and that was really good because it meant that they are serious and open. It made you realize that you are part of the company – there was a real buzz after that.' The other half of employees were more sceptical and took a 'wait and see' attitude. A shopfloor worker commented: 'I got the impression that people didn't believe them, there was no reason to believe it.' The dichotomy in those believing appeared to be based on a management–shopfloor divide. This division was to continue to some extent throughout the entire acquisition.

The first phase of the implementation plan commenced immediately. The directors as well as many middle managers were highly involved with the collection and correlation of the information demanded by Anglo-American's head office; this placed a heavy burden on the finance department. This time proved to be trying for many of those employees due to the long hours and workload required. On top of this, the year end accounts had to conform with those of Anglo-American's other subsidiaries. A new budget was also renegotiated which placed an additional burden on those directors. One director commented: 'They gave me great wads of books to fill out with information and I could see all the stuff we had got to do, preliminary research data forms. It was a great concern because of the sheer amount of work needed and the timescale given.' The commercial director resigned citing incompatible management styles. The rest of the senior and middle management team, however, remained intact despite the workload.

The importance of budget negotiation became apparent during this phase of the acquisition. It was clear that the budget negotiation process was an integral part of the management process at Anglo-American. Gas Appliances renegotiated a new budget for the upcoming year, projecting greater profit than they had ever made. The pressure on senior management to exceed budget was seen as extreme. The unconfirmed rumours suggested that managers who failed to reach budget did so only once; upon the second failure they were made redundant, placing great pressure on the existing management to perform.

Other departments were equally busy attempting to catalogue their entire product range and each product's profit margins. This culminated in a presentation to the Anglo-American management team. In the case of one product, a Gas Appliances manager rounded the figure off incorrectly which was picked up before the meeting by one of the Anglo-American acquisition team members. The corrections were made with the strong suggestion that inaccuracies would not be tolerated and that all the figures should be double checked. The exercise, however, was deemed by those involved as highly valuable. A director commented: 'I can't say it was an experience one wants to go through but I think we were all richer for having done it, you come out of it more focused.' The product lines were rationalized in line with the margin and profitability findings as suggested by the Anglo-American team.

While the internal information gathering phase was occurring all other employees were responsible for cleaning up their work areas with the acquisition team supervising. Several Gas Appliances employees in each area of the facility were assigned to help. Many employees were approached by acquisition team members and quizzed about the origin of unclaimed papers and items. The cardboard which had previously served as unofficial demarcation dividers on the shopfloor was discarded. If items weren't claimed within a day or deemed important, they were thrown out. This method was highly effective. One manager commented: 'Everyone really pitched in and threw everything out and I suppose it was like sweeping out the old Gas Appliances and welcoming in the new. It was very symbolic.' Those documents which were considered important were stored in a new archive centre on the premises.

When this phase was complete, the second phase of office refurbishment began. The corporate builders and decorators arrived on site and began reorganizing the layout in line with other Anglo-American subsidiaries. Several key middle managers including the office manager from Gas Appliances were given responsibility for the office layout and design. One manager commented: 'We had a corridor down the middle and it was a waste of time walking in and out. Now we just shout across the office, the physical lines of communication are so much shorter, you know where everybody is or where they should be.' While several employees affected by the changes complained that they didn't like open plan offices it appeared to be more efficient and, in the end, even those reluctant employees admitted that the new layout and style were far preferable to the previous style. In addition, offices were furnished with new furniture and equipment which included computerizing all offices. The latter point was also well received by employees. One manager said: 'They bought all the secretaries word processors instead of typewriters. Then a few months later I had a typed letter come in that was tatty and you realize that you have moved on and that this is state of the art now. Customers see the value of buying Gas Appliances' quality.'

During this phase, the communal areas were also redecorated. A plush new reception area was added in which several of the products were sympathetically displayed. A bright new canteen with seating area was also added where all employees would dine and where group meetings would also be held. A product demonstration building was also erected on the site in which all the company's products were displayed. The site including the shopfloor area was painted. The change was remarkable; photographs of the premises prior to and after the refurbishment were taken and displayed and the results were well received. One marketing manager commented: 'If you had come here as a visitor two years ago you would have sat here under the stairs whereas now you feel as if you are walking into the number one gas appliances manufacturer. We wouldn't have done that because there was no return on that; we didn't exploit our position.' The plan to this stage had taken several months to complete.

It was only after the initial stages of refurbishment were completed that the final phase of reorganizing the shopfloor commenced. The main issues to be addressed were the poor quality record in manufacturing and seasonality of the product. These two issues were factors in the unsatisfactorily high percentage of finished goods in inventory which needed to be reworked prior to sale.

The newly appointed operations director shared a vision for the shopfloor which was similar to that of Anglo-American. This included the reorganization of the floor into production cells, the introduction of just-in-time inventory and finished goods, zero defects manufacturing and a flatter organizational structure. In addition, the pay schedules and the use of sub-contracted labour were to come under review. Many of the shopfloor employees interviewed were wary but resigned to the changes; they did not resist the introduction of the new working practices. As one shopfloor worker said: 'It was a gradual thing with the shopfloor as well as me. It made me trust them [Anglo-American] because what they said they were going to do, they did. The old management was, "Oh yes, we are going to do it", but they never did.'

The first task was to renegotiate the current employment contracts with the shopfloor employees. With the co-operation of the trade unions the employee contracts were renegotiated. The employees were previously on a variety of different pay grades based on a piecework system which made short cycle production management an impossibility. The pay rates were increased and levelled with no loss of earnings into two different pay grades on the shopfloor, one for cell leaders and another for cell members. Performance-based pay was abolished. Because of the historical use of seasonal workers, it was not necessary to make any of the existing shopfloor employees redundant. In addition, Gas Appliances had begun a delayering process two months prior to the acquisition and had made redundant or redeployed several of the production managers. In spite of this, some middle management redundancies in production were needed in order to further flatten the organizational hierarchy; they were enacted without issue or long-term detriment to the organization.

The employees were then given the opportunity to determine how to cope with the seasonality of the products. Management, via the personnel department, asked employees for ideas on how to deal with the manufacturing seasonality. Management received a variety of responses, the majority of which were helpful, although a few were sarcastic. One suggestion put forward by management was that the existing work force would work shorter hours in the slower summer months and longer hours in the peak winter months. This translated into a 35-hour week in the summer and a 45-hour week in the winter months. This response was accepted by the trade unions on behalf of the employees and the affected employees voted again on the preferred start and finish times. There was some cynicism over this solution. One worker commented: 'The shopfloor felt as if they were threatened into accepting the new hours, most of them had their arm twisted into accepting it and they resent being threatened into changing their hours.' This view was not held by all employees, however. One explained the cynical attitude: 'There was a small faction here that would never accept that things were going to work, doom and gloom, and you could never get through to them.'

The acquisition team then began the shopfloor transformation. The process by now had engendered a positive attitude in most of managers involved. One director commented: 'When we started reorganizing the offices, I thought, this is terrific. We would have never done this, the factory I could have always got through but when they started on the offices and I saw how we could get so many good things, I thought this is wonderful so we were on a bit of a buzz.' All those in senior and middle production management positions felt involved in the process and felt that they had received enough information about the changes. One manager said: 'The fact that Alistair Anderson and the entourage came in and were walking around asking what is this and what is that, if I hadn't been involved some of the impact would have been lost.' Some of those lower-level employees, however, did not receive as much information as they would have liked and did not feel involved. One shopfloor employee commented: 'They didn't really let us know, the attitude I get is it doesn't concern you, just come here and do the job that you are supposed to do and that is it.' The sporadic nature of communication to the shopfloor was caused in part by the still existing layers of production management; some of the shopfloor employees indicated that they felt their managers were fully informed yet failed to pass on that information. Others felt that Anglo-American's and Gas Appliances' own management had been good communicators during this process. Of those employees who did not receive sufficient information, anxiety levels were greater during the changes.

The shifting of the shopfloor lines into production cells with greater responsibility, combined with the flatter production structure, required the promotion of certain shopfloor employees into cell leader and production manager positions. It was a management decision to promote and train current employees rather than hire externally. Of those employees promoted, the majority initially found the increased responsibility difficult. In some cases, they weren't sure if they were performing their job to the satisfaction of Anglo-

American's management. In most cases, however, employees were informed of changes and encouraged to pursue their new roles. One newly appointed manager commented: 'I was very nervous [of being promoted] but Anglo-American were very good and they all helped me, once I made the move it was quite good and I surprised myself that I could do what they thought I could do.' Because of the good and long-standing working relationships between the production managers and the cell leaders, the cell leaders trusted their production managers and appeared to be well informed about job changes and performance.

This same degree of trust was not universal between all shopfloor employees and the acquisition team, nor with the operations director. Perhaps the lack of interaction combined with the power wielded by the acquisition team led a few of the cell leaders interviewed to indicate they were anxious when confronted with team members. In some cases it was just the manner of the acquisition team members on the shopfloor. One shopfloor worker commented: 'It is the fear and the image, they are standing just watching you and not speaking. You would feel a lot better if they would speak to you and put you at your ease. That is done for about fifteen minutes and then they walk to another line and do the same thing, asking questions. You feel like you are on trial.' Most employees, however, found them extremely helpful and straightforward. One worker commented: 'I did speak to one of them [an acquisition team member] a couple of times and found him very pleasant and completely different to the impression he was giving. I found him very nice and you could talk to him, I didn't realize because for a few weeks I was really afraid of him.' Another commented: 'The outside worked hard at this myth "Oh, Anglo-American, the sports cars" but there wasn't that at all, no uncomfortableness at all.'

The objective of the new cell structure was to achieve maximum responsiveness to production needs, including functional flexibility within their cells which was achieved via training within the cells. In addition, they were measured on their ability to achieve zero quality defects. Finally, cells were responsible for maintaining a low finished goods inventory. The process of transforming the lines and achieving these objectives was moderately painful for the shopfloor. In one afternoon, the entire shopfloor was turned around; where the lines had previously run the length of the factory, they now ran width-wise. While the changes were addressed adequately to the senior and middle managers, some of the cell leaders continued to feel that they were not included in the sharing of information. One shopfloor worker commented: 'We don't get any information at all, you just get rumours but you can't get them substantiated or anything like that.' This was manifest in some friction on the shopfloor. At the height of the changes a senior acquisition team member supervising the transition commented to a director: 'I have just been around the factory and the atmosphere is terrible. They hate you, the operations director, and they especially hate Anglo-American.' With substantial input from the Anglo-American acquisition team, however, this problem was to pass within weeks as the shopfloor became more accustomed to the changes and could see that they were a radical improvement.

In support of the actual shopfloor changes, there were procedural changes implemented which were designed to facilitate the achieving of high commitment management practices. Each cell had a large display board on which to report its weekly quality levels. In addition, charts and graphs indicating production goals and objectives were displayed throughout the shopfloor. The information concerning production figures, inventory and finished goods warehousing targets, and profits and loss were also readily available and on display on the shopfloor along with 'before' and 'after' photographs of the site to remind employees how much the site had improved. This was greeted positively by most of the shopfloor employees.

In spite of the initial problems, the changes did take hold and production efficiency increased. Employee morale increased as the employees began to feel comfortable with the new working practices and routines. The process had required an enormous amount of change for certain employees, most notably the shopfloor, but had had no long-term negative effects. The changes took approximately seven months to fully implement from 'Day One' of the acquisition. When the acquisition team finally left the site at the end of the seven months, it had been transformed by the new facilities and work techniques. The company launched a new product later that year which became a marketing success. The company also tripled profits to record levels, and had laid the foundations for achieving even higher profits. Employees interviewed were unanimous in their conclusion that the acquisition was a success. One shopfloor worker said:

> Anglo-American should be proud of what it has actually done, I am amazed by the transition period and how it has gone through in such a short period of time. People who have been out in the past seven or eight years come back and can't even recognize the place, I wouldn't.

STABILIZATION PERIOD

After the acquisition team left the site, there was a genuine attempt to keep the momentum achieved in communication flowing, especially with the shopfloor. Daily debriefing meetings were held in order to discuss the day's production. Monthly management meetings were also held in which the production managers were invited to participate, and it was the responsibility of those attending to brief their subordinates as to the meetings' outcomes. Although the forums were in place to facilitate communication, the actual constructive flow of information both upward and downward was impeded in some cases by undertones within the company culture. There persisted a strong management–employee divide which impeded some upward communication. There was also an amount of fear in some directors caused by the perceived profit/budget emphasis of the highly financially driven parent company. Thus, it appeared that some employees tried to protect themselves by 'pointing the finger' at departments or individuals if problems arose. This attitude impeded the free flow of information and the general problem solving attitude needed for maximum efficiency. Several employees interviewed commented that prior to the interviews, one of the directors instructed them not to lie but to be optimistic when discussing the changes at Gas Appliances.

The massive changes brought on by the acquisition created a normal degree of uncertainty amongst the acquired employees. They had no reason to trust or believe Anglo-American at the beginning of the acquisition. In spite of this, the management team lost only one director during the process and virtually none of middle management other than through redundancy. Many employees commented that while they didn't initially believe Anglo-American, the fact that they fulfilled employee expectations lowered their initial concerns and enhanced Anglo-American's believability in an upward spiralling effect. This process included accurately communicating the planned changes to employees prior to their implementation and following through with the implementation as discussed. This was enhanced by the positive leadership demonstrated by Alistair Anderson and the acquisition team, especially in their help in defining job roles during shopfloor changes as well as the positive impact that the acquisition had on Gas Appliances' facilities.

In conclusion, the acquisition was considered a success by employees and management by virtue of achieving the stated acquisition objectives with the least amount of long-term disruption. Gas Appliances recently received a national business award for its quality production initiatives which had been implemented during the acquisition.

CONCLUSION

Of the five cases studied, Anglo-American most clearly followed the process of acquisition implementation and, in doing so, successfully managed employee expectations. They had a very detailed and thorough plan, they communicated that plan to the affected employees and then implemented it as communicated in a fair and logical manner.

Perhaps the greatest strength of Anglo-American was their pre-acquisition planning. Nothing was left to chance. While they had operated in this manner since their inception, their tried and tested formula worked very well. As a consequence, on the day of announcement, communication was comprehensive, consistent and unequivocally accurate. This made an enormous impact on the directors during their initial contact with Anglo-American by creating the impression of a thorough and professional management team. The plan was then able to be enacted in precisely the manner in which it was communicated and based upon years of professional acquisition experience.

The way in which Anglo-American communicated the formulated plan so publicly gave employees a chance to assess their abilities as managers; when the plan was consistently executed it led to an increased respect of their leadership and management abilities. Inherent to this is the practice of building in 'quick wins'. Employees were told of key (and very public) milestones prior to their occurrence; when they inevitably happened, employees saw that Anglo-American could be believed. The different messages appropriate for the different audiences (directors, managers and shopfloor) were also evident in the different presentations. Employees were left in no doubt as to what was going to happen; it was then up to Anglo-American to deliver the changes in a fair and logical manner, which they did. Anglo-American also used more than one communication medium to ensure that messages were given to all employees. As some shopfloor employees did not receive adequate briefings from their managers, this precaution proved sensible.

The participation of many directors and managers in implementing the general corporate decisions was also seen as crucial to the acceptance of those decisions. Although the major decisions had been made in accordance with the company policies, the way in which they were implemented was not. This compares favourably with the amount of employee participation and the time element during acquisition implementation, as discussed in Chapter 5. Employees could also see the benefits and logic of Anglo-American's actions which further enhanced their credibility, especially in light of Gas Appliances' previous management style of promising and not delivering. All in all, Anglo-American were able to introduce far-reaching changes with little or no long-term disruption by successfully following the outlined process and managing employee expectations.

Anglo-American also followed the acquisition policy of integrative separation which clearly made the process less complicated and served as a distinct advantage. They also carefully vetted potential acquisition targets and chose only those to which they felt they could add value during the 'restructuring' phase of the acquisition, thereby providing an opportunity to improve the target and enhance earnings without disrupting the other Anglo-American businesses. This remained a critical and fundamental element of their pre-acquisition planning and ensured that they were seen to bring value to the companies they acquired.

8 Service Conglomerate and Quality Guarding

INTRODUCTION

This case involves the subsidiary sale of a major contract guarding company (for the sake of the case study, called Quality Guarding) from a British-based global conglomerate (called Global Services plc) to a UK-related service conglomerate (referred to as Service Conglomerate). Quality Guarding's managing director is Quentin Graham; the name of the Service Conglomerate chief executive is Sam Cummings.

The modus operandi of Service Conglomerate was very similar to that of Anglo-American in the previous chapter: to buy assets which were not being used to their full effectiveness and, with assistance if necessary, elicit a greater return. This style lent itself well to the change and then arm's-length management style with financial controls also employed by Anglo-American. As will be seen in this chapter, while both companies had the same acquisition objectives and degree of integration, their relative implementation successes varied greatly.

BACKGROUND TO THE ACQUISITION

Quality Guarding's head office was a stately home in Southeast England. It had six decentralized, limited liability operating companies operating throughout the UK. Each operating company had its own managing director, usually two or three operations directors, a finance director, a marketing director and the reporting staff, as seen in the organizational chart (See Figure 8.1). Regional companies were responsible for the guarding contracts and employees in their region which numbered 1000 and 15 000 in total for the company, respectively. Quality Guarding was amongst the top four guarding firms in the UK based on the number of contracts held. It specialized in providing high-quality male and female office reception and security personnel for prestigious clients throughout the UK. By virtue of the nature

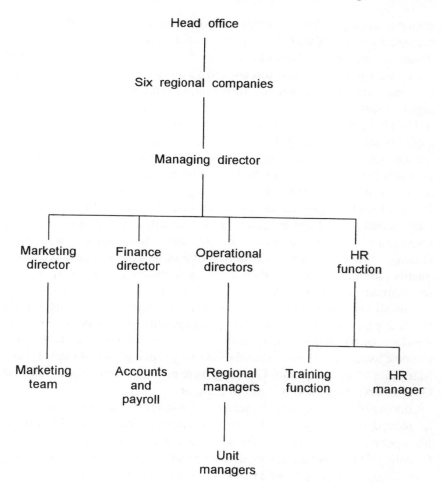

Fig. 8.1   *Organizational chart of Quality Guarding*

of the business, the organization was highly decentralized with many locations supporting only a few members of staff.

Regional managers were assigned to monitor units in their specific area in terms of financial performance, to ensure an adequate service level was being provided to the customer, to aid in budgeting and to act as client liaison. Each manager was assigned approximately twelve contracts depending on the geographical spread and size of the units as well as the capabilities of both the individual regional and unit managers. Three years prior to the acquisition, Quality Guarding had discontinued a position known as the senior regional manager. This position was to allow exceptional managers to manage 24 contracts with the help of an assistant provided by the company; it was also seen as good training for those who excelled to become operational directors. The position was discontinued as senior management deemed it important for the organization to become flatter and in order to ensure regional managers provided a quality service to clients.

The philosophy at Quality Guarding was to retain contracts by delivering a quality service at a slightly premium price. According to the trade press, the business was perceived in the market place as providing good value for the money paid. Staff were of the highest quality and integrity; their loyalty to clients was seen by Quality Guarding's management as being a key success factor in ensuring the provision of a superior service. Staff were well trained by the large in-house training department and, in fact, Quality Guarding had recently received a national award for its training initiatives. Quality Guarding's employees were proud of its deserved reputation as a quality provider and its record on retaining contracts; it was not uncommon for contracts to have been with Quality Guarding for over 20 years.

The quality image sat well with the owners of Quality Guarding, Global Services plc, which encouraged the quality culture as it 'fitted' with Global Services' own commitment to service. It was Global Services' intention to promote long-term growth within the Group by seeking to build market share. Many employees at Quality Guarding were proud of their connection with Global Services plc and its blue chip image.

Global Services plc management was not interested in short-term profit, or, indeed, on making the assets work particularly hard. Global Services' management was happy with the 4 per cent margins generated by Quality Guarding. One director recounted how he had suggested ways of improving profit margins only to be told the 4 per cent return was adequate.

Two months prior to the acquisition, there had been rumours at Quality Guarding that Global Services would like to expand other areas of its business and that it needed to raise capital to do so. While attending one of the frequent management training courses these rumours reached the attention of Quality Guarding's management, whereupon it questioned the chairman of Global Services. The message received by one director was clear: 'He [the Chairman] said, "No, Quality Guarding is an important part of this Group and it is becoming part of our core business and is a very successful company". I was looking at him straight in the eye so that made it twice as hard to take.' This reassuring message was relayed back to staff at the regional offices and operating units. Eight weeks later, Quality Guarding was sold to Service Conglomerate.

THE ACQUISITION

The sale of Quality Guarding came as a complete shock to its management team, even Quentin Graham, the managing director. On the morning of the sale, the Quality Guarding senior board was told to report to Global Services' London office at 8:30 a.m. where they were told for the first time that they had been sold to Service Conglomerate. The directors of Service Conglomerate were present and introduced; the board of Quality Guarding was told to report to its new owner's head office nearby. The regional directors heard the news through various means, including through the parent company, via junior colleagues or through the media. Everyone interviewed remembered how they heard the news and stories went around the organization as to how the various directors had heard. The most notable story was that one director heard the news on the radio as he drove to work that morning and promptly smashed into the car in front of him.

Initial reactions to the acquisition by those interviewed tended to be negative. The acquiring organization's chief executive, Sam Cummings, had a fierce reputation in the industry, having been managing director of a competitor, and through drastic cuts in staffing and service had dramatically doubled their profit margins. In doing so, he had maximized short-term profits but, in the opinion of some Quality Guarding employees, had done so at the expense of a quality service.

Most employees felt a great sense of betrayal and loss, not only because of the actual acquisition but also because of the way it had been announced. Many felt angry about the chairman's comments made only two months earlier. This was exemplified by one director's comments: 'Figure I was just shocked, I thought "I don't believe it." I never even had an inkling that they had even given it a thought, so it was a shock. Then I was angry, I felt betrayed and let down by Global Services.'

Others spoke of a great sense of loss as they felt Service Conglomerate did not have the same quality reputation as Global Services. Whereas they were proud to be a part of Global, many of those interviewed were embarrassed about their new ownership by Service Conglomerate. One manager commented: 'The difference I see is it is going from a premier division company to a second division company ... I was concerned that we weren't linked with a premier company any more. Service Conglomerate's services aren't very good and their image isn't as good.'

The immediate press response surrounding the sale was more positive, certainly for Service Conglomerate. Press comments referred to Sam Cummings' reputation and track record in the industry. Cummings was quoted as saying that, as in the previous guarding company, a similar doubling of profit margins would occur at Quality Guarding from 4 per cent to 10 per cent.

Service Conglomerate moved quickly in an attempt to allay the concerns of Quality Guarding's senior management by holding a reception and presentation for the board and regional managing directors on the night of the acquisition. The personnel director of Service Conglomerate distributed a detailed question and answer sheet which tackled many of the tough issues raised by the acquisition, such as reasons for the sale and the outlining of terms and conditions. Both the question and answer sheet and the personnel director were well received by those interviewed who attended. One senior manager commented: 'The question and answer was very important, we learned a lot about Service Conglomerate. Also the personnel director was the human face of capitalism ... very professional and discreet.' The effectiveness of this, however, was somewhat mitigated by the presentation which followed. It contained spelling mistakes and had suffered from the rather uncomfortable presentation style of Sam Cummings. Furthermore, the security personnel for the Service Conglomerate building were perceived to be of a lower standard than those of Quality Guarding.

A follow-up letter from Service Conglomerate was immediately sent to all Quality Guarding staff which welcomed them to the new organization and suggested that visits to the newly acquired sites would be occurring in the near future. In addition, the regional managing directors were given a similar question and answer sheet to distribute amongst their staff; however, very few staff members actually saw the document other than those attending the original meeting. All staff were also later to receive a Service Conglomerate discount card which offered 10 per cent off all Service Conglomerate services, although this was delayed until staffing cuts had been made.

Within three days, staff received a letter from Quentin Graham saying 'business as usual' and that he would keep staff informed of all changes if and when they occurred. In addition, Graham said that if any staff had questions they could speak to him directly. This last element of the letter was received with mixed results; some employees felt it was a reassuring gesture, while others felt it was a gimmick. The 'business as usual' comment was believed by some employees, but questioned by most other employees who found that this conflicted with the press statements of Sam Cummings. The subsequent inconsistency of information created a healthy degree of cynicism amongst many employees. One manager commented: 'We laughed at Quentin's memo, I was cynical of the situation of "business as usual" because you have to achieve the 10 per cent [profit margins] somehow, you either sting the clients which is high risk, bump up unit prices which is the same, or you cut your overheads dramatically, so I didn't lend much credence to it.'

The initial meeting between the Quality Guarding and Service Conglomerate boards occurred very soon thereafter. The Quality Guarding board was given six weeks to prepare a business plan for Service Conglomerate outlining anticipated profit improvement savings at Quality Guarding. Service Conglomerate handed the responsibility directly to Quality Guarding; this in essence became the acquisition's pre-acquisition plan. Although no figures were actually given, the media reports gave a good indication of what was wanted, namely large-scale profit improvement and little need for structural integration with Service Conglomerate. While it was not equivocally stated, it was clear that if the plan was not acceptable the directors would be made redundant.

For six weeks the three most senior directors (managing, marketing and finance) worked out a profit improvement plan for Sam Cummings. The cost savings were to be phased over three years with the initial reductions to occur immediately. The operational plan was drawn up with the peripheral help of the personnel function but not the regional directors, who knew of the plan's formulation but were not included in it. This bothered many of the regional directors who felt that they were having decisions made about their futures without their knowledge or consent. It placed these directors who were used to being 'negotiators' in a position where they had become 'enactors'. One such affected director commented:

> The bit that really hurt and was very divisive was that there were three or four guys who were on the inside track when the rest of us were on the outside. It creates a different culture post-decision time because there were those who were there and those who were not.

Middle managers also knew that the most senior directors were formulating the plan without the other employees' input. One manager commented:

> It was obvious that something was going on, we knew what was happening but when we asked questions, we got no replies because they couldn't tell us. I don't understand why they had to be so secretive, the results were the same and we all expected it anyway.

ACQUISITION IMPLEMENTATION

The profit improvement plan was accepted by Service Conglomerate and directors were given approval for its implementation. At this point the

Quality Guarding directors were not only relieved that they had kept their jobs but also they were impressed with the management style of Sam Cummings. Cummings let the directors know what was expected of them and gave them his support to go out and achieve their objectives. One director commented:

> Still one of the most pleasant surprises of the whole lot [is Cumming's management style]. We thought we would have all sorts of interference and the reverse has been the case. His style has been, 'You are the board and just deliver – manage your business.'

The essence of the plan was to cut costs, the greatest being labour costs, ideally without affecting the operating units themselves. Because of this, few changes were to affect the units directly, but savings had to be made in restructuring and reducing costs in the management of those units. This included changing the company's regional limited companies into subsidiaries and reducing the number of regional offices from six to four with the absorption of the two offices into the remaining regions. The head office was moved from the stately home back into the unassuming West London office they previously occupied two years prior to the acquisition. The training function was to be drastically cut and moved to computerized training units, which were at various locations throughout the regions. Training was to be done predominantly in the employee's own time instead of the company's, as it had been previously. Those remaining trainers were to help with the installation of new technology into the business units and the training of staff to use the technology. The number of regional managers was to be cut by around 20 per cent and those remaining were to take on the contracts of those being made redundant. Whereas the average number of contracts held by regional managers prior to the acquisition was 12, this was intended to rise to an average of 16 after the reorganization. The position of senior regional manager was reinstated for those who managed over 24 contracts; those managers would in principle be aided in their workload by a part-time unit manager. The cost of the part-time unit manager, however, was to be borne by the contracts and not by Quality Guarding, as it had in the past. In addition, the number of operational directors was to be cut to one for each region. The marketing department was left virtually alone. The finance department was to centralize accounts in their northern region; payroll was to be centralized nine months later, although this was not made public in the first announcement. It was envisaged that all employees being made redundant would be offered an alternative position in the organization where possible, although in most cases these positions were a demotion in status and responsibility and, therefore, not attractive alternatives to those affected.

When it came to the plan's implementation, the three Quality Guarding directors who wrote the plan decided that the regional managing directors should be included. Two managing directors who were to be made redundant, one from a disappearing region and another from a remaining region, were not included in the meetings but, according to colleagues, knew these meetings were taking place. The date of the implementation was postponed in order to include the remaining managing directors; this occurred three weeks before the revised date of implementation. All the regional managing directors signed confidentiality agreements in which, on the penalty of dismissal, they would not disclose any of the meetings' proceedings or contents to any employees. Some employees knew of these agreements and found them unnecessary and a sign of the low trust Quality Guarding placed even in their most senior employees.

A couple of weeks prior to the implementation announcement a reshuffle was to occur in which some of the managing directors were to be assigned to new regions in order to compensate for the dismissals being made. This plan was thrown into disarray when the first managing director approached to move refused the transfer to another region. The situation was exacerbated when another managing director resigned in order to rejoin the Global Services management team. Ultimately, a managing director who was to be made redundant was drafted in to replace the resigning managing director and the others remained in their previous positions.

With the plan implementation a couple of weeks off, the head office personnel department used centrally held personnel files to calculate the terms and conditions of the employees targeted for redundancy; in many cases the information was out of date and incorrect. When this information was not available the regional human resource departments were asked for the information concerning the affected employees. They were not told why the information was needed as it had been decided by head office that as few people as possible should know of the impending changes.

No more formal communication was sent to employees from Quentin Graham's 'business as usual' letter to the time of the redundancy announcements. All employees were told that in a fortnight or so they were to report to their regional offices at a specified time but were not told what the meetings would cover. This created a great deal of speculation as to the nature of the meetings. All employees being made redundant were to be seen individually by the regional managing directors, while those remaining were seen singly or in small work groups. With such a large number of employees to be seen, the meetings began very early in the morning; in one region the first meeting was scheduled for 6:30 a.m.

The scheduling of employees' meetings was a source of worry for many of the employees interviewed. In most regions, the employees remaining were seen earlier in the day and those being made redundant were seen in the afternoon. Employees began comparing interview times and wondering about the discrepancies. It proved to be the topic of speculation for the two weeks prior to the meetings. One middle manager said:

> We all knew of the meeting with [our managing director] for a full week and two weekends so we were all sweating bullets and were talking about the meetings in the toilet. Every time [the MD] would walk by it was dead quiet acting like we weren't talking about anything but it was a long time to wait.

The employees knew of the meetings occurring at head office and consequently suspected that changes may occur; the redundancy meetings, therefore, did not come as a surprise. What did come as a total surprise was the severity of the redundancies. One manager commented: 'We knew something was going to happen but it was far worse than I anticipated; I didn't think we would lose our operations director, we thought maybe one regional manager would go, but not two.'

On the announcement day, the personnel managers were appraised of the situation half an hour before they were supposed to assist in the process which included counselling and outplacement. Due to the gathering of employee information from head office records, many cases were inaccurate, with employees' redundancy pay calculations, job titles and even names incorrect. Personnel managers spent much of their time in the meetings trying to recalculate the figures. One human resource manager commented: 'We realized that most of the information was wrong: names, titles, years of service. We had to spend most of the time correcting the mistakes rather than offering comfort or advice.'

The length and content of the individual meetings varied from region to region. In some cases, the managing director spent some time with the remaining employees explaining the changes. In others, the meeting consisted of a sentence such as: 'Don't worry, your job is safe.' Meetings with the employees being made redundant were inconsistent as to their content and the sensitivity with which they were handled, again depending on the individual managing directors. Employee reactions to the redundancies varied from resignation and acceptance to upset and anger. One managing director commented: 'A lot of people cried in here on that day, girls particularly were very upset. It was inhumane not to give more time to those people, to comfort them and counsel them.'

Employees from the disappearing regions reported to their regional offices as requested where a notice told them to report to the nearest remaining office, which they did. At the new offices some of those employees were told that they had new operational directors or territories and that their regions were disappearing; others were made redundant by people they had never met before.

Across all regions the interviews took longer than expected and delays occurred of up to five hours in some cases. One employee who experienced long delays commented: 'We were left in reception sitting in seats around 11.00 a.m. and some people had already been seen and people kept walking by with sympathetic looks and tutting and that was our first realization that something drastic was happening.'

In several cases, different directors came in to interrupt meetings and rehire employees as they were being made redundant. Other employees were informed that they didn't have a job at one office, and they should go to another office to see if there was a job for them there. Another human resource manager recounted the scene:

> The organization [of the day] was dreadful, we had one regional manager down from [a disappearing region] who was in discussing his package and another operations director burst in and pulled him out saying, 'We could use you and you aren't redundant.' Another was made redundant then called back the next day to say he had a job but he didn't take it. Another from [a disappearing region] came to us and then was told we didn't have a job for him but if he went to another office they may have something for him. It was so callous, we were telling people we had never met before that they were being made redundant in a strange office, it was just awful, it stunk, it was totally wrong.

In one region, two operational directors were given the opportunity to take demotions to regional managers' jobs or face redundancy. If they were to take the jobs, four of their regional managers would be made redundant. The directors chose redundancy. Later that afternoon, the regional managing director briefed the remaining employees of the new organizational structure. The managing director had not anticipated the operational directors' departure and, therefore, the organizational structure had not been amended to reflect this: the four regional managers' names who were present at the meeting were not on the chart. Employees witnessing this found it upsetting; one such employee commented: 'The regional managers who were retained, their

self-esteem must have been the pits; when their names were left off the organizational chart the comment was made that it had changed slightly since
this morning. These are people's lives.' Another commented: 'When that
came out a lot of people said, "That is a sick thing to do, you can't ask people
to make that kind of choice, it is not fair." '

Another incident highlighted further problems. A trainer was transferred
by her regional managing director from one sub-office to another sub-
office a week prior to the day of redundancies. As a consequence of the
restructuring only the most senior trainer in each office remained with the
company while all others were made redundant. If that trainer had remained
at the original sub-office for just a week longer, her job would have been
secure but because of the move the prior week she was made redundant.
Others in the region found this action most cruel and unfair, especially as
the managing director knew of the impending changes. A colleague
commented: 'There were certain people that should have been shocked,
particularly the girl in training who was surprised by it, they had just
relocated her. I couldn't come to terms with that one at all.'

Most employees being made redundant left the offices immediately with
little ceremony or comment to those remaining. Some of the remaining
employees interviewed didn't know how to react to those being made
redundant. One manager said: '[My boss] came out here and cleared his desk;
I didn't even go in and see him because there was nothing I could say to
that guy. What you do say when someone is made redundant?'

This day has come to be known within the company as 'Black Monday'
and the technique of the fast and painful execution of redundancies as the
'abattoir effect'.[1] Although some regional managing directors handled it better
than others, the brutality of the day and company's actions shocked not only
those employees being made redundant but also those remaining. One
manager commented:

> I thought it was appalling the way colleagues were handled. How could
> they just get rid of people with no justifiable reason? My job was safe
> but I just felt terrible about my colleagues and that was the overriding
> thing. It did worry me that the company was starting to change like that.

Shortly thereafter, the accounts department was told that it would be
centralized in the North and that those in the other regions would be made

---

1. This term was coined by a director during the director feedback session. The director suggested that
the abattoir effect of quick, sharp and unsuspected execution of redundancies was far more humane
than telling employees prior to the day that the process was going to occur.

redundant. While this move did have some initial problems, it did eventually settle. Those in the payroll departments which remained in the regions, however, became uneasy sensing the logic in centralizing their function as well. The payroll employees along with all other employees were told by senior Quality Guarding management that there would be no further changes. This bothered some senior directors who knew of future changes and the impending plan. One commented:

> We now have a situation where Quentin is saying no further changes planned and I know there are and we are trying to implement it without letting people know. We will be made to look silly.

The payroll function was centralized less than a year later.

Many of the remaining employees believed, despite management protestations, that another wave of redundancies was imminent, which would further deplete their numbers and increase their workloads. This worry was especially notable in the regional managers. Those interviewed referred to the published figure of 16 contracts per regional manager – they could not understand how this figure could be achieved without further staffing cuts. In fact it was the intention of Quality Guarding management to reach this figure by natural attrition; however, this had never been made public.

In addition to the reductions in staffing, further changes were made in order to cut costs and enhance profits. While the training department was radically reduced, customers continued to pay a training levy. This created a great deal of role conflict and ambiguity for the regional managers interviewed whose previous job performance had been based on giving a total quality service to clients in order to build and retain a long-term client relationship. In effect, those managers were now being required to hide the fact that the training department was now not as effective as it had been previously, while their customers continued to pay a training levy. In the opinions of those regional managers interviewed, this disparity would ultimately jeopardize those client relationships.

New technology charges were also a source of role conflict for many of the regional managers. Quality Guarding was to initiate a programme of installing technology in the units in order to maximize efficiency, the cost of which was to be passed on to the clients. But because of the greater price sensitivity many clients demonstrated during the recession, as well as the new profit maximization plan, managers in some regions were told not to increase any levies to their units. In those cases managers were told to 'hide' the technology costs in their wage bill rather than pass on the levy to customers in a more visible manner. This deception resulted in increased

role conflict for some middle managers who had previously maintained a
very open and honest relationship with their clients. One client-facing
manager commented:

> They want us to bury the costs in the units, it is just fraud. We are
> supposed to look after the client and they expect us to stand up in front
> of the client and lie. Quality Guarding aren't paying for it [the technology]
> and what else can you say? It is just really bad.

Of those remaining employees, many demonstrated a high intention to
leave averaging approximately half of all employees across the regions and
over three-quarters of regional managers. The latter employees also continued
to suffer badly from survivor guilt due to the lack of explanation or
understanding as to why colleagues were chosen for redundancy. One
manager commented:

> There didn't seem to be any logic in who went and who stayed. We were
> never told why those people were chosen. I had to sit with those people
> and they would ask me why and I couldn't begin to answer them, none
> of us knew. There was no rationale on who went and who stayed.

Another commented:

> There was no sense of relief, I felt guilty. I am married to a professional
> so it wasn't life or death if I had a job and my colleague who sat in this
> office with me went. He had two children. I was so shocked when he told
> me that I went straight to my husband's office in floods of tears.

Three months after 'Black Monday' many middle managers continued
to feel a great sense of role ambiguity as they tried to cope with dramatically
increased workloads – often with new colleagues, directors, subordinates,
customers and territories. Whereas previously there had been enough time
to deliver a quality service, many managers felt that they could no longer
do their jobs in the same way and deliver the same standard of service –
some compensated by working 70-hour weeks. This was exacerbated by
the lack of job redefinition from either Quality Guarding's or Service
Conglomerate's senior management who had not provided any input on how
the regional managers should now perform their jobs in the light of the
increased workload. One manager said:

I have more work than I can actually cope with. I have been 'mega-stressed' and I don't think the company realizes what they are asking people to do. Some of that is self-inflicted because I want to get the job done, but that is the way we are. They are not aware that you work 15-hour days.

The changing role of the regional manager began to impact on some individual contracts. One unit manager, when discussing her trainer, commented: 'You can't even get her on the phone when you have a question, how is she supposed to help you with the health and safety training when she is so busy? She can't do it so you give up.' Other unit managers interviewed were less affected – many felt little change in their work routines once they had been assured of the security of their jobs and their staff. Another unit manager commented: 'At grass roots they are just getting on with it, we still feel part of Quality Guarding. We will do our thing until we are told to do something different.'

At approximately this time, the chairman of Service Conglomerate visited one of the regional offices. His visit was very well received as he took time to speak to all the employees on site. This impressed those attending; one worker said:

[The chairman] came here ... and went around every single member of staff and asked who we were, how long we had been with the company. He seemed genuinely interested, he asked questions and seemed interested in our responses. It was so refreshing; after he went we all said he wasn't so bad – we all expected a monster.

Other regions had yet to have the promised visit from senior Service Conglomerate personnel. This perplexed many of those interviewed who couldn't understand why they had not been to visit. As one manager said:

We have talked about broken promises, one thing that Sam Cummings said was, 'When we come to see you in your offices', and of course, he never has. They have never come down here and they said they would; I don't think it will make a great deal of difference now, other than they said they would and they didn't.

Most employees commented that they would have welcomed a visit from Service Conglomerate personnel at an early stage in the acquisition. Many felt that because they had had no contact with Service Conglomerate employees, they did not know any more about the company than they did when they were first acquired.

STABILIZATION PERIOD

Even during the stabilization period, it became apparent that morale was still low and many employees felt a lingering sense of betrayal over the way the redundancies had been handled. A further 15 per cent of middle managers had left the company voluntarily during the months following 'Black Monday'. This was due to two reasons. Some employees felt it unfair the way their colleagues had been treated, and others left because of the disillusionment caused and ethical issues raised by the role conflict and prevailing company attitude. One manager who was contemplating leaving summed up his feelings by saying: 'Many of us will leave just for the sake of that scalpel cut being a touch too deep.'

Further resignations were not calculated in the manpower planning strategy and some of those made redundant had to be rehired as consultants to replace those subsequently leaving. Others made redundant when approached would not return to the company. One middle manager described a colleague who was approached for rehire:

I had a colleague who was with us for many years, who was offered a job in the reshuffle and it wasn't a good job so he left. He has subsequently been offered other jobs and point blank he won't come back to the company. This just sums it up; this person gave 14 years to the company, every day of the week, broke up his marriage as a result and was blown out on Monday.

The main beneficiaries of the Quality Guarding employee exodus were their competitors. One redundant operations director set up a rival guarding firm and began recruiting his team from the Quality Guarding survivors. Those employees remaining with Quality Guarding were under constant threat from head hunters; one client-facing manager had been approached by eight recruitment consultants in as many weeks. He suggested that those remaining regional managers were being targeted because it was felt those who had survived 'Black Monday' were perceived as being very good in the market due to their high levels of training, superb client relationships and professionalism.

Employees at head office were seen as not fully understanding the impact of the plan's implementation in the regions, although they did seem to sense some disenchantment. This misalignment was exacerbated by the senior directors actually enjoying the changes brought on by the acquisition, most notably the management style at Service Conglomerate, which they found open and straightforward. While having to move offices, head office staff had not gone through the radical changes felt by the regions. This in itself caused some degree of resentment in the regions; one regional manager commented: 'It does appear that the top has been looked after – if you work for Group you are okay. People just don't trust Group any more.'

The effects of the redundancies were being felt in the regional offices six months after 'Black Monday'. Managers commented that whereas previously the offices were busy well past regular work hours, the atmosphere now was likened 'to a morgue' by several employees in different regions. This feeling of fear and apprehension was heightened by the lack of notice given regarding 'Black Monday'. Common responses made by many employees was that they were 'watching their backs' and 'keeping their heads down' in order to avoid bringing attention to themselves in an attempt to escape from any future cuts. Employees noted that as the previous cuts were made without prior employee warning, they felt that any future cuts would also be done the same way. Several managers interviewed were told by their directors to keep their comments 'low key' in the interviews. One such affected employee commented:

I think they [Group management] are not unbelievable but their credibility in terms of believability has been damaged from all of this. Before this interview, someone [a senior enactor] said to me, 'You won't say anything controversial will you?', and that itself is an interesting viewpoint.

This feeling had yet to abate by the end of the case study research.

POSTSCRIPT

After this research had been conducted the results and alternative means of implementation were discussed in detail with the directors, and feedback given to the employees who participated. The feedback was very honest and all participants received a written report outlining the findings above. The directors were very open in discussing the acquisition problems and recommendations; they were clearly interested in learning from the experience. In the light of the results, changes were made as the payroll redundancies were handled in a much more sympathetic fashion with the human resource function heavily involved in the process from the outset. One human resource manager involved confirmed that the payroll redundancies were far better handled and much less traumatic than those of 'Black Monday'.

Soon thereafter, Quality Guarding was one of five companies bidding for another contract guarding firm that was highly unionized. The human resource director requested, and was given, the responsibility for the acquisition and its implementation. His main objective for the sale was to manage stakeholders' expectations from the very beginning. A provisional acquisition plan was drawn up and communicated to the target company prior to the acquisition. The director was very honest with the unions prior to the acquisition as to the extent of centralizing key functions and related redundancies. He also outlined the acquisition implementation plan and corresponding communication strategy and how this would affect all the acquired employees. The unions chose Quality Guarding as their preferred choice in the sale as it was deemed to have the most coherent and sympathetic acquisition implementation plan. The sale proceeded with full union approval with the implementation mirroring the stated communication and being considered highly successful. The damage done by 'Black Monday' to the existing workforce, however, had yet to fully abate. As one manager so aptly put it: 'Open heart surgery without anaesthetic takes a long time to heal. I have known worse situations and I think it can improve but I have never known a situation which could have been handled so much better and was so badly bungled.'

CONCLUSION

In terms of the process of managing the acquisition, this case illustrates several points. First, the target management at Quality Guarding was given an inordinately large amount of leeway in enacting its plan by Service Conglomerate. In some ways, this mirrored Anglo-American; Sam Cummings made it very clear what his objective was – it was up to the acquired management to see that those targets were reached and he empowered them to do so. The down-side of this is that they were not given enough guidance on how this should be accomplished: in many ways they went too far, too fast, and, unlike with Anglo-American, were not given the guidance necessary, nor did they have the experience, to ensure it was done properly.

Another major difficulty arose because the target management was not given the opportunity to perform any pre-acquisition planning due to the surprise nature of the sale. This combination of events meant that pre-acquisition planning had to occur after the event. While this is unfortunate, it didn't necessarily spell disaster for the acquisition. Within these constraints, Quality Guarding senior management had an adequate, if not good, acquisition plan that was 'implementable'. The only criticism of their process of planning was the exclusion of other senior directors from the process; this was a situation that some affected regional directors found divisive.

There were two major areas, however, where the process was seen as lacking: the communication of the plan to the affected employees and the implementation of that plan in a 'fair and reasonable' manner.

Communication was poor on three fronts. First, the surprise nature of the acquisition meant that not enough employees were given sufficient information on 'Day One' of the transaction. The way that the deal was announced only exacerbated employee concerns. Thus, for the first week or so, employees from directors downward were dealing with their own sense of shock as well as having to try and field customer enquiries without having adequate information to do so. This should have been better orchestrated by both Service Conglomerate and Global Services plc to ensure timely information to all employees. The position of the Quality Guarding directors further hindered communication – their shock and the tenuousness of their own positions meant that they, too, were not as effective in management as they could have been.

Second, the 'business as usual' comments were seen as grossly misleading, and were exacerbated by the inconsistency between internal communication and media comments. Sam Cummings' statement of a doubling of profit margins did much to appease the financiers of the deal but also did much to alarm employees and customers. When this interpretation of the future was seen as being more accurate, the credibility of internal communication sources was damaged.

The final deficiency in communication occurred when employees were told that they would be kept informed and they should wait for future communication, yet none was forthcoming prior to the day of redundancies. By 'Black Monday', employees knew that redundancies and changes were going to happen. A more realistic and open approach to announcing that changes would occur would have caused less long-term damage within the company. In addition, announcing the changes of the coming year would also have caused less long-term disruption than the 'drip effect' of bad news every few months. The end result was a chronic sense of unease in employees as they waited for the next wave of bad news.

In terms of enacting the pre-acquisition plan, the lack of logic and fairness in its implementation was what caused the bulk of the concern in most employees. What occurred was called the 'abattoir effect' by one director, where the changes were to be quick and painless. Instead, what happened was shocking to those employees who did not anticipate the changes or could not see the logic of their severity. Perceived cruelty, such as the actions towards the trainer and the operations directors, only fuelled these feelings. The result was a large degree of 'survivor guilt' where those employees remaining at Quality Guarding did not know or understand the selection for retaining their positions and, because of this, felt guilty. This questioning of the plan's imple- mentation intensified as the plan was fully implemented including the training and technology levies and increased workload; employees simply could not see the logic of endangering what they saw as the mainstay of their business, their customer relationships. The end result was an overall questioning of the company, its culture and management, which culminated in additional employees leaving the organization voluntarily – causing further problems for Quality Guarding.

Instead, the logic behind the employee redundancies should have been made public – keeping employee disruption to a minimum is a perfectly acceptable reason for retaining employees. By not making this known, employees reached their own conclusions, which were generally negative and flawed.

Finally, Quality Guarding did not take into account the inevitable increase in employee turnover after acquisition. Instead, they made too many people redundant and had to try and rehire employees as natural attrition took its toll. Ironically, had they handled the redundancies better, the level of voluntary resignations would assuredly have been much lower.

9   Global Products and its Acquisition Strategy

INTRODUCTION

This case analyses the acquisition strategy of a blue chip American-based company called Global which specialized in fast-moving consumer goods. It had a reputation for ethical and moral business beliefs and highly sophisticated policies and procedures. This case examines Global's acquisitions during a seven-year period in which four large acquisitions occurred. This case differs to the other cases in that the research examines the company's actions over a series of acquisitions. The first acquisition occurred in the late 1980s and the remaining three acquisitions occurred in the early to mid-1990s.

The approach taken by Global was to merge the acquired businesses into their existing operation thereby creating value by economies of scale and synergies. This required a different approach to Anglo-American and Service Conglomerate as it involved the combining of functions and personnel via wholesale organizational change. In cases of integration, one would normally expect employees from both the acquirer and target to be affected; this was minimized in Global to a greater extent due to their unusual culture which is discussed below.

BACKGROUND TO THE ACQUISITION

Global was a truly multinational organization with operations in virtually every country in the world. It maintained what was perceived to be a very high ethical and moral standard in both its treatment of employees and its business practices. It operated a sophisticated human resource strategy in order to perpetuate a highly stylized organization-wide culture based heavily on written procedures. In order to preserve this culture, the company had previously avoided growth via acquisition and concentrated on organic growth, a policy which had led to no acquisitions in their European operations from 1934 to the late 1980s.

The human resource strategy at Global included hiring top-notch graduates directly from university, adhering strictly to an internal labour market, extensively training those 'fast track' employees and the careful plotting of their career paths, including two- to three-year tours of duty in various functions and locations. Because of the policy of hiring only from the top 10 per cent of graduates of first-class universities, there was a great deal of competition both in being selected and in pursuing a career once inside the organization; recruits were considered to be both highly competent and ambitious. In order to retain these employees, Global was known in the industry as being a good employer offering generous compensation supported by superb training and career development.

THE JOHNSON ACQUISITION

In the late 1980s, the company which was to become Global's first major European acquisition in 50 years was under threat of hostile acquisition by a keen competitor of Global. The target, known as Johnson Products, was a US quoted company although the Johnson family controlled almost 50 per cent of the shares. Johnson Products had retained its family culture in spite of its growth over the years; the Johnson family still sat on the company's board and their children spent their summers working in Johnson's European head office in London, England. Johnson had been in a joint venture in certain regions of the world with the now hostile suitor and had operated a 'gentlemen's agreement' whereby the acquisitive company would not attempt to acquire Johnson, a promise which clearly had been broken. With Johnson under threat, a couple of other large multinationals entered into the fray in an attempt to win Johnson's household brand names. In order to stave off the unwanted advances of the acquirers, the Johnson family turned to Global with whom they had maintained contact over the years; it was not uncommon for ex-Global executives to sit on the Johnson Products' board of directors. Global agreed to act as a 'white knight' for Johnson. In the process, Global acquired a far larger range of products for its European division than it had owned previously, as Johnson had outperformed Global in terms of both brand ownership and volume in the European sector.

The Johnson employees interviewed were shocked by the sale of the company, not only because of the family ownership but also because of the transaction's speed; the time from the initial hostile approach to the sale's approval to Global was only six weeks. The press welcomed the transaction which was consistently deemed a merger by both the Johnson family and Global.

Global had done a degree of pre-acquisition planning based on 'target tracking', a process of monitoring all interesting potential acquisition targets. Because of this and the long-standing relationship with Johnson, Global knew a fair amount about Johnson; what they didn't know was what they were going to do with it. This lack of future intention was caused to a large extent by the speed of the transaction. Global were known internally as good communicators – these skills were called into play to produce communication on 'Day One'.

The Johnson employees in the UK were told they would receive updates from the US headquarters as to the merger. One of their first contacts with Global was through the chairman who stood on the balcony of Johnson's US head office and made a speech to all acquired employees which was then videotaped and sent to the UK. The speech sent some mixed messages. While it warmly welcomed all the newly joining employees and stated that Global needed them for future success, it referred to the transaction as an acquisition rather than a merger. The chairman also said there would be no changes and that it would be 'business as usual' at Johnson. Finally, he said the employees would not feel a great sense of change as the company cultures were so similar. One employee recounted the scene:

> I can see the chairman now, stood on the balcony of the Johnson headquarters in the US with all the employees gathered down below and he made the statement, 'No one would be thrown out on the streets, this is a marriage made in heaven, we love you and need you more than you need us.' I wouldn't go as far as to say I believed him but it offered a large degree of reassurance at the time. But always in the back of one's mind is a sort of sneaky feeling of, 'Was this really true?'

It wasn't. While the initial plans to buy the business had been made, there was little substance to what would happen to the businesses in the foreseeable future. Instead, employees were led to believe it would continue as it had in the past.

ACQUISITION IMPLEMENTATION

Approximately half of the employees believed the chairman while the other half did not. One employee commented: 'We had no experience of what happened in a takeover so when someone tells us that everything will carry on the same, in our innocence, we believed him.' While no transfer of business occurred immediately, things did change quickly in some respects.

In line with other Global operations, the company began moving some of the senior Johnson employees, including the managing director of Johnson Europe, to the United States for 'training'. It was thought he would some day return and run his former division, but that never occurred. In his place, a Global manager was to head up the Johnson operations. He was not considered a terribly good choice by those with whom he had to work closely. One director said:

> Their management team came down here to become chiefs so we suddenly had imposed on us the Global management structure with Global people ... the people we were assigned to run Johnson at the time were totally insensitive and were probably two of the worst people they could have sent down to us.

The Global procedures were implemented immediately underpinning the highly stylized and written culture. Senior executives were sent on a two-day memo-writing course as it was deemed that this was the most important communication skill within the company; this, however, did not fully prepare them for the impact of the Global culture. Another director said: 'I started getting more confused about my own status and procedures and I suppose started to feel cynical about the initial statements about company culture.' Managers and workforce employees were not given any formal training whatsoever, but instead had to rely on learning from sympathetic colleagues. Some of those Global employees brought into the Johnson organizational structure were less than sympathetic to the newly acquired employees. One middle manager commented:

> The thing that really amazed me was that it was very much a 'find out for yourself' culture. I had to find out the hard way with my first recommendation being torn apart and with me being told, 'What is this? This isn't the way we put forward a recommendation in Global, this is not the way to make things happen at Global.' You had to find out the hard way so I had a few scars and bruises to show for it.

This inability to communicate effectively was exacerbated by the inexperience of Global employees in dealing with 'outsiders' in a business context. The overwhelming majority of Global employees had never worked anywhere else and, therefore, were not used to dealing with different cultures and employee diversity. In fact, it appeared many did not realize that their own culture was so unique.

During this time, it was assumed that all employees would begin operating a 'Global style' of doing business: a heavily written culture, a unique language and unusual procedures. Johnson procedures were discarded without consideration of their merit or appropriateness. By this stage, no one had been told that Global was integrating Johnson into their operation; instead, Global people took prime positions of power within the company to ensure that it complied with the 'Global Way'. By now the Johnson directors and managers were bewildered by the new procedures at Global. The company-specific language, mannerisms, reliance on written documentation, and perceived lack of patience or even understanding of these differences all served to confuse many of the acquired employees. In addition, Global employees were gradually being slotted into almost all the top jobs at Johnson with the existing Johnson employees being either demoted or moved laterally. This led to many employees being confused and upset by the message sent by the Global chairman and the subsequent actions in the UK. One director described his feelings:

> I couldn't even drive the car into the company, I just couldn't get there in mind and body, I just couldn't get that car in so I would circle around for two or three times. Those things haunt you for quite a long time. You never know how much it is influencing your thinking and eating away inside of you.

It was during these first few months that the acquired Johnson employees were being assessed as to their ability and suitability in their current positions. It was not taken into account that many of the managers were uncomfortable with the new working environment and didn't understand the corporate procedures or culture. Thus, in almost all cases, the Johnson managers were demoted at least one level in Global based on their performance in the new company. While the Johnson employees could accept that the Global managers were excellent, it was difficult for them to understand that they were better than every single Johnson manager. Others were lucky just to keep their jobs. One director tells of a colleague who found the new regime very hard to grasp:

> After the acquisition, Global expected all the [work] to be presented in a form that Global provides and we didn't know it and they certainly didn't tell us. It was a terrible, terrible time and my boss would come in there and say quite often, 'I want that man fired [the director's subordinate].' Today that man is still heading up his department and his performance

appraisals are outstanding, but the knee-jerk reaction was to get rid of him.

During this first year, some employees were fortunate enough to have sympathetic bosses or colleagues; in a few cases, Global employees were brought in to serve as 'translators' for the Johnson employees. This proved highly valuable to some affected employees. One commented:

> We got a Global lady who had taken some time off and she came in as sort of a consultant to everybody for several months. She had an office and if anyone had a memo to write they would go to her and find out how to write it, or say, 'I have written this document, is it in Global language?' She was a great help actually, it sounds extraordinary.

Several aspects of the acquisition were handled very quickly and professionally in the eyes of the acquired employees, highlighting the quality of staff and some procedures at Global. The harmonization of the Johnson employees' terms and conditions was considered a difficult and time-consuming task, yet was handled quickly and with little problem. One manager commented: 'We had a sales guy in Johnson and he regarded himself as a good organizational strategist and planner but his methods were back of the envelope compared with the Global method and attention to detail.' Many Johnson employees commented that it was the brilliance of the individuals at Global which impressed them and not necessarily the logic of their procedures. These events, however, did make the Johnson employees acknowledge that Global was a professionally run company.

Most employees' jobs were secure during the integration, including those of the workforce. Where redundancy was inevitable, those affected were told with plenty of notice, given very generous terms and handled in a fashion considered to be very fair. Communication concerning employees' personal job situations was considered good, with excellent management of expectations in this area.

Generally, it was considered that communication within Global was good. Employees felt they were getting enough information concerning their own personal security and that of their colleagues as well as day-to-day information needed for the running of the company. What was lacking, however, were any maps or guidelines on how to understand the Global culture or procedures. Many managers found this highly frustrating. One commented: 'The longer you go post-acquisition you pick it up, but you pick up the ways to behave and to say things and what is the right answer to the questions by trial and error and not by someone sitting you down and telling you.'

Support staff, on the other hand, while finding some of the routines illogical, were less affected by changes in procedures and status and were therefore able to adapt more quickly.

Within a year it became apparent that the English offices would become the European headquarters for that Global division. It was decided that it was more efficient to merge the existing smaller Global operation into the larger Johnson site in London. Thus, the Global employees moved from their offices in the north of the country down to the Johnson site. Several of the Johnson employees said that they would have resigned if they had been asked to move north.

During the twelve months preceding the acquisition, and despite the initial comments from the chairman, Johnson Products had ceased to exist and was subsumed into Global in the UK. Many at Global insisted that this was not going to happen in the US, although it did the following year. While many at the UK operation believed the chairman's initial comments, his inaccuracies were to be memorable for many employees. One employee commented: 'Maybe I was being naive but I think I was believing the messages coming down from on high that the cultures were very similar and we had similar values – I found out the real news later on.'

The reaction of employees was by no means purely negative. In fact, virtually all those Johnson employees still with Global commented that on the whole it was a good employer. Global was considered a well paying and ethical organization. In almost all cases, employees did not suffer a drop in salary which mirrored their drop in status. Several of the Johnson employees cited instances where during the acquisition Global had been very understanding in terms of personal issues. In terms of status and procedures and cultural issues, however, Global had been less forthright.

Global had done a good job in implementing personal and group changes, including redundancies, in a fair manner. Employees, however, recalled the chairman's initial comments that it was to be a merger rather than an acquisition with varying degrees of cynicism. Global was perceived as doing an awful job managing the company-wide issues of culture, status and procedures. Whereas new 'fast track' employees are given extensive training and indoctrination into the 'Global Way', acquired employees received virtually no training – with the exception of the directors' memo-writing course. Whether this was down to not wanting acquired employees to stay with the company (and not caring what they thought) or down to sheer ignorance of the differences, the end result was the same – many talented employees left Global rather than stay and be frustrated.

Within a short amount of time, almost all the acquired directors had been removed from mainstream jobs and placed into lateral managerial positions, their previous positions being reserved for 'fast track' Global employees. As with their bosses, most managers were moved into non-career positions or laterally within the organization. The more ambitious managers became disillusioned and left the organization, stating in their exit interviews their dismay at the discrepancies in expectations over career path and the lack of help in understanding given by Global. One director said:

> There were people I would have preferred not to see leave the organization and some who have left and I thought, 'That is a waste that has been mismanaged and could have been avoided.' It is Global's loss and a loss that they would feel.

Middle managers appeared to suffer the most during the transition, receiving little training or help, and were most concerned with differences in organizational culture tangibly expressed in the procedural differences. Many found the lack of career management and direction and the lack of help from Global employees frustrating. The directors, many of whom were in the latter stages of their career, were resigned to their positions within the organization and because of their ages felt they could not move jobs as easily. In addition, they felt Global's terms and conditions were very good and it was worthwhile to remain. The staff, mostly in support, technical and research positions, were for the most part happy after the acquisition and were not unduly affected by the procedural changes. According to company survey material, acquired support staff were happier overall with Global than with their previous company.

THE OTHER ACQUISITIONS

Global acquired three other organizations within 18 months in quick succession: one family owned and two subsidiary sales. The three acquisitions and respective implementations share a great deal in common with the acquisition of Johnson Products; each will be outlined in turn.

The first acquisition occurred when Global acquired a large family-owned enterprise in the US. The company had a small overseas operation which made a moderate profit, although the operation was never able to exploit the US operation's well-respected brand names. The family had made it clear over the years that as the business was family owned, it was secure and there was no worry about its being sold. Thus, when the sale was announced, it came as a complete surprise to all employees, even the world-wide managing director. In spite of this, Global made it clear that they understood the newly acquired company's culture and that the two company cultures were not dissimilar, which provided some initial, if short-lived, relief to the target employees.

A considerable amount of planning had gone into the acquisition as it enjoyed a longer lead time than the Johnson acquisition. Employees were told early on that the acquired company's head office in Bristol would be closed and integrated with Global's London operation. As with Johnson, very attractive redundancy packages and outplacements were offered to those employees not being asked to relocate and who were consequently made redundant. Managers were encouraged to relocate to the London offices and Global provided relocation officers to aid those managers in moving to the new area. Employees were given ample time and information in order to help them to make up their minds as to the relocation. Global handled the personal and group issues in this acquisition with great sensitivity, fairness and professionalism. One manager commented: 'Global were extremely patient with me – I actually said "No, I don't want to come" maybe twice and they were happy for me to change my mind and were pretty understanding in that situation.'

As in the Johnson acquisition, however, the organizational issues of procedures and culture were insufficiently addressed. Managers were not given adequate training on how to perform in their new company. The target's systems and procedures were abandoned entirely in favour of Global's, with affected employees receiving no training or encouragement to understand the new environment. At the same time, managers were being assessed within the Global system and systematically found wanting. One middle manager said:

> I think early on you need to be given a thorough dose of the new culture, how things are done and why, anything. You really need to be dipped in the water because you don't want to be, you should be forced to and they didn't do that.

Another employee commented:

> There seemed to be an inability to understand how do you communicate with people you have taken over who didn't understand the Global system, so the expectation wasn't there for providing reasons for doing things or providing data in the way that Global wanted it. And you didn't do it because you hadn't had the training or any advice or direction. They then think this guy doesn't know how to do his job, so that was a problem.

Some relocated managers indicated that certain promises had been made to staff presumably in order to encourage them to relocate; this included promotion opportunities and an agreement to harmonize employment terms and conditions with the higher Global packages. Three years after the acquisition, these had failed to materialize. On two separate occasions employees had been told that the harmonization of terms and conditions would occur, only to have it postponed both times. This was seen as a result of two factors. First, Global had undertaken three major acquisitions in a short amount of time, thus creating a large number of employees affected by harmonization issues. Second, the factor of the increased costs caused by harmonization was given as a reason that it could not go forward. This was considered an illogical reason considering the company's predilection for long-term planning; these costs had not been factored into the acquisition budgeting process. This left a negative impression on the employees interviewed, with one director commenting:

> The harmonization of contracts doesn't mean an awful lot but it is the principle of the thing. The excuse is that we can't afford it; when you are Global and you acquire companies, to my mind, you then deal with the people, they plan for everything and they should have costed that in their plan. It is supposed to happen next year but we will see, there have been a couple of false alarms where they have said they will do it by a certain date and they haven't.

In this acquisition, like the others, almost all the employees who did relocate were moved laterally or demoted from their mainstream jobs to peripheral roles within Global. In many cases their previous positions were now occupied by Global 'fast track' employees. This created problems for some of the acquired employees, especially those who were given indications of career advancement. Once again, this led to some of the more talented employees leaving Global for other companies, a situation which would serve to the company's detriment in the near future.

The second acquisition involved a small 'product group' company which was sold as a subsidiary to Global. The target employees knew of the impending sale and were mentally prepared for it. Global appointed an acquisition implementation team headed by a well-respected survivor of the Johnson acquisition to manage the integration. He was deemed as being invaluable to many employees in terms of explaining the 'Global Way'. One manager commented, 'The head of the taskforce was a Johnson acquiree and an absolutely charming man and a perfect person for that ... he had this wonderful paternal soothing approach, it was a clever move on Global's part.'

Others on the team were not as highly thought of; that same manager continued: 'There were other people under the head who didn't seem to engender the same sense of respect, one was described as unfair and looking after himself.' In the end, not many of the managers from the target were needed and the bulk were made redundant. The redundancies were made with generous packages and handled in a way considered very fair. In addition, all employees, whether or not they were to stay, went on a mandatory counselling course which was considered very worthwhile. One employee commented:

> The outplacement counselling I found very helpful because I had never had any counselling, and I thought it was very good because it wasn't as if it was the loser's consolation prize – everyone went on this. They took the view that if you choose to leave or if you stay it would be useful and I learned a lot and I thought it was terrific.

As in the previous acquisitions, however, the newly acquired employees were confused and bewildered by the procedures at Global. One employee recounted:

> For the first six months I had to keep stopping and asking people what they meant – and acronyms, they love acronyms. I would say, 'I am sorry but what does that mean?' They give you a glossary when you join but it doesn't include any of the interesting words which are absolutely essential. The important ones are not in the book so I got no training on that at all and had to learn it by fire. I laugh about it now but you have to pick your way and for the people who don't have the energy, confidence or resilience to see the trees through the woods, it must be very demoralizing.

Other than a manual and any help given by the acquisition integration team, very little information was forthcoming which would have enabled the target employees to negotiate their way around Global. As in the previous acquisitions, it was during this time of procedural ambiguity that employees were being assessed as to their ability. As in the previous acquisitions, almost all acquired employees were moved into lateral management positions rather than remaining in 'fast track' positions on the career ladder. Most of the middle managers either left voluntarily or were encouraged to leave by Global, leaving only a handful of managers still remaining at Global from this acquisition.

The final acquisition followed the third acquisition quite closely, being completed only six months later. The sale was a subsidiary sale from a US company which, due to financial pressures, was forced to sell off its various European brands to several buyers. The employees, therefore, were well prepared for the sale which took over a year to complete due to its complex structure. It proved to be a highly complicated acquisition as several of the brands were manufactured at two plants; employee contracts were also confused as employees originally contracted to one brand worked for other brands as well. The first part of the acquisition was spent determining which employees would be acquired and which would remain employees of the original company. Global was seen to behave in a highly ethical manner during this procedure by not attempting to steal key employees from the parent company.

Like the previous acquisitions, acquired employees found the cultural and procedural issues very different from their own backgrounds. In addition, no training was given to acquired employees to enable them to deal with the radical changes in working practices. Employees reacted differently. One employee organized his own informal training via reading the company biography and as much information as he could find on the cultural issues at Global. He sought out advice and training on the written culture and how to succeed in the environment. Others were less proactive. One director commented that the cultural issues were a barrier to optimum performance, and said:

> I am still very, very cross that the only Global training we got was only learning how to write memos 'Global style' and that was it. Once you have been here a bit and see what the training programmes look like, I don't think they put any real effort into the training at all [for acquired employees].

Because of the lack of training and understanding of procedural and cultural issues, Global lost many good employees who left voluntarily rather than endure the unpleasant socialization process.

Like the other rapid acquisitions, the terms and conditions for the final acquisition had yet to be harmonized for staff or plant employees. Again financial constraints were given as the reason why it could not occur; a date of one year hence was given as the date on which harmonization would eventually occur.

A large-scale study was then conducted to determine if there was manufacturing over-capacity due to the recent acquisitions of related product manufacturing. The objective was to determine if production could be rationalized. The study and findings were well publicized within the company. Employees were told that Global would try to ensure other positions within the company for those working in plants earmarked for closure. As a result of the study two of the acquired plants were closed. Employees from the sites were made redundant and in some cases offered comparable positions at other Global sites, all of which required relocation as the new sites were between 100 and 200 miles away. This led to some of the employees taking a more cynical view and suggesting that this aspect of the relocation should have been pointed out prior to the promises being made. Some employees felt company rhetoric in 'being seen to do the right thing' often outweighed the actual benefit to employees.

The attitude of Global in making those acquired employees redundant as well as encouraging employees to leave also led to some problems when manufacturing was shifted to the new locations. One employee said: 'The start-up of the new plant was a disaster because not enough people with the relevant skills were put in there; that was due to people leaving and people knowing better who didn't go and that cost Global a fortune in the short term.' Once again, the mass exodus of acquired employees had cost Global financially.

STABILIZATION PERIOD

A considerable amount of time had elapsed from the initial Johnson acquisition and its subsequent transactions. While each was different, these four acquisitions shared striking similarities of a pattern at Global.

Global's response to personal and group issues was considered very fair. Employees were given indications early on during the implementation period that their jobs as well as their colleagues' jobs were, or were not, secure. In many cases, employees were given mandatory counselling whether they chose to go or to stay. When employees and colleagues were made redundant, the parting was treated in a humane and professional manner – employees were given generous packages and in all cases outplacement was offered. If employees were encouraged to stay with Global and needed to relocate, considerable resources were employed to help with their move. Employees were given a great deal of latitude in deciding whether or not to stay and were treated very professionally by Global. It appears that Global managed their acquired employees' two areas of concerns very well.

An employee opinion survey was conducted in 1995 at Global (see Table 9.1). A total of 351 employees responded, including 66 acquired employees. Acquired employees demonstrated high levels of satisfaction vis-à-vis their jobs and towards the organization as a whole; in fact, in many cases their responses were higher than indigenous Global employees. These areas included pay and benefits, job satisfaction and rating one's immediate manager. Three other findings were of note. First, employees were asked to rate their satisfaction with their career with Global. Managers were far less satisfied than their Global colleagues, with 41 per cent indicating unfavourable career satisfaction compared to 29 per cent of Global employees.

Table 9.1 Global opinion survey results for acquired and Global employees

Career satisfaction	Favourable (%)	Neutral (%)	Unfavourable (%)
Global managers	44	27	29
Acquired managers	27	32	41
Contribution	**Favourable (%)**	**Neutral (%)**	**Unfavourable (%)**
Global managers	50*	26*	23*
Acquired managers	60	26	14
Training	**Favourable (%)**	**Neutral (%)**	**Unfavourable (%)**
Global managers	50	29	21
Acquired managers	60	20	20

* The sum does not total 100 per cent due to rounding of figures in the survey.

The contribution element of the survey measured 'how employees view their ability to make a contribution' to Global while the training index measures 'how employees view the training they receive'. The survey suggests, second, that acquired employees feel they have a significant contribution to make to Global and are not being given the opportunity to demonstrate their abilities. Third, the favourable perception of training seems only to serve to frustrate acquired employees as they see what Global could have done for them in terms of training if they had been inclined to do so.

Perhaps because of this lack of awareness concerning the cultural and procedural differences, acquired employees were not given the socialization programme necessary for a working understanding of Global. Global was willing to expend considerable resources on training their new graduates and indoctrinating them into the Global culture, but were unwilling to train newly acquired employees in their methods and procedures – yet it was during the first several months of tenure that these employees were being assessed as to their capability and suitability within Global, often while struggling to adapt to these changes. This may have contributed to these employees being assessed less favourably and consequently moved laterally or demoted based on their perceived ability. It was as if they were inconsistent – while they did not want acquired employees as a whole to remain, they still wanted affected employees to be treated fairly. One director described his experience:

> I told my people this by way of warning: Imagine you are a polar bear and a pretty good polar bear, you know where the holes are in the ice, you know how to get the seals out and you are the king of the ice. Imagine you the polar bear have just been parachuted into the middle of the Malayan jungle; you are still a big tough polar bear and this little thing wriggles in front you, it is brown and green and you take a swipe at it and it bites you and you are a dead polar bear. That is what it is like at Global – you must come out of your polar bear culture and enter the Malayan jungle culture. It isn't necessarily any more hostile than the culture you are coming from but it is entirely different and that is what I began to realize those months later. We are talking about a very, very different culture and we were a long way off from Global's.

Those Johnson employees who chose to stay have become resigned to their positions within Global. Many of the directors and managers who remained felt that the benefits of remaining at Global outweighed the disadvantages. Many chose to stay rather than look for other jobs during a time in their career when age may become a factor affecting employability. In general, Global was a good employer, and ultimately they became comfortable with the culture and procedures. One director summed it up:

> It wasn't very long before you realized that Global is a very good company and I count myself lucky today that I was bought by Global and survived the initial two years ... I just look back at that period as a dark abyss which I came through.

Once the shopfloor employees felt comfortable with the changes in working practices, all enjoyed the increased benefits of working for Global. Those employees from the more recent acquisitions had not reached this point of acceptance or rejection of the organization.

Global, however, was less successful in managing group concerns of procedural and cultural changes in their newly acquired employees. This was for two reasons. First, it was seen as a genuine inability on the part of Global employees to realize just how unique the Global culture was in an industrial context. This was exacerbated by the lack of diverse organizational backgrounds experienced by Global employees – the vast majority of Global 'fast track' employees in the UK had worked only for Global since leaving university. They had not therefore experienced other organizational cultures in any depth. They were, in essence, 'culturally blind' – to them Global was 'normal'. Second, their lack of effort was seen as a sign of arrogance in many Global employees when comparing themselves to other, non-Global employees. Many of the acquired employees readily acknowledged that the majority of Global employees were exceptional, which is not surprising given the Global policy of recruiting top graduates. What was seen as the problem was the lack of credence given to those employees who came from acquired or diverse backgrounds. What made acquired employees even more sensitive was that often their target company brands had outperformed Global's in the European arena prior to their acquisition. This was especially disillusioning for some acquired employees as the Global business literature states that Global values diversity of experience – many felt this was just rhetoric. This finding was supported by the internal survey which asked all employees whether they believed that diversity was encouraged in Global; managers and directors within the organization felt that while the company states that it values diversity, the truth is that there remains a 'glass ceiling' for acquired employees (see Table 9.1).

CONCLUSION

This case was unusual in that it was highly successful in some areas and unsuccessful in others. In terms of the acquisition process, it was seen that in their first acquisition Global did not have a sufficient acquisition plan, no doubt due to the immediate nature of their 'white knight' involvement. In their subsequent acquisitions, it was seen that Global did have an acquisition plan but one which only covered issues such as redundancies and relocations sufficiently. It did not cover the more complex issues of procedural and cultural differences.

Global communicated aspects of its acquisition plan well, especially when it involved practices it had encountered previously, such as redundancies and office relocations. As any cultural or procedural anomalies were not considered, they were not communicated (nor were their ramifications considered in an operational context) with regard to the target employees.

Global enacted the elements of its acquisition implementation plan which dealt with individual and group issues with great professionalism and empathy for those affected employees. This served to confuse some of the employees who could not understand how an acquirer could be so professional in one aspect of its implementation and so callous in another – the fact that they did not even understand the cultural differences was not taken into account by either side. The irony is that Global management did not realize that this dealt with only part of the problem.

Curiously, in all four acquisitions, Global's approach to the implementation process differed; in one case it used an acquisition manager and, although successful, it did not use this approach in subsequent acquisitions. It was as if Global didn't learn from each acquisition but instead 'reinvented the wheel'. Those areas in which it did well, such as implementing redundancies, it continued to do well. Those which it handled poorly, such as dealing with procedural and cultural change, it continued to handle poorly.

Finally, this case highlights the difficulties in communicating an organization's inherent traits because it requires the acquirer to be aware of its own unique cultural and procedural qualities. In the case of Global, this self-knowledge was seriously hampered by the lack of corporate diversification experienced by its own personnel – it appeared that Global didn't even realize it was so culturally and procedurally different to those companies it acquired. This was highlighted by Global's repeated claims to its targets that their companies' cultures were similar, when in fact the similarities were few. Furthermore, as an organization's culture is, by its nature, unwritten, the ability to explain this to a newcomer is made even more difficult. This notwithstanding, it would have been possible for Global to introduce acquired employees to the culture in a more comprehensive manner, as seen in the extensive training programmes offered to new recruits at Global. What then becomes the issue is whether or not the acquirer feels this expense in terms of time and money is worth the long-term benefit. If the acquirer expects the bulk of target employees to leave over time (or even *wants* them to), this expense is largely unnecessary. This then becomes a calculated business decision and not a cultural fluke. However, this needs to be spelled out for certain acquired employees (managers and directors) – you may have a job but you do not have a career with Global, but if you go you will be treated fairly in the process.

10   Discovery and the Scottish Yeast Company

INTRODUCTION

This acquisition demonstrates how the companies' previous histories can dramatically affect the current acquisition. Whereas the previous chapters looked at targets with no history of being acquired, Discovery took over a company with a long and traumatic history of being a target. On top of this, Discovery wanted to make far-reaching changes which would cause further upheaval within the workforce. Like Service Conglomerate and Anglo-American, Discovery wanted to make operating changes, then run the company via financial controls without merging the business into existing functions or units. What is interesting is that while Discovery introduced changes far more revolutionary and negative in terms of redundancies than those at Quality Guarding, the long-term effects on the workforce were not nearly as potent.

This case study examines Scottish Yeast, originally a subsidiary of a large Scottish conglomerate (which will be called Scottish Conglomerate in this case study), which was involved in one of the most acrimonious hostile takeovers in British history. Drinks Company plc was brought in as a 'white knight' to rescue Scottish Conglomerate from another predatory conglomerate, which resulted in a fraught and unethical bidding war which was to last almost 18 months. In the end, amid allegations of illegal actions, Drinks Company acquired Scottish Conglomerate. It was made quite clear early on that Drinks Company was interested only in those Scottish Conglomerate companies which were key to their core businesses of drinks and alcohol; all other companies including Scottish Yeast would be divested. Scottish Yeast was then sold to a division of Giant Foods, a European conglomerate, and, 18 months after that acquisition, 'sold' to another division of Giant Foods.

Where the historical implications of this case are important in analysing the current acquisition, they will be touched upon. The case, however, will concentrate on the last subsidiary transfer which occurred internally at Giant. This is for several reasons. First, it was during this transfer that the greatest changes took place. Second, it is the most recent of the acquisitions and, therefore, fresh in people's minds. Finally, the fact that it was a 'sale' from one subsidiary to another highlights some interesting points which will be discussed.

BACKGROUND TO THE ACQUISITION

Scottish Yeast was founded by Scottish Conglomerate in the early 1800s to provide a source of fine yeast for Scottish Conglomerate's high-quality whisky distilleries. Because of this, Scottish Yeast had been left to run reasonably autonomously and was seen more as a stand alone operation than a profit centre; Scottish Yeast hadn't made a profit during the last 20 years. The overall production of Scottish Yeast had dwindled in size during this time. Whereas previously there had been four yeast production facilities, only two existed at the time of the Drinks Company takeover, one in England as well as the Scottish facility.

Scottish Yeast was situated in a small rural location in mid-Scotland in an area which has previously been known for its woollen factories; the recession and changes in textile manufacturing, however, had greatly reduced that industry's impact and now Scottish Yeast was the immediate vicinity's largest employer. Because of this, it was not uncommon to find Scottish Yeast employees who had been with the company for over 30 years. It was also common to find entire families working at the facility as well as several generations of relatives.

The culture at the site was one of tradition and long-standing practices. There were some prejudices in the working environment, including a management–worker schism which operated with only a low degree of trust. This was seen most noticeably in the older and longer-serving shopfloor employees. There was also little understanding between the site's large R&D team and the non-managerial staff. Thus, the site was not one of harmonious unitarism but instead a collection of distinct groups, each with their own sub-cultures and agendas.

Over the years, Scottish Yeast had developed two distinct areas of business, an active yeast side which, until the purchase by Giant Foods, constituted the greater part of the business, and an inactives side. Active yeast was used for the production of whisky and, therefore, was considered the primary product for manufacturing. Inactives were used in the production of predominately beef food flavourings and was the much smaller and less strategically important portion of the business for their earlier acquirers.

Scottish Conglomerate was one of the last large independent Scottish-headquartered multinationals and its sale was a source of nationalistic concern for many of those affected. During the takeover fight and in order to play on the nationalistic concerns, the Drinks Company chief executive made several promises, including retaining a Scottish chairman, most of the Scottish board of directors and the Scottish head office. His pro-Scottish attitude made many of the Scottish Yeast employees initially supportive of Drinks Company as opposed to the other contender during the acquisition negotiation.

Once the acquisition battle was actually concluded and Drinks Company had secured Scottish Conglomerate, the Drinks Company chief executive's pro-Scottish attitude quickly changed. The Scottish head office was closed and the Scottish chairman and board of directors fired. The tension escalated as the Drinks Company CEO and several other Drinks Company directors were found to have behaved criminally in the takeover bid and were subsequently jailed. Even though Scottish Yeast was left virtually untouched during this time, it was a time of great stress for the Scottish Yeast employees as it was seen as the demise of one of the last great Scottish conglomerates compounded by the fact that it was 'lost' in an unfair fight. Many of the site's employees suffered marital problems and several had nervous breakdowns. One employee described it by saying: 'I was totally devastated by that takeover because for Scotland, Scottish Conglomerate was the biggest and best-known company and I felt really secure and when they were sold to Drinks Company, I felt shot in the foot.'

Because of the other 'anti-Scottish' decisions taken, Drinks Company suffered a Scottish backlash and was forced to offer some minor concessions. It was during this time that it became apparent that either Scottish Yeast or its sister company in England was under threat of closure due to a decline in demand for active yeast products. An intensive internal audit left those employees in Scotland sure of their closure. However, the Scottish plant remained open while the English operation closed. While not all employees knew of the situation, rumours concerning the potential closure were rife. Those employees who knew were greatly relieved; it was perceived that the pro-Scottish sensitivities helped. One director commented:

It didn't look very good closing a factory in Scotland during all of this because a big part of this was the Scottish ownership factor and Drinks Company sought to allay that, so it was because of the takeover that the closure didn't take place. Not everyone here was aware of that, only some of us, but it was a lucky escape.

While activity was occurring at the corporate level, the Scottish Yeast site was left virtually untouched by Drinks Company. Employees received no information nor any indication from Drinks Company as to what their fate would be. Although Drinks Company management indicated in the media that all non-core businesses would be divested, no action had been taken to either confirm or deny this. In fact, very little had actually changed under Drinks Company ownership, which in itself created unease as employees waited to find out what would happen to their subsidiary.

Approximately 18 months after the Drinks Company takeover, prospective purchasers began to view the factory. Senior management was aware of the intended sale but middle managers and shopfloor employees had to rely on reasonably accurate rumours for information. This time proved to be very worrying for the Scottish Yeast employees. One shopfloor worker commented:

All these people were walking around and we didn't know anything, that was the worst bit of it, the lack of information and we all wanted information but management weren't saying a thing.

There were four potential buyers: a US brewer, a British bakery, French Foods and Willmot Foods, a subsidiary of Giant Foods. The former two were interested in the active yeast side for beer and bread, respectively. French Foods was also interested in the active side as it was a leading French yeast producer. It was rumoured that French Foods wanted the brand name and would close down the plant and move the capacity to its existing French operation. Willmot was not a logical fit, being a margarine and related foodstuffs producer, but it was rumoured that the marketing team felt it could cross-sell the inactive yeast flavourings to its existing customer base. In the end, Willmot was successful in acquiring Scottish Yeast. Most of the employees, however, did not understand the rationale behind the purchase.

Giant Foods plc, in turn, was a massive and highly successful player in the global food industry, owning many of the top brands sold throughout the world. Giant was characterized by a decentralized organizational structure held together by a very well developed and sophisticated human resource function. Giant practised a well-established internal labour market for managers which encouraged upward promotion through the organizational ranks and frequent company transfers. When a new company was acquired, it was common practice to import Giant employees to occupy some of the top spots in the new organization; seen as key were the managing director, financial and personnel specialists. Giant took a long-term perspective with its acquisitions. Because of this, it was common practice at Giant to do nothing as far as integration with a newly acquired business other than to install a few key managers, familiarize itself with the operation and get to know its strengths and weaknesses for a period of up to two years. It was this approach that their subsidiary, Willmot, took with Scottish Yeast.

The site did not see a great deal of change after the sale by Drinks Company. The management team remained unchanged with the addition of Willmot personnel, finance and managing directors overseeing the site and some initial investment; the finance and personnel directors retired early and the managing director stayed on as a deputy to the new managing director. Most employees did not know the reasons for the purchase nor did they receive any information concerning changes after the acquisition. They also did not know of Giant's 'wait and see' practice in the early stages of acquisition because employees were not told of this; there was a high degree of restlessness and uncertainty. The situation remained 'business as usual'. Because of the uncertainty and lack of formal communication, the site had a highly active and relatively accurate informal 'grapevine' which fuelled speculation even more. Willmot did invest some initial capital to modernize aspects of the plant but left the majority of the site untouched. Many employees, especially middle managers, were concerned. One commented:

> It got better in the sense that Giant is a huge company and they started to invest some money, but we also found it more difficult because we were waiting for some kind of direction, some kind of leadership and wanting to know where we fit in the company because it didn't really make sense to us with Willmot. They make margarine and that didn't seem to tie in with yeast. It was better in the sense that we were part of Giant but there was always this underlying concern of where we fit in with Willmot.

It was during this time that Discovery Foods, another division of Giant, became involved with the Scottish Yeast site. Discovery was a flavourings manufacturer and was very interested in the inactives business for beef flavourings and consequently began working on site with Willmot. French Foods also began purchasing large quantities of active yeast from Scottish Yeast to bolster their own production and within a short amount of time became Scottish Yeast's largest active yeast customer, along with Drinks Company who continued to use Scottish Yeast for their whisky production. In spite of this increased demand, Scottish Yeast had yet to make a profit.

Approximately one year into Willmot's ownership, a salmonella outbreak occurred in the inactives side of Scottish Yeast. Giant's response was decisive; it arrived with a full team of professionals, found the source of the problem and eradicated it swiftly. Employees found it a unifying experience where the plant united against a common problem, with the R&D

team, shopfloor and management all working closely together. One shopfloor employee summed it up by saying:

> It was unifying and everyone had to pull together; I don't often agree with everything management do but I think they did a good job there. The guy who was in charge did a really good job, he carries a lot of responsibility for what happened at the time and he did it well.

Several employees commented that if they had been part of a smaller or short-term orientated organization, the salmonella event would have marked the end for the plant. Another shopfloor worker agreed: 'Giant being the big company it is, it played it down and managed to contain it. If we were owned by anybody else we would not have survived that.'

Approximately ten months after the salmonella outbreak, it became clear that the plant was still not operating at a profit and that the marketing synergies envisaged by Willmot management were not materializing. It became clear that the plant was under review for sale. While only the senior management knew of the sale, middle management and the shopfloor heard rumours via the well-established grapevine. The prime candidate to purchase the site was French Foods, which remained the largest client of the actives business. Discovery, however, was very interested in pursuing the inactives business which had been expanding under their guidance. It was even considered that the site should be split in half and fenced off accordingly, with Discovery taking total control of the inactives business and French Foods buying the actives side of the business. Ultimately, the business was 'sold' to Discovery who assumed total control of the site while French Foods remained a large customer with a long-term supply contract running until mid-1999. Scottish Yeast had acquired its fourth owner in less than five years. The employees were becoming almost blasé about the changes in ownership; one employee commented: 'We don't know what to call each other half the time, everyone keeps changing names around here.'

DISCOVERY'S ACQUISITION AND IMPLEMENTATION

Immediately upon acquiring the site, Discovery sent three new managers including Scott Young, the site's new general manager. Young was in his mid-thirties and a Giant 'fast track' employee brimming with enthusiasm for the newly acquired site. His natural exuberance was seen in two different lights at Scottish Yeast; some employees found him a natural leader while others found him impetuous and brash. Because Young had had to prepare a business plan internally in order to secure the site, he had some idea of its strategic direction. He had also secured agreement for a substantial sum for capital investment to modernize the facilities if he could finalize a business plan detailing the expenditure.

Young immediately called together the existing management and hosted a dinner off site during which he outlined his vision for the future. He, with the existing Scottish Yeast team which had remained virtually intact since the Drinks Company acquisition, then put together a plan for the site's development. The team worked for several weeks pulling together the details of the high level operational plan. While Young had Giant's approval, he knew little about the site and had to rely on the local management for advice and guidance.

It was during this time that Young's and the other Discovery directors' enthusiasm began to win support from some of the senior Scottish Yeast directors. One negotiator involved in the process said:

> It was striking when the Discovery directors came here, I imagined their attitude would be one of, 'We have got this place and we own it to stop French Foods from being in inactives so we had to keep control of it. What do we do with it?' But in fact, they were self-evidently enthusiastic so those of us who were involved in this particular meeting were very struck. I was very, very struck by that. Then after that we were involved with the senior people before the announcement was made [to the rest of the workforce] and we knew what they were going to do with the site and the investment on the site and in producing the plan for the site.

The plan for the site's development was approved by Giant, as was the considerable investment in plant and equipment. Because the new equipment was more automated, there would need to be substantial staffing reductions throughout the organizational hierarchy. In order to announce the changes and impending workforce redundancies, Young called a meeting off site in a Glasgow hotel in order to hold an open forum and discuss the changes with the entire management team. Managers received this well – he was trying to keep them informed of changes even if they were not directly involved in the decision making themselves.

Very soon after briefing the management team, he called a meeting within the factory to discuss the situation with the workforce which he encouraged everyone to attend. Young began the meeting by saying he was in favour of open communication and people could ask any questions they wished. He then went on to say that, in turn, he would be totally honest, and he proceeded to tell them about the plans. He said that there would be good news and bad – the good news being that Giant was willing to invest tens of millions of pounds in order to make Scottish Yeast a world leader in yeast production. The bad news was that only 60 per cent of the current staffing level was needed in order to run the new facilities. Young then elaborated on Giant's investment intentions and the ramifications for staffing numbers on the site. The overwhelming response of the managers and shopfloor employees present was approval of the honest approach taken by Young in spite of the negative message. One shopfloor worker commented:

I thought it was a good meeting because after it everyone knew exactly what was happening. That was one thing, there weren't a lot of rumours coming out of it and that was good. It put everyone straight and then they were aware, everyone said it was great and that it was the best meeting we had ever had. Young didn't hum and haw, he got to the point and said this is the way it is and I had to admire him for that. He was the first person who had been straight with us and he managed to speak his mind and knew exactly what he was going to say, and he said it.

The site investment commenced immediately and was concentrated on the inactives business in order to cope with the increased product demand. Young continued to try and keep communication lines open and encourage feedback; however, his efforts were met with a mixed response. Most employees warmed to his loud and spontaneous management style while a few found him overpowering. One employee commented: 'Young bubbles with enthusiasm even in meetings, the energy is there. It is tangible because he bubbles so much.' A minority were less receptive to his style of management – another employee commented:

I don't trust him and what he says, I find him difficult. You really try to avoid him because you don't know what he is going to say or shout across the office. Most people tend to steer clear rather than get involved with him.

This difference in employee views impaired Young's ability to achieve open communication with all employees; in general, however, most employees found his style acceptable. As a result, the overactive 'grapevine' had actually diminished in frequency and breadth of gossip since the formal communication had increased in volume, frequency and honesty.

Work on site was progressing with changes taking place at a rapid pace. Many of the managers were involved in teams working in specific projects, although time constraints and perhaps a skill shortage meant there had been inadequate planning and project management. In some cases, works had to be modified because it appeared that the original plans had not taken all factors into account. This led some employees to question Discovery's management credibility. Young admitted that he 'sailed a bit close to the wind' but suggested that one always had to take chances in order to achieve. This was not a feeling shared by some of the more conservative Scottish Yeast employees. One employee commented: 'It doesn't seem like they think things through. It seems like they say, "Oh that sounds like a good idea, let's do it." '

In line with the advances in automation, redundancies commenced. It was Giant's policy to offer voluntary redundancies and early retirement as initial steps and only to use mandatory redundancies if absolutely necessary. It was also Giant's policy to allow as much as a year to elapse between the redundancy announcement and occurrence and to offer as much assistance as possible to those affected employees. In the event, mandatory redundancies were necessary for the shopfloor staff but not the management staff. Although the latter's numbers were cut by a third, it was possible to achieve the appropriate management staffing levels via early retirement and voluntary redundancy. Discovery actually reduced the management staffing levels by too much to cope with a concurrent upturn in demand which required the rehiring of several of the managers as short-term consultants; this was done without communicating the reason to all employees. Some of the shopfloor viewed this with cynicism and one shopfloor employee said: 'It wasn't fair, they cut the lower people but not anyone above – they just bring them back as consultants.' In the light of the highly cynical workforce, this should have been communicated more effectively.

Even after voluntary redundancies, it was necessary to make additional shopfloor employees redundant via mandatory redundancies. The management at Discovery did not want to use the traditional last in first out method of determining shopfloor redundancies as the facility was heavily staffed by older employees. They also wanted to keep the best performers, who were not necessarily the longest servers. There was no formal evaluation procedure in place so the Discovery personnel manager met with the site's trade union in order to determine a formula for picking the best employees. The formula agreed included a certain scoring for each time an employee arrived late for work, for sick days, and for formal warnings they had received. An employee ranking was then drawn up and those worst offenders were the first to be given mandatory redundancy. The greatest problem from Discovery's point of view was that some of the best operators were top of the redundancy list. One manager commented:

The people who were selected by this formula unfortunately were some of my best operators and the most skilled and capable persons amongst the group. You have to have some basis and that was the basis chosen but it was hard for me and very difficult to explain to my people.

Only about twelve employees from the list had to be made redundant. In the middle of the redundancy process, the anticipated product demand increased and several employees who were to be made redundant were offered the choice of rolling three-month contracts rather than outright redundancy. The situation continued for almost a year. This was not perceived as fair by the remaining shopfloor employees who, in general, felt that these employees should be fully reinstated rather than face the uncertainty of three-month contracts.

Even though the plan was agreed by the employees' trade union which was involved throughout the process, most of the shopfloor felt that the selection process was unfair. This was due largely to the fact that employees' performances were being judged retrospectively without their knowledge of the assessment. One affected employee commented:

I can understand why they had redundancies because in the long run it is better for the company because it gives it some chance for survival, but it is just the way they did it that was a bit unsettling for everyone. These are our friends. First and foremost you worry about your own job and then you worry about your mates.

In addition, one employee claimed to have seen documentation stating that management had targeted certain troublemakers in the plant and were using this process to eliminate them. While this appears illogical given the trade union's involvement, it highlights the continuing problem at Scottish Yeast of a lack of trust between the shopfloor and management which a faulty selection process exacerbated.

Many of the older shopfloor employees felt a very strong, almost irrational, distrust for management in general and certain managers in particular. It was the classic 'them and us' worker–management relationship. With some employees, no matter what positive things one could say about the acquisition and the improvements to the site, the response was always negative; in some cases this was very pronounced. This distrust of management could only have been greatly exacerbated by the rapid succession of owners during the previous four years, the reprehensible actions of the Drinks Company executives, the broken promises made by Drinks Company and the failure of previous owners to do anything with Scottish Yeast's facilities. In addition, the perceived 'chance taking' attitude of Scott Young didn't convince some of the shopfloor of the abilities of management as a whole. These combined to give some employees a highly cynical view of management's capabilities.

This was highlighted by the leadership programme initiated by Scott Young in which middle and lower managers were encouraged to take a greater role in communicating to their subordinates. In order to promote this, some of the employees were to be taken on a short course to learn communication facilitation. At first, only middle managers were invited, and then (it appeared grudgingly to some employees) the scope was widened to include lower-level managers. This created the impression amongst some of the shopfloor that management was just trying to get more work out of them for less money. One employee so inclined commented: 'We have tried this team stuff two or three times and I don't believe in it and they don't pay us any more for it – they are really tight with the pound note.'

STABILIZATION PERIOD

Two years after the acquisition, the year's results were posted and Scottish Yeast made a profit for the first time in 20 years, due largely to the increased volume generated by the inactives business and the newly automated manufacturing efficiencies. Scott Young, having served his two-year stint at Scottish Yeast, was about to move into a new role within Giant and a new manager was to take over the site. The employees were thus about to be faced with another change in management style.

The employees were divided on the success brought on by the acquisition, including the changes in communication style. The vast majority of employees, including the shopfloor, felt the acquisition to be a success, with the majority feeling that a useful by-product was communication under the Discovery regime being much better than it had been previously. In addition, the capital investment and increased product demand gave some degree of employment security for those employees still working at Scottish Yeast. There is little that Discovery can do, however, about the turbulent past it inherited in Scottish Yeast. It is doubtful that those employed at Scottish Yeast will recover quickly or totally from the five years of ownership turmoil.

Employees who were working for the inactives business were more bullish about the future as they could see the demand for their product continuing to increase. In addition, they had seen a large portion of the capital expenditure go to improvement in their half of the business. Those employees who were involved in the actives business were less enthusiastic; they had seen the demand for their product fall during the past five years relative to the inactives business. In addition, French Foods remained their biggest client – although their long-term contract was to expire soon, thereby creating a further degree of uncertainty in those employees. It was feared French Foods would buy that portion of the site, or that if the contract was not renewed more redundancies would follow. Every time a French Foods executive visited the site, rumours would spread quickly around the shopfloor. The frequent changes in ownership seemed to make employees only more sensitive to ownership speculation. This had not abated; however, management was making a concerted effort to address employee fears and build upon the site's improvement. As one director commented:

> Our biggest problem we have is getting them excited and earning their trust, also getting rid of the hidden agenda. That is very difficult and some people will never accept it, but from now on it will be better.

CONCLUSION

Scottish Yeast should be considered a successful acquisition for Discovery. When one considers the mindset of the workforce in light of previous experiences, as well as the difficulty of having to make large-scale redundancies, Discovery fared better than the vast majority would have expected. It is interesting to note the differences in change impact between Quality Guarding and Scottish Yeast. Redundancies and job role changes were less far-reaching at Quality Guarding yet the workforce was more traumatized by the implementation process. At Scottish Yeast, on the other hand, almost half of the workforce was made redundant and those who remained saw major changes in how they were to perform their jobs. The difference in approach by the two managements highlights the result of an effective implementation process.

Discovery's management had a clear objective after the acquisition which was supported by solid pre-acquisition planning. The vision was very clearly discussed and further developed by local management prior to its final approval, therefore creating a shared sense of ownership. It was then openly outlined to the various interest groups of senior and middle management and the shopfloor. The plan was considered rational and logical and, although it included the painful element of wide-scale redundancies, it was accepted as making sound business sense.

The communication of the plan to all employees was handled in a way which was markedly different from Scottish Yeast's previous employers.

The fact that the communication was handled in an open manner meant that employees were more receptive to the message, even though it wasn't a particularly pleasant one. The ongoing communication initiative meant a drop in informal means such as the 'grapevine'. In spite of this, Discovery would have benefited from even more communication, especially regarding the logic behind some decisions taken, in order to further reduce speculation regarding the logic of some decisions and outcomes.

What further differentiated Discovery and Quality Guarding was the manner in which the plan was implemented. The implementation of the plan was considered fair except for the issue of mandatory redundancies. Redundancies and changes in working roles were handled in an open and timely manner; uncertainty was kept to a minimum as employees were told of the changes well before they were to occur. One of the only shortcomings of Discovery in this process was to fall short in a project planning and management sense. Discovery would have been better served to explain the logic behind some of the decisions more carefully than it did (bearing in mind the mindset of the workforce).

The mandatory redundancy issue highlights an interesting part of Discovery's implementation plan. Even though employees participated in the criteria for redundancy selection via their trade union, they still considered it unfair due to its retrospective nature. This illustrates the problem of having the perceptions of the process affect the perceived outcome in employees' views of what is fair and unfair (as was discussed in Chapter 5). It is clearly a pitfall facing many acquirers, especially during times of low trust which certainly exists during the implementation process. Another example of this will be seen in the TeleCable acquisition of Infosys, discussed in Chapter 11.

11   TeleCable Group and Infosys

'This could have been a perfect acquisition.'
(Acquired Manager)

INTRODUCTION

The fifth case study involves the acquisition of a market-leading information technology company by a large UK telecommunications group which, in turn, is owned by a larger global conglomerate. These companies will be called Infosys Ltd, TeleCable Group and Conglom plc, respectively. The managing director of Infosys Ltd is named Isabelle Saunders; the chief executive of TeleCable Group is Tom Green.

BACKGROUND TO THE ACQUISITION

TeleCable Group was a large and rapidly expanding company in the cable and television industry. It was part of a larger conglomerate, Conglom plc, which had made acquisitions in recent years and possessed a series of market leading and highly respected brands. It was known in the industry for being a paternalistic company with long-serving employees. TeleCable Group was one of its flagship companies; its brand was well known and it was considered a leader in its industry. It was intended to enlarge the division and resources were earmarked to fund that expansion.

The area that TeleCable Group planned on expanding was the fast growing business information market. The business information market was based on key data being input onto a system and then disseminated to its subscribers. Fast-breaking company news, annual reports and other company information was also available. The service was costly but considered essential by many of the users based in financial markets throughout the world. A key to its success was having accurate company information in a timely fashion, usually within twelve hours of the news breaking.

TeleCable Group's growth strategy included making several key acquisitions through which to gain critical mass. TeleCable Group had made some smaller acquisitions previously which had not been particularly

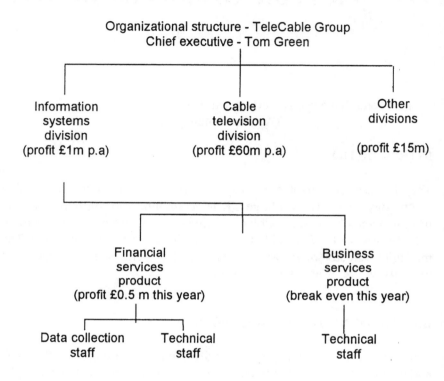

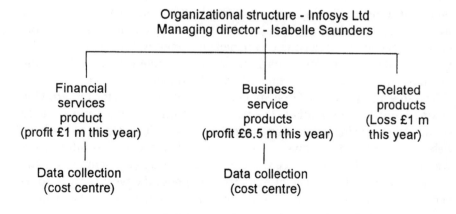

Fig. 11.1 *Organizational structure of TeleCable Group and Infosys*

successful; the new acquisitions being considered were far larger and were deemed critical for success. TeleCable Group's newly appointed chief executive, Tom Green, brought in an external information systems director, Glenn Johnson, to become the divisional managing director and to locate, analyse, acquire and integrate the chosen strategic acquisitions. Several targets were highlighted and approached; however, no targets prior to Infosys had been successfully acquired under Johnson's tutelage.

TeleCable Group had several offices, including its head office in London, marketing and technical offices with 80 employees on the outskirts of London, and a data collection office with 60 employees on the south coast of England. Infosys had one large site in London which housed their administrative staff (200 employees), their marketing and technical staff (100 employees), and their data collection unit, also with 100 employees. The companies' respective organizational charts are shown above (see Figure 11.1).

The strengths of each company were seen to complement each other. The TeleCable Group name was seen to have a good brand image, although not seen thus far in the information systems industry. They had an able and aggressive marketing function headed by a recently appointed charismatic marketing director who had been instrumental in turning that division around. Its weakness was in its data collection. The information collected by TeleCable Group entailed approximately 100 pieces of business information which were then sent out to subscribers. The turnover of staff was high at their south coast office and the job of data analysis and input was considered a moderately skilled but low-paid, transient position. This, combined with a new office location, led to TeleCable Group having no employees with over three years' data collection experience on staff.

TeleCable's new divisional managing director, Glenn Johnson, began investigating which targets could add immediate value to TeleCable Group. Infosys' name naturally came up. Infosys Ltd had market-leading products in its specific niches. While a small player, it achieved growth due to its innovative and profitable products; its top management team worked closely together and as a result was a very cohesive group. Isabelle Saunders, the managing director, had previously worked at TeleCable Group and had resigned to lead Infosys. Because of its success, the components of that product were highly rated: its in-house technical staff, product development and data collection and analysis departments. The data collection for the Infosys products, while similar to TeleCable Group's, was far more complicated as they collected over 700 pieces of information on each category profile. The data collection and editing positions were viewed as career opportunities and, as a result, Infosys had employees with over twelve years' experience editing the information. Infosys' weakness was seen by the TeleCable

Group managers to be its rather narrow management focus and lack of marketing aggressiveness. There was also the opportunity to grow internationally as only 20 per cent of Infosys' sales were outside the UK. One TeleCable Group director commented that: 'from our side it looked good ... our view was that Infosys' weaknesses were sales and marketing and its strengths are in the data.'

It became known that Infosys Ltd was being sold by its owners, who maintained a very 'hands off' financially controlled approach with the company. Four potential purchasers came to the forefront of the subsidiary sale: a European publishing house, an American conglomerate, a UK-based company similar to TeleCable Group, and TeleCable Group. The Infosys employees, with the exception of the directors, didn't know for certain the company was for sale, although rumours concerning the sale were rife.

The directors of Infosys Ltd were asked to prepare and discuss a presentation for the various potential buyers. When meeting the various buyers, a clear preference by the directors was shown for the European publishing house which offered a 'hands off' integration strategy similar to Infosys' existing owners. TeleCable Group was viewed slightly warily because it was thought that if it purchased Infosys Ltd, there would be a duplication of services and that because of this, rationalization in some form would occur.

THE ACQUISITION

Infosys Ltd was acquired by TeleCable Group for approximately £75 million, the Group's most ambitious divisional acquisition to date. Conglom plc made it clear to TeleCable's management that it expected the acquisition to be a great success, justifying itself in terms of its integration and quickly resulting in enhanced profits. A degree of high-level acquisition planning had occurred prior to the purchase, although this information was not made available to all the employees. A great deal of detail was left undecided; Tom Green wanted to take some time and get to know Infosys without rushing in and making changes and potentially mistakes. Instead, he wanted to retain the top team and slowly integrate it into the existing operation.

Tom Green of TeleCable Group and Isabelle Saunders of Infosys knew each other from Saunders' time at TeleCable Group and they met several times prior to the acquisition to discuss issues and strategy. It had been made clear prior to the acquisition to Glenn Johnson, the information systems director, that he was to be in charge of integrating Infosys into the existing TeleCable Group information division and that Isabelle Saunders would ultimately report to him.

The day after the acquisition, Tom Green of TeleCable Group went to the office of Infosys Ltd to talk to the newly acquired employees. In total, almost all 400 Infosys employees were present. His talk was very well received as he laid out the vision of the new organization and the way forward. One Infosys manager commented:

> Tom Green, incredibly, he got a round of applause; it went down extremely well and not what people are used to around here, but they just appreciated that ... he had actually taken the time out and the trouble to come here.

Another manager added: 'Tom Green's talk was excellent, the vision, it was really good and well delivered; he got across the message better than anyone else had.'

The new employees found the vision exciting and as a result felt positively towards the acquisition. Tom Green told the employees that the operational plan would be developed by a joint operating committee which would include himself and the directors from both TeleCable Group and Infosys. All major decisions would be taken by this committee, with final approval being granted by the executive steering committee which comprised Tom Green, the TeleCable Group finance and personnel directors, along with Glenn Johnson and Isabelle Saunders. Tom Green stressed that no major decisions had been made as to how the vision would be accomplished and that the TeleCable Group management had entered into the acquisition with a totally open mind. It was to be a joint effort by both companies in determining the way forward operationally. In addition, employees would be kept informed of the impending changes by an acquisition newsletter which would come out regularly.

The acquisition plan originally agreed by Tom Green and Glenn Johnson was changed within a week of the acquisition. Whereas Isabelle Saunders was supposed to report to Tom Green via Glenn Johnson, Saunders was now to report directly to Tom Green with only an informal reporting line to Glenn Johnson. Saunders had made it clear she would be unhappy reporting via Johnson and because Tom Green did not want to lose any of the key acquired directors including Saunders, the changes were made. The rationale for Tom Green's decision was that Infosys was bigger and more profitable than TeleCable Group's existing division and, therefore, warranted a direct reporting line. An organizational chart was drawn up illustrating the new arrangement but was seen only on a 'need to know basis' and thus was not distributed freely.

Instead, the new roles of the two directors were to require a great deal of liaising and information sharing as they were to manage the business split along functional lines. Isabelle Saunders would be in charge of the day-to-day running of the operation which was ultimately to include TeleCable Group's former marketing operations. Glenn Johnson would now be in less of an operational role and in more of a line position, being in charge of divisional strategy, technology and data collection. The new organizational structure created confusion in both organizations as it was deemed illogical – it was seen that there was clearly only one job and two suitors. It created a great deal of uncertainty in both those directors – as they saw there was only one job – and in the other directors, and the managers who reported to them. This was most acute in TeleCable Group where, up until that time, they had felt they were the acquirers and were not going to be unduly affected by the acquisition.

The initial contacts between TeleCable Group and Infosys highlighted different organizational cultures. TeleCable Group was a more relaxed, relationship-driven organization in which decisions were taken by committee and in an environment in which politics played a part. Lateral communication and matrix-style management were not only accepted, but encouraged in order to facilitate the building of relationships within the organization. Infosys was seen as a rigid hierarchical structure which was unable to deal with the flowing matrix-style of management used at TeleCable Group. Instead, information flowed from the top either downward or laterally to the appropriate employees.

In addition, even though the organizations overlapped in many areas, it became evident that they didn't have the same industrial vocabulary. This was demonstrated during the first joint meeting in which the directors presented their companies' respective strategies. An Infosys director noticed the different styles and languages, commenting: 'The biggest mistake was they were giving us a presentation in their own language and jargon and they weren't talking the same language – they call it intellectual property rights and we call it copyright.'

THE ACQUISITION IMPLEMENTATION

Shortly thereafter, operational meetings began in an attempt to solve the various integration issues. In each case, the affected directors from both organizations were told by Glenn Johnson to go away and formulate a joint strategy, often with the involvement of middle managers. The decisions were made behind closed doors and the process of decision making was not formally or openly debated, with only the final decision being made public.

The first group meeting concerned the merging of the respective business products divisions. It was amicably and unanimously agreed that the much smaller TeleCable Group operation should merge into the much larger and more profitable Infosys division. The division was to continue to run on an independent basis including keeping its own data collection service intact. The decision was agreed by the steering committee on the recommendation of the affected directors.

The second operational decision involved the integration of the remaining two data collection systems from the respective financial services product divisions and proved not to be as straightforward. Infosys' in-house data collection service was based in London and was operated by its large and well-established staff. TeleCable Group's smaller and less experienced staff was based in its new office on the south coast. Infosys had already discussed the possibility of outsourcing their data collection to a cheaper location, such as the Far East, but this had been rejected as the accuracy and breadth of data collection was seen as the competitive advantage of Infosys' product. It had also considered moving the data collection unit outside London to Essex or Kent where most of their employees resided, although no decision had been taken by the time the acquisition had occurred.

No consensus as to the combined location of the site could be reached amongst the participating managers. Both felt the data collection unit should stay with them; those involved also realized that if their unit closed, they and their teams would lose their jobs. Instead, both teams were told by Glenn Johnson to formulate presentations for the joint operating committee as to why the site should be given to the respective groups. This meeting was scheduled involving not only Saunders and Johnson but also the affected managers, including the potential 'winner' and 'loser'.

The general feeling of both sides was that the logical choice for the data collection facility, and therefore the favourite, was the Infosys collection centre. This was due primarily to its longer-serving, more experienced employee base and more complicated data input process.

The data collection meeting was chaired by Glenn Johnson and attended by all senior people from both sides, as well as the managers; 30 people were present. Prior to the presentations, the manager in charge of TeleCable Group's south coast data collection operation made some 'off the cuff' remarks directed towards the Infosys directors. One included a comment suggesting that substantial cost savings could be achieved merely by firing Isabelle Saunders. Glenn Johnson was used to the manager's quips and did not reprimand him unduly; however, he did ask him to apologize at the end of the meeting. When the presentations were finally made, TeleCable Group's presentation relied on some costings which were subsequently hard to verify; its presentation, however, emphasized the cost savings of combining the operations on the south coast. The TeleCable Group manager was better prepared, understood the criteria used by TeleCable Group in decisions such as this and his presentation style was perceived as being more dynamic. One TeleCable Group director attending the meeting said:

> [The TeleCable Group manager] is a brilliant presenter and [the Infosys manager] isn't, and on that basis of [the TeleCable Group manager] being a better presenter, the meeting took a decision that we go with TeleCable Group's proposition.

Glenn Johnson moved that the data collection should be centralized at the TeleCable Group's south coast offices. The Infosys directors, while not agreeing with the decision, felt their own jobs were not secure, and therefore felt they were not in a position to voice their objections loudly. One Infosys manager present commented:

> [The TeleCable Group manager] insulted everyone, 'like a loose cannon' firing off everywhere, but if we had attacked him, then we would have been attacking Glenn Johnson and you can't do that so we were on a hiding to nothing.

The steering committee agreed that the data collection facility should move to the TeleCable Group's south coast operation.

Accounts of the meeting's outcome and the way in which it was handled circulated around the respective companies' rumour mills quickly. The decision brought an outcry from the Infosys employees for several reasons. First and foremost, they were upset by the perceived inequality of the meeting and the abrasive personality of the TeleCable Group manager. It was seen that the clear beneficiary of the decision was the same rude and highly political manager who was in charge of the site. The signal perceived by Infosys employees was that TeleCable Group was a highly political organization where personalities count for more than ability or logic. One Infosys employee who attended the meeting said: '[The TeleCable Group manager] should have been fired on the spot but he has seemed to gain everything; he is the blue-eyed boy, he is the one who has gained the most from the data collection move.' Second, it was perceived that if TeleCable Group had fully understood Infosys' collection system, it would have not made the decision that it did. It was the case that TeleCable Group's management did not fully understand the complexity of the Infosys data input process at the time when the decision was made. Third, Infosys employees felt that data collection was key to their product's success and control of this was now being taken away from them and given to an abrasive and inexperienced manager. The reaction engendered such distrust that one employee said:

> Infosys have had no say whatsoever on who the senior manager should be in the organization managing something that is fundamental to their revenue stream ... managed by someone whom people here will feel very unhappy and uncomfortable working with.

Finally, the rationale for the decision was never made public and the bulk of the Infosys employees did not know why they or their colleagues were losing their jobs. Rumours and explanations as to why Infosys had 'lost' were rife and varied from the TeleCable Group manager being Tom Green's favourite, to TeleCable Group having just signed a very disadvantageous 30-year lease. The real reason for the decision was never made known.

Likewise, the decision wasn't perceived as making total sense to some of the TeleCable Group employees attending the meeting. One of them recounted:

> Whether the Infosys presentation was better or worse, time is now indicating it was all in the wash, it is costing us as much to move to the south coast as it would up to here as far as I can tell ... when that meeting closed I said to Glenn Johnson, 'Look, this just doesn't make sense.'

The situation was exacerbated by post-decision actions. Although certain Infosys data collection managers were to be made redundant as a result of the decision, no one actually informed some of them of their terms and conditions, nor the timescale; in fact, in certain cases, they were not formally told that they were going to be made redundant for several months after the decision. The result was heavy survival guilt in many colleagues of the affected employees. One such affected manager said:

> I am the invisible man in that some people knowing I am going are embarrassed to come and talk to me because they think, 'Why him and not me?', and they feel guilty; some people think 'I'd better not tell him' because this is about our future and he is not part of it or that maybe I will go work for a competitor.

All of this heightened the Infosys employees' distrust towards the TeleCable Group as they felt the treatment of fellow employees was unjust. The option

of relocating to the south coast was offered to the operationally based
Infosys data collection managers; their participation and experience was
considered key in maintaining product consistency during the location
changeover. TeleCable Group stressed that these managers were critical to
the success of the move and openly asked them to consider moving to the
south coast. While twelve managers expressed an interest when they visited
the site, nine were put off by the mixed stories they were receiving about
their terms and status as well the abrasive nature of the TeleCable manager
in charge of the site. TeleCable Group was not willing to keep the Infosys
managers' current terms and conditions because they would have been far
higher paid than their TeleCable counterparts. If this differential had been
eroded, it would have negated some of the cost savings effects of the move
out of London.

In the end only three managers relocated and with a drop in salary of 20
per cent; 95 employees were made redundant. One affected Infosys manager
commented: 'If they had really wanted me to move down there, they would
have had their story straight about my status and not dropped my salary by
20 per cent.'

The third major implementation decision taken was the decision regarding
the degree of integration of the two marketing departments. While it was
agreed that they wouldn't cross-sell each other's products immediately, it
was decided that they should be integrated onto the same site. Despite
protestations from the TeleCable Group's marketing director, the steering
committee's decision went to Infosys. The TeleCable Group's marketing
and technical teams were moved from their office outside London into
Infosys' central London location. While the decision itself was not necessarily
seen as a poor one, the handling of it was seen as lacking for several reasons.
First, Isabelle Saunders viewed the Infosys marketing director as her protégé
and it was rumoured that she campaigned very hard for Infosys to retain
the marketing function. This caused some Infosys employees to suggest that
she sacrificed the data collection decision in order to secure the marketing
department. Second, the TeleCable Group employees had no idea that the
acquisition would affect them in such a way and, consequently, the move
came as a shock. In spite of the data processing decision, employees were
saying that the acquisition was really a reverse takeover. Third, no explanation
was given to those employees being forced to relocate as to why the move
was necessary. A TeleCable Group manager commented: 'A lot more people
would have moved if they had handled the communication better because
people were assuming that it was just a temporary thing and then they will
get rid of us.' Finally, the moved marketing employees received salary

reviews to reflect central London wages while the technical staff did not, causing further resentment on the part of the latter.

Both moves highlighted the unexpected yet considerable costs of harmonization during acquisition implementation. Both the moves to the south coast and central London included uniting employees with different pay levels. In the case of the south coast move, Infosys employees were forced to accept the lower salaries in an attempt to justify the cost savings for which the move occurred. This only exacerbated the managers' disinclination to accept the move offer, potentially damaging the product's consistency and organization in the long term. In the move to central London, the harmonization costs were substantial, including increased salaries for all the marketing staff to reflect central London terms and conditions. The extent of these costs was not fully understood nor taken into account by TeleCable Group at the acquisition's outset.

All in all, it was seen that there were two difficult decisions to be made during integration – marketing and data collection – and a decision had to go each way in order to keep some semblance of 'fairness', regardless of what was best for the organization. The net result was that most of the employees involved, including those who had 'won' their positions, felt a sense of loss and, to some extent, resentment. The lack of coherent or logical management action made them question the abilities of TeleCable's and Infosys' senior management teams.

As a result of the decisions taken, a reshuffle occurred at director level. The Infosys finance director was no longer needed in his job so he replaced the retiring Infosys technical director; in line with the Johnson–Saunders role changes, he was to report to Glenn Johnson as opposed to the previous arrangement of reporting to Isabelle Saunders. His office, however, remained in the Infosys building. This created some confusion on two levels. First, the finance director, while perceived as being extremely competent in his previous job, had little technical experience. As a result, his ability to add technical expertise was questioned by the technical staff who reported to him. Second, his lateral reporting change also bothered some Infosys directors who felt he was an integral part of the Infosys decision making process. The fact that his office remained at Infosys only exacerbated the natural inclination to stay involved in the operations at Infosys.

The same was happening at TeleCable Group. Because of the marketing decision, the TeleCable Group marketing director was to join Infosys' marketing director on its board of directors and report to Isabelle Saunders. While this in itself was not a problem, the TeleCable Group marketing director still appeared confused and hostile about the marketing decision going against TeleCable Group and was less than co-operative. Instead, he continued to report informally to Glenn Johnson and refused to operate within the organizational system as it had been decided.

Although the major decisions had been made during the first three months of the acquisition, the situation remained uncertain. To the employees, the process appeared to be unmanaged. The major problem was seen as the unresolved organizational structure – it relied heavily on co-operation and the lateral flow of information between Isabelle Saunders and Glenn Johnson. The nebulous situation surrounding Saunders' and Johnson's appointments appeared only to heighten their unwillingness to interact. There was only one job to do and until their line of authority was settled the situation remained unresolved and untenable. This was exacerbated by the two leaders' personalities; while both were highly competent in a technical sense, neither were naturally outgoing or communicative. One TeleCable Group manager commented: 'With that inherent conflict at the top, it is like they can't decide between these two people so how are the rest of us supposed to decide between them?' As a consequence, the two directors did not liaise and, in fact, avoided each other by their own admission, thus inhibiting their own job performance, each other's and that of those around them.

This highlighted the cultural problems between the two companies. Another example occurred when Glenn Johnson approached an Infosys director directly concerning a technical problem. As Johnson was in charge of that line function, his approach was totally justified. The Infosys director felt this direct approach undermined Isabelle Saunders' authority and felt uncomfortable in operating in this matrix style of management. Instead, he felt that the approach should come down the organizational hierarchy from Saunders, but as the two leaders were not openly working together this would have proved difficult. In addition, in the TeleCable Group context it would also have been very bureaucratic as this hierarchical attitude was foreign to the TeleCable Group management who operated in a more open, flexible style. One Infosys director commented on the situation:

> We don't work for Glenn Johnson, we work for Isabelle Saunders who is on a level with Glenn, so Isabelle says, 'Why is Glenn asking you for information, why isn't he asking me for it?' [Isabelle] didn't know what to do – she was bothered by it, but if she spoke to Glenn, Glenn would say, 'Why are you so protective of your domain?', so she is caught in a dilemma.

While this role ambiguity and conflict was occurring at the top of the organization, employee concerns magnified further down the organization, especially at Infosys. There was no communication coming from the directors, presumably because they had not yet resolved their own personal conflicts. Middle managers were aware of the directors' problems yet unable to give their own subordinates any additional information. Employees were seeing their colleagues being made redundant, yet not being handled in what they considered to be a logical or fair manner.

The Business Products divisional director at Infosys tried to rectify the situation by holding an open forum discussion session with his 125 divisional employees. There he provided as much information as he could and was open and honest about what he did not know; in some cases he said he would try to find out information and tell them subsequently, which he did. While his division had not been unduly affected, his employees were highly concerned about their colleagues in the other divisions. It was clear that employees were less concerned about any residual uncertainty affecting them but were more worried about their colleagues in other divisions.

Six months after the acquisition, a shock announcement was made: Glenn Johnson had secretly been asked to resign by Tom Green. It was felt that Johnson had not been performing his line function as he should have been by liaising with the appropriate Infosys directors. Isabelle Saunders became the sole head of the information systems division. The TeleCable Group employees were stunned. They spoke of it being a reverse takeover and that they had been misled by TeleCable Group. One manager commented: 'We didn't expect to have the same concerns [as the Infosys employees] because we were the acquiring company, we shouldn't have so many concerns.'

STABILIZATION PERIOD

Within the first six months of the acquisition, the number of Infosys employee resignations increased dramatically to an annualized rate of 37 per cent, where previously the figure had been far lower. The intention to leave was reported to be much higher at around 65 per cent which was caused, according to employees, by the acquisition implementation process. This was more alarming when considering the length of employment of those employees – many had been with Infosys for over 15 years. Many employees commented that the unfair and mismanaged implementation process was even more disappointing after they had received such a positive and uplifting vision by Tom Green on 'Day One' of the acquisition.

Employees from affected functions of the TeleCable Group were also demonstrating a high intention to leave, although not as high as at Infosys. A concern voiced by most employees was that they were unaware that the acquisition would affect them directly and when it did, it was entirely unexpected. This made the subsequent changes harder to accept and created 'expectation dissonance', as discussed in Chapter 2.

Tom Green was isolated from criticism as his vision of the acquisition and the way forward were clear and encouraging. Instead, criticism was levelled at those in charge of changing the vision into an operational plan. An Infosys employee said: 'My impression is of a strong visionary head of the company [Tom Green] surrounded by people who don't match up to that vision.'

The strategic reasons given for the acquisition were to allow TeleCable Group to combine and strengthen its own technological and data collection provision (economies of scale) and gain added market share and entrée to new customers (both market penetration). In return, TeleCable Group directors felt they could add to Infosys in terms of brand name – especially overseas – marketing prowess and general management aggressiveness. The acquisition implementation led to TeleCable Group losing control over the marketing function and overall management of the information system division. In contrast, it gained control over an area which was not its expertise, data collection. Instead, Infosys lost control over its area of expertise which was critical to the success of Infosys' products, but gained control over an area in which it was considered weak. In essence, it appears that the post-acquisition plan changed from its pre-acquisition state during the acquisition due to people, not business issues, and to the strategic detriment of the combined organization.

CONCLUSION

This case is an illustration of when the best strategies can often be dramatically altered during the acquisition process. While Tom Green at TeleCable delivered a vision for the acquisition, he did not have a detailed enough acquisition plan to make it viable. While the original organizational structure may have been sustainable, the subsequent structure chosen was flawed. Although it was important to retain key employees in the target, changing the structure into something unworkable to ensure this happened was probably not a good idea.

The decision making process was also seen as flawed. In fact, many commented that they would have preferred to have their fates dictated to them by TeleCable rather than go through the decision making process and feel it was irrational. This highlights several key points. First, the plan should take into account the workloads of the individuals upon whom it relies; Tom Green could not possibly manage the acquisition and his hectic schedule, so he had to delegate. Yet he delegated to an individual who was directly affected by changes and decisions being taken as well as being subsumed in his own problems created by the new structure. Thus, there was no independent adjudicator to ensure decisions taken helped achieve the acquisition's objectives. The head of Infosys was in a similar position. She was so worried about the tenuousness of her own position that she felt unable to speak out at the illogical outcome of the data processing decision. Those in charge of the acquisition implementation process must be secure in their own positions or they will be too busy fighting their own battles to manage the process effectively.

Second, the acquisition plan and structure put employees in highly con-frontational situations – few ambitious employees will talk themselves out of a job if they can avoid it. The data processing decision pitted employees 'head to head' in which they were arguing ultimately over their own orga-nizational survival and not what was best for the company. It is natural; it is human behaviour. But the repercussions can take a long time to heal. As discussed in Chapter 5, conflict during acquisition does happen but it needs to be channelled and managed, not left to develop and fester on its own.

Third, decisions needed to be enforced. It is how one deals with the conflict and negative behaviour which sets the scene, not the behaviour itself. The TeleCable manager's offensive quips during the data collection meeting went virtually unpunished. There were other examples: TeleCable Group's marketing director refusing to work within the structure, the Infosys directors not co-operating with Johnson, and so on. Yet there was no one to enforce a code of behaviour because there was no one person who was unaffected and therefore able to rise above it. In addition, there was no attempt to avoid having such situations arise (for example, keeping the Infosys IT director's office in situ).

Fourth, cultural differences were not taken into account. The different management styles played a role in encouraging greater distrust between employees. The manager's comments in the data processing meeting were almost acceptable in the TeleCable culture, yet not within that of Infosys. The free-flowing matrix style of management of TeleCable was anathema to Infosys' managers; Infosys' hierarchical structure was seen as over-bureaucratic and protective at TeleCable. Because these issues were not addressed, they remained irritants and became examples of negative behaviour in a downward spiral of distrust, when really they were nothing more sinister than cultural misunderstandings.

Finally, the process appeared unmanaged. Tom Green was genuinely trying to let Infosys employees participate in merging the businesses together. In order to do that, it required a great deal of fluidity in decision making;

this, in turn, required trust which did not exist, nor was it encouraged by Johnson and Saunders due to the ambiguous organizational structure. As seen in Chapter 3, having high degrees of employee participation so soon after acquisition can lead to an inherent distrust of the processes and decisions, especially if they are patently not fair; this is clearly what happened.

In summing up, the Infosys acquisition had the hallmarks of a top acquisition – a brilliant fit, willing parties and strong leadership. Its downfall was a lack of planning, inadequate communication and a poorly managed implementation process – in effect, everything that the process outlined in this book says *not* to do. Perhaps that is why it was such a failure, and that is truly a wasted opportunity.

Conclusion

The five case studies offer some stark comparisons on how five different blue chip companies approached their acquisitions. In terms of the process described in this book, two were moderately successful in following it, two were unsuccessful and one only partially successful (see Table C.1). Both Anglo-American and Discovery followed the process well and had successful acquisitions; TeleCable Group followed the process the least and had their acquisition fail to achieve its full potential.

Table C.1 Comparing the five cases at each stage of the acquisition process

Case study	Pre-acquisition planning	Communication	Implementation	Stabilization and monitoring
Anglo-American/ Gas Appliances	Very well	Very well	Very well	Very well
Service Conglomerate/ Quality Guarding	Good	Poor	Poor	Very well
Global	Moderate	Very well about some things and poor about others	Very well about some things and poor about others	Moderate
Discovery/ Scottish Yeast	Very well	Very well	Very well (with a small hiccup)	Good
TeleCable Group and Infosys	Poor	Poor (except for 'Day One' presentation)	Poor	Poor

I hope one does not infer from this book that I encourage acquirers to manage employee expectations for the sake of being nice. By managing expectations I mean having a plan, communicating the plan, implementing it fairly and monitoring its progress. I promote this approach because it is by far the most successful way of achieving one's objectives as an acquirer. If an acquirer wants to be in control of which employees stay and which leave, the process needs to be handled in a certain way – one where employees want to stay. In those rare acquisitions where the acquirer truly does not need the existing workforce to be productive or to preserve customer relationships, a more aggressive stance can be taken.

One can use Anglo-American as an example. It could never be considered a paternalistic organization which 'mollycoddles' its employees, but it clearly follows this process of managing expectations in order to optimize its acquisitions. Thus, managing expectations is not about being 'soft' on employees, it is about being professional. The outcome is increased control over the process and a sense of 'goodwill' in acquired employees – it buys one time to prove that one is worth working for. It also means a far quicker return to normalcy and 'back to business'.

I hope this book has been helpful in understanding the complexities of acquisition and goes some way in explaining why so many get it wrong. Successful acquiring is paradoxical – so simple, yet so complicated: simple in that to do it right requires no more than to plan thoroughly, communicate effectively and implement professionally while monitoring the situation; and complicated because to do this is much harder than it appears on the surface – if it were not, the success rate would be far higher. For those involved, acquisitions require vision, stamina, discipline, empathy, honesty, patience, attention to detail, charisma, communication skills, determination, objectivity, professionalism and, of course, leadership. This isn't too much to ask for in a business manager! And acquisition requires not just one manager to have these traits but an entire team of like-minded individuals all working towards the same objective.

Each acquisition will differ. They will depend on a lot of different factors which are unique to every acquisition. But they share some striking similarities. A simple framework illustrates the similar aspects of acquisition (see Figure C.1). The first category is the individual. Some individuals have certain career or personal characteristics which make them more or less receptive to being acquired – perhaps they have a sought-after skill which makes them more mobile than other employees or career aspirations. The second area of the framework is the overlap of the individual and the organization representing the employee's relationship with that company. An individual's position within an organization influences his or her concerns during acquisition. Directors will have different agendas than middle managers and the shopfloor, all of which need to be managed in order for the acquisition to be successful. The third area of the framework is the organization's history which influences the receptiveness of employees to the acquirer. If the companies have been fierce rivals in the past, this may make employees less receptive to being acquired by them in the future. The fourth area is the relationship between the organization and acquisition. A prior organizational history of being acquired may influence the workforce and its receptiveness to being acquired again. If the process had gone smoothly, another acquisition may be greeted positively; if it had gone badly, the reaction may be negative. The fifth area of the framework is the acquisition itself and the reasoning behind the deal. This includes the degree of integration required in order to fulfill the acquisition objectives – the greater the degree of integration, the more complex the implementation process. The sixth area is the relationship of the acquisition and individuals. Previous acquisition experience influences some employees' concerns and degree of pragmatism. Finally, the convergence of the individual, organization and acquisition is the specific set of circumstances which makes every acquisition unique.

The process of acquiring also remains basically the same. Employees expect change after being acquired – it is a golden opportunity to address many of the long-standing 'taboo subjects' of a business because of this expectation for change. It is how the change issues are handled which determines acquisition success, not the changes themselves. After acquisition, employees will accept massive change if only they are told what is happening prior to its occurrence and treated fairly when it is implemented. One only has to

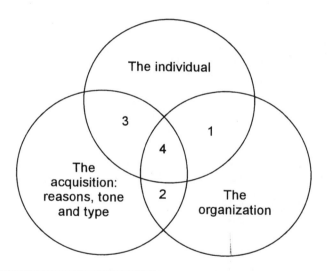

1	The individual in the organization
2	The organization's acquisition history
3	The individual's prior acquisition experiences
4	The acquisition

Fig. C.1 *Acquisition framework*

remember Scottish Yeast to see this. But in order to do this, one must plan, communicate and effectively manage the process. This lies almost entirely within the acquirer's control. So if it mismanages the acquisition, it has no one to blame but itself.

It is also worth remembering that once one acquires, nothing remains the same. The company culture, top team, management style and workload never go back to the way they were before the deal. One can look fondly back at those days but it will never be like that again.

I recently met the director in charge of integrating a 'mega-merger' and asked him what his advice was for managing acquisitions. He smiled and replied: 'Acquisitions are not for the faint-hearted but it is worth it in the end.' In many ways, this sums it up.

Bibliography and Suggested Further Reading

Acquisitions Monthly. 'Cashing in on Britannia'. 1998 Jan: 32–34.

Acquisitions Monthly. 'Break for the Border'. 1998 Feb: 42–45.

AMR International. *Successful Acquiring*. London: 1998.

Armstrong-Stassen, M. 'Coping with transition: A study of layoff survivors'. *Journal of Organizational Behavior*. 1994 Dec; 15(4): 597–621.

Arnold, H. J.; Feldman, D. C. 'A multivariate analysis of the determinants of job turnover'. *Journal of Applied Psychology*. 1982; 67: 350–360.

Auerback, A. J.; Reishus, D. 'Taxes and the Merger Decision'. *Take-overs and Contests for Corporate Control*. Coffee, J.; Lowenstein, L., eds. Oxford: Oxford University Press; 1987.

Baker, H. K.; Miller, T. O.; Ramsberger, B. J. 'An Inside Look at Corporate Mergers and Acquisitions'. *MSU Topics*. 1981 Winter: 49–57.

Barnatt, C.; Wong, P. 'Acquisition activity and organizational structure'. *Journal of General Management*. 1992 Spring; 17(3): 1–15.

Barney, J. B.; Hansen, M. K. 'Trustworthiness as a source of competitive advantage'. *Strategic Management Journal*. 1994 Winter; 15: 175–190.

Bartolome, F. 'Nobody trusts the boss completely – Now what?' *Harvard Business Review*. 1989 Mar; 67(2): 134–142.

Bastien, D. T. 'Common patterns of behavior and communication in corporate mergers and acquisitions'. *Human Resource Management*. 1987 Spring; 26(1): 17–33.

Bies, R. H. 'The Predicament of Injustice: The Management of Morale Outrage'. *Research in Organizational Behavior*. Cummings, L. L.; Straw, B. M., eds. Greenwich, CT: JAI Press; 1987.

Bies, R. J.; Moag, J. S. 'Interactional Justice: Communication Criteria of Fairness'. *Research on Negotiation in Organizations*. Lewicki, R. J., Sheppard, B. H., Bazerman, B. H., eds. Greenwich, CT: JAI Press; 1986.

Brockner, J.; Davy, J.; Carter, C. 'Layoffs, self-esteem, and survivor guilt: Motivational, affective, and attitudinal consequences'. *Organizational Behavior and Human Decision Processes*. 1985; 36(2): 229–244.

Buono, A. F., Bowditch, J. L. *The Human Side of Mergers and Acquisitions*. San Francisco: Jossey-Bass Publishers; 1989.

Buono, A. F.; Bowditch, J. L.; Lewis III, J. W. 'When cultures collide: The anatomy of a merger'. *Human Relations*. 1985; 538(5): 477–500.

Caplow, T. *The Sociology of Work*. New York: McGraw-Hill; 1964.

Carbrera, J. C. 'Take-overs ... the risks of the game and how to get around them'. *Management Review*. 1971; 71(11).

Cartwright, S.; Cooper, C. *Mergers and Acquisitions: The Human Factor*. Oxford: Butterworth-Heinemann Ltd; 1992.

Cartwright, S.; Cooper, C. 'The psychological impact of merger and acquisition on the individual: A study of building society managers'. *Human Relations*. 1993 Mar; 46(3):327–347.

Chatterjee, S. 'Types of synergies and economic value: The impact of acquisitions on merging and rival firms'. *Strategic Management Journal*. 1986 Jul:119–140.

Christensen, H. K.; Montgomery, C. A. 'Corporate economic performances: Diversification strategy versus market structure'. *Strategic Management Journal*. 1981; 2:327–343.

Coopers & Lybrand. *Why Do Acquisitions Fail?* London: 1992.

Cruise O'Brien, R. 'Is trust a calculable asset in the firm?' *Business Strategy Review*. 1995 Winter; 6(4):39–54.

Daly, J. P.; Geyer, P. D. 'The role of fairness in implementing large-scale change: Employee evaluations of process and outcome in seven facility relocations'. *Journal of Organizational Behavior*. 1994 Dec; 15(7):623–628.

Datta, D. K.; Grant, J. H. 'Relationships between type of acquisition, the autonomy given to the acquired firm, and acquisition success: An empirical analysis'. *Journal of Management*. 1990 Mar; 16(1):29–44.

Davis, K. *Human Behavior at Work*. New York: McGraw-Hill;1977.

Davy, J. A.; Kinicki, A. J.; Scheck, C. L. 'After the merger: Dealing with people's uncertainty'. *Training & Development Journal*. 1988 Nov; 42(11):56–61.

Dean, R. A.; Wanous, J. P. 'Effects of realistic job previews on hiring bank tellers'. *Journal of Applied Psychology*. 1984; 69: 61–68.

DeNoble, A. F.; Gustafson, L. T.; Hergert, M. 'Planning for post-merger integration – Eight lessons for merger success'. *Long Range Planning*. 1988 Aug; 21(4):82–85.

DiFonzo, N.; Bordia, P.; Rosnow, R. 'Reining in rumors'. *Organizational Dynamics*. 1994 Summer; 23(1):47–62.

Dubin, R. ed. *Handbook of Work, Organization and Society*. Chicago: Rand-McNally; 1976.

Dunnette, M.; Avrey, R.; Banas, P. 'Why do They Leave?' Unpublished paper. Minneapolis, Minnesota: University of Minnesota; 1973.

Feldman, D. C. 'The multiple socialization of organizational members'. *Academy of Management Review*. 1981; 6(2):309–318.

Festinger, L. *A Theory of Cognitive Dissonance*. Stanford, Ca.: Stanford University; 1957.

Folger, R.; Bies, R. J. 'Managerial responsibilities and procedural justice'. *Employee Responsibilities and Rights Journal*. 1989 Feb; 2.

Folger, R.; Konovsky, M. K. 'Effects of procedural and distributive justice on reactions to pay raise decisions'. *Academy of Management Journal*. 1989; 32:115–130.

Fowler, K. L.; Schmidt, D. R. 'Determinants of tender offer post-acquisition financial performance'. *Strategic Management Journal*. 1989 Jul; 10(4):339–350.

Franck, G. 'Mergers and acquisitions: Competitive advantage and cultural fit'. *European Management Journal*. 1990 Mar; 8(1):40–43.

Gill, J.; Foulder, I. 'Managing a merger: The acquisition and the aftermath'. *Personnel Today*. 1978; 10(1):14–17.

Goold, M.; Luchs, K. 'Why diversify? Four decades of management thinking'. *Academy of Management Executive*. 1993 Aug; 7(3):7–25.

Grant, R. M. 'The resource-based theory of competitive advantage: Implications for strategy formulation'. *California Management Review*. 1991 Spring; 33(3): 114–135.

Graves, D. 'Individual reactions to a merger of two small brokers in the re-insurance industry: A total population survey'. *Journal of Management Studies*. 1975; 18(1):89–113.

Greenberg, J. 'Determinants of perceived fairness of performance evaluations'. *Journal of Applied Psychology*. 1986; 71:340–342.

Greenberg, J. 'A taxonomy of organizational justice theories'. *Academy of Management Review*. 1987 Dec; 12:9–12.

Greenberg, J. 'Employee theft as a reaction to underpayment inequity: The hidden cost of pay cuts'. *Journal of Applied Psychology*. 1990 Oct; 75(5):561–568.

Greenberg, J.; Folger, R. 'Procedural Justice, Participation, and the Fair Process Effect in Groups and Organizations'. *Basic Group Process*. Paulus, P., ed. New York: Springer-Verlag; 1983: 235–256.

Habbe, quoted in Handy, C. B. *Understanding Organizations*. Middlesex: Penguin; 1976.

Haspeslagh, P. C.; Jemison, D. B. *Managing Acquisitions*. New York: Free Press; 1991.

Hellriegel, D.; Slocum, J. W. 'Organizational climate: Measures research and contingencies'. *Academy of Management Journal*. 1974; 17(2):255–280.

Herzberg, F. *Work and the Nature of Man*. Cleveland: World Publishing Co.; 1966.

Hill, C. W. L.; Pickering, J. F. 'Divisionalization, decentralization and performance of large United Kingdom companies'. *Journal of Management Studies*. 1986 Jan; 23(1):26–50.

Hise, R. T. 'Evaluating marketing assets in mergers and acquisitions'. *Journal of Business Strategy*. 1991 Jul; 12(4):46–51.

Hitt, M. A.; Hoskisson, R. E.; Ireland, R. D.; Harrison, J. S. 'Effects of acquisitions on R&D inputs and outputs'. *Strategic Management Journal*. 1991 Sep; 34(3):693–706.

Hom, P. W.; Griffeth, R. W. 'An experimental evaluation of the effects of a realistic job preview on nursing turnover'. *Academy of Management Proceedings*. 1985.

Horner, S.; Mobley, W.; Meglino, B. 'An Experimental Evaluation of the Effects of a Realistic Job Preview on Marine Recruit Affect, Intentions, and Behavior'. Columbia, S.C.: Center for Management and Organizational Research; 1979; Technical Report 9.

Hubbard, N. 'Downsizing: Managing to motivate'. *Acquisitions Monthly*. 1995; April:56–57.

Hubbard, N. 'The Role of Managing Employee Expectations in Acquisition Implementation'. (Unpublished doctoral thesis.) Oxford: University of Oxford; 1997.

Hubbard, N. 'Why mergers can be murder' *Human Resources*. 1998 Sep:56–60.

Hubbard, N.; Purcell, J. *Acquisition: A Paradox of Synergies*. Oxford: Templeton College; 1993 Dec; Working paper 93/29.

Hunt, J.; Turner, D. 'Hidden extras: How people get overlooked in take-overs'. *Personnel Management*. 1987 Jul; 19(7):24–26, 28.

Hunt, J. W.; Lees, S.; Grumbar, J. J.; Vivian, P. D. *Acquisitions: The Human Factor*. London: London Business School and Egon Zehnder International; 1987.

Ilgen, D. R.; Seely, W. 'Realistic expectations as an aid in reducing voluntary resignations'. *Journal of Applied Psychology*. 1974; 59:452–455.

Ivancevich, J. M.; Matteson, M. T.; Preston, C. 'Occupational stress, type A behavior, and physical well being'. *Academy of Management Journal*. 1982; 25(2):373–391.

Ivancevich, J. M.; Schweiger, D. M.; Power, F. R. 'Strategies for managing human resources during mergers and acquisitions'. *Human Resource Planning*. 1987; 10(1):19–35.

Jarrell, G. A. 'The returns to acquiring firms in takeovers: Evidence from three decades'. *Financial Management*. 1989 Autumn; 18(3):12–19.

Jarrell, G. A.; Brickley, J. A.; Netter, J. M. 'The market for corporate control: The empirical evidence since 1980'. *Journal of Economic Perspectives*. 1988 Dec; 2(1).

Jemison, D. B.; Sitkin, S. B. 'Acquisitions: The process can be a problem'. *Harvard Business Review*. 1986 Mar; 64(2):107–116.

Jensen, M. C. 'Takeovers: Their causes and consequences'. *Journal of Economic Perspectives*. 1988; 2(1):21–48.

Jones, C. S. 'Integrating acquired companies'. *Management Accounting*. 1986 Apr: 13.

Kanter, R. M. *Men and Women of the Corporation*. New York: Basic Books; 1977.

Katzell, M. E. 'Expectations and dropouts in schools of nursing'. *Journal of Applied Psychology*. 1968: 52.

Keller, R. T. 'Role conflict and ambiguity: Correlates with job satisfaction and values'. *Personnel Psychology*. 1972; 85.

Kelman, H. C. 'Compliance, identification and internalization: Three processes of attitude change'. *Conflict Resolution*. 1958; 2:51–60.

Kitching, J. 'Why do mergers miscarry?' *Harvard Business Review*. 1967 Nov:84–101.

Konovsky, M. A.; Cropanzano, R. 'Perceived fairness of employee drug testing as a predictor of employee attitudes and job performance'. *Journal of Applied Psychology*. 1991; 76(5):698–707.

Korsgaard, M. A.; Schweiger, D. M.; Sapienza, H. J. 'Building commitment, attachment, and trust in strategic decision-making teams: The role of procedural justice'. *Academy of Management Journal*. 1995 Feb; 38(1):60–84.

Kouzes, J. M.; Posner, B. Z. 'The credibility factor: What followers expect from their leaders'. *Business Credit*. 1990 Jul; 92(5):24–28.

KPMG Management Consulting. *Colouring the Map: Mergers & Acquisitions in Europe*. Research Report. London; 1997.

Kubler-Ross, E. *On Death and Dying*. New York: Macmillan; 1969.

Kusewitt, J. B. 'An exploratory study of strategic acquisition factors relating to performance'. *Strategic Management Journal*. 1985 Apr; 6(2):151–170.

Lamalie Associates (1985) in Siehl, C. and Smith, D. 'Avoiding the loss of a gain: Retaining top managers in an acquisition'. *Human Resource Management*. 1990 Summer; 29(2): 167–185.

Leana, C. R.; Feldman, D. C. 'Individual responses to job loss: Perceptions, reactions and coping behaviors'. *Journal of Management*. 1988 Sep; 14(3):375–389.

Leana, C. R.; Feldman, D. C. 'When mergers force layoffs: Some lessons about managing the human resource problems'. *Human Resource Planning*. 1989; 12(2):123–140.

Lee, T. W.; Mowday, R. T. 'Voluntarily leaving an organization: An empirical investigation of Steers and Mowday's model of turnover'. *Academy of Management Journal*. 1987; 30:721–743.

Lefkoe, M. 'Why so many mergers fail'. *Fortune*. 1987: 20 Jul; 116(2):113–114.

Legge, K. 'Managing Culture: Fact or Fiction?' *Personnel Management*. K. Sisson ed. Oxford: Blackwell; 1994.

Leung, K.; Li, W. 'Psychological mechanisms of process-control effects'. *Journal of Applied Psychology*. 1990; 75(6):613–620.

Lewis, W.; Harris, C. 'The year to end all years.' *Financial Times*. 26 June 1998.

Lind, E. A.; Tyler, T. R. *The Social Psychology of Procedural Justice*. New York: Plenum Press; 1988.

Lubatkin, M. 'Mergers, strategies and stockholder value'. *Strategic Management Journal*. 1987 Jan; 8(1):39–53.

Macedonia, R. M. 'Expectation – Press and Survival'. Unpublished doctoral dissertation. New York: New York Graduate School of Public Administration, New York University; 1969.

Magnet, M. 'Acquiring without smothering'. *Fortune*. Feb 3 1984:22.

Malekzadeh, A. R.; Nahavandi, A. 'Making mergers work by managing cultures'. *Journal of Business Strategy*. 1990 May; 11(3):55–57.

Maletesta, P. H. 'The wealth effect of merger activity and the objective functions of merging firms'. *Journal of Financial Economics*. 1983 Apr; 11:155–182.

Marks, M. L.; Mirvis, P. H. 'Mergers syndrome: Stress and uncertainty'. *Mergers & Acquisitions*. 1985 Summer:50–55.

Marks, M. L.; Cutcliffe, J. G. 'Making mergers work'. *Training & Development Journal*. 1988 Apr; 42(4):30–36.

Marks, M. L.; Mirvis, P. H. 'Track the impact of mergers and acquisitions'. *Personnel Journal*. 1992 Apr; 71(4):70–79.

Marriot, C. 'Boom Time is Back'. *Acquisitions Monthly*. 1996 Jan.

Meeks, G.; Meeks, J. G. 'Profitability measures as indicators of post-merger efficiency'. *Journal of Industrial Economics.* 1981 Jun:335–344.

Meglino, B. M.; DeNisi, A. S. 'Realistic job previews: Some thoughts on their more effective use in managing the flow of human resources'. *Human Resource Planning.* 1987; 10(3):157–167.

Meglino, B. M.; DeNisi, A. S.; Youngblood, S. A.; Williams, K. J. 'Effects of realistic job previews: A comparison using an "enhancement" and a "reduction" preview'. *Journal of Applied Psychology.* 1988; 73(2):259–266.

Michel, A.; Shaked, I. 'Evaluating merger performance'. *California Management Review.* 1985 Mar; 27(3).

Mirvis, P. H. 'Negotiations after the sale: The roots and ramifications of conflict in acquisition'. *Journal of Occupational Behavior.* 1985; 6:65–84.

Mitchell, D; Holmes, G. *Making Acquisitions Work: Learning from companies' successes and failures.* Research report. London: 1996.

Mowday, R. T.; Steers, R. M.; Porter, L.W. 'The measurement of organizational commitment'. *Journal of Vocational Behavior.* 1979; 14:224–247.

Mueller, D. C. 'Mergers and market share'. *Journal of Economics and Statistics.* 1985:259–267.

Napier, N. K. 'Mergers and acquisitions, human issues and outcomes: A review and suggested typology'. *Journal of Management Studies.* 1989; 26(3):271–289.

Napier, N.; Simmons, G.; Stratton, K. 'Communicating during a merger: Experience of two banks'. *Human Resource Planning.* 1989; 12(2):105–122.

Nicholson, N.; Arnold, J. 'From expectation to experience: Graduates entering a large corporation'. *Journal of Organizational Behavior.* 1991 Sep; 12(5):413–429.

O'Driscoll, M. P.; Beehr, T. A. 'Supervisor behaviors, role stressors and uncertainty as predictors of personal outcomes for subordinates'. *Journal of Organizational Behavior.* 1994; 15:141–155.

Pablo, A. L. 'Determinants of acquisition integration: A decision-making perspective'. *Academy of Management Journal.* 1994 Aug; 37(4):803–836.

Patch, F.; Rice, D.; Dreilinger, C. 'A contract for commitment'. *Training & Development.* 1992 Nov; 46(11):47–51.

Pitts, R. A. 'Diversification strategies and organizational policies of large diversified firms'. *Journal of Economics and Business.* 1976 Mar; 28(3):181–188.

Porter, L.; Lawler III, E.; Hachman, J. R., eds. *Behavior in Organizations.* New York: McGraw-Hill; 1975.

Porter, L. W.; Steers, R. M. 'Organizational, work, and personal factors in employee turnover and absenteeism'. *Psychological Bulletin.* 1973; 80:151–176.

Porter, M. E. 'From competitive advantage to corporate strategy'. *Harvard Business Review.* 1987 May; 65(3): 43–59.

Premack, S. L.; Wanous, J. P. 'A meta-analysis of realistic job preview experiments'. *Journal of Applied Psychology.* 1985; 70:706–719.

Purcell, J.; Marginson, P.; Armstrong. P.; Edwards, P.; Hubbard, N. 'The control of industrial relations in large enterprises: Initial analysis of the 2nd Company

Level Industrial Relations Survey'. Warwick: Warwick University; 1993; Report Vol. 45.

Ravenscraft, D.; Scherer, F. M., *Mergers, Sell-Offs, and Economic Efficiency*. Washington, D.C.: Brookings Institution; 1987.

Rizzo, J. R.; House, R. J.; Lirtzman, S. I. 'Role conflict and ambiguity in complex organizations'. *Administrative Science Quarterly*. 1970; 15:150–163.

Robinson, S.L. 'Trust and the breach of the psychological contract'. *Administrative Science Quarterly*. 1996 Dec; 41(4):574–599.

Robinson, S. L.; Rousseau, D. M. 'Violating the psychological contract: Not the exception but the norm'. *Journal of Organizational Behavior*. 1994 May; 15(3):245–259.

Roethlisberger, F. J. 'The foreman: Master and victim of double talk'. *Harvard Business Review*. 1965; 45:22.

Roll, R. 'The hubris hypothesis of corporate takeovers'. *Journal of Business*. 1986 Apr; 59(2):197–216.

Roskies, E.; Louis-Green, C.; Fournier, C. 'Coping with job insecurity: How does personality make a difference?' *Journal of Organizational Behavior*. 1993 Dec; 14(7):617–630.

Ryan; Oesterich, quoted in 'A contract for commitment'. Patch, F.; Rice, M. P.; Dreilinger, C. *Training & Development*. 1992 Nov; 46(11):47–51.

Saks, A.; Cronshaw, S. 'A process investigation of realistic job previews: Mediating variables and channels of communication'. *Journal of Organizational Behavior*. 1990 May; 11(3):221–236.

Saks, A. N. 'A psychological process investigation for the effects of recruitment source and organization information on job survival'. *Journal of Organizational Behavior*. 1994 May; 15(3):225–244.

Schuler, R. S. 'Role perceptions, satisfaction and performance moderated by organization level and participation in decision making'. *Academy of Management Journal*. 1977 Mar; 20(1): 159–164.

Schwartz, H.; Davis, S. M. 'Matching corporate culture and business strategy'. *Organizational Dynamics*. 1981 Jun; 60:30–48.

Schweiger, D. M.; DeNisi, A. S. 'Communication with employees following a merger: A longitudinal field experiment'. *Academy of Management Journal*. 1991 Mar; 34(1):110–135.

Schweiger, D. M.; Ivancevich, J. M.; Power, F. R. 'Strategies for managing human resources during mergers and acquisitions'. *Human Resource Planning*. 1987; 10(1):127–138.

Schweiger, D. M.; Weber, Y. 'Strategies for managing human resources during mergers and acquisitions: An empirical investigation'. *Human Resource Planning*. 1989; 12(2):69–86.

Shanley, M. T.; Correa, M. E. 'Agreement between top management teams and expectations for post acquisition performance'. *Strategic Management Journal*. 1992 May; 13(4):245–266.

Shaskin, M.; Williams, R. L. 'Does fairness make a difference?' *Organizational Dynamics*. 1993.

Shibutani, T. *Improvised News*. Indianapolis: Bobbs-Merrill; 1966.

Shrivastava, P. 'Post-merger integration'. *Journal of Business Strategy*. 1986 Jun; 7(1):65–76.

Siehl, C.; Ledford, G.; Silverman, R.; Fay, R. 'Preventing culture clashes from botching a merger'. *Mergers & Acquisitions*. 1988 Mar; 22(5):51–57.

Singh, H.; Montgomery, C. 'Corporate acquisition strategies and economic performance'. *Strategic Management Journal*. 1987 Jul; 8(4):377–386.

Smeltzer, L. R. 'An analysis of strategies for announcing organization-wide change'. *Group & Organization Studies*. 1991 Mar; 16(1):5–24.

Smye, M. D.; Grant, A. 'The personnel challenges of mergers and acquisitions'. *Canadian Banker*. 1989 Jan; 96(1):44–49.

Trautwein, F. 'Merger motives and merger prescriptions'. *Strategic Management Journal*. 1990 Nov; 11(4):283–295.

Troy, K. 'Restructuring: Good and bad news for employee communications'. *Public Relations Journal*. 1992 Apr; 45(4):51.

Van Maanen, J. 'Breaking In: A Consideration of Organizational Socialization'. *Handbook of Work, Organization and Society*. Dubin, R., ed. Chicago: Rand-McNally; 1976:67–130.

Walsh, J. P. 'Top management turnover following mergers and acquisitions'. *Strategic Management Journal*. 1988 Mar; 9(2):173–183.

Walsh, J. P.; Ellwood, J. W. 'Mergers, acquisitions and the pruning of managerial deadwood'. *Strategic Management Journal*. 1991 Mar; 12(3):201–217.

Wanous, J. P. 'Organizational entry: From naive expectations to realistic beliefs'. *Journal of Applied Psychology*. 1976; 61(1).

Wanous, J. P.; Poland, T. D.; Premack, S. L.; Davis, K. S. 'The effects of met expectations on newcomer attitudes and behaviours: A review and meta-analysis'. *Journal of Applied Psychology*. 1992 Jun; 77(3):286–297.

Weitz, M. 'Job expectancy and survival'. *Journal of Applied and Social Psychology*. 1956; 40:245–247.

Welter, T. R. 'Reducing employee fear'. *Small Business Reports*. 1991 Apr; 16(4):15–18.

Weston, J. F.; Chung, K. S. 'Takeovers and corporate restructuring: An overview'. *Business Economics*. 1990 Apr; 25(2):6–11.

Wishard, B. J. 'The human dimension'. *The Magazine Bank Administration*. 1985; 61.

Index

Entries in 'inverted commas' refer to fictional names of people and companies in the case studies.

267

Index compiled by Sue Carlton